Read Canadian

Read Canadian:
A Book about
Canadian Books

**Edited by Robert Fulford, David Godfrey
and Abraham Rotstein**

Toronto: James Lewis & Samuel   1972

Published with the assistance of the Canadian Horizons program of the Canada Council.

ISBN 0-88862-018-7 (cloth)
     0-88862-019-5 (paper)

Library of Congress Catalogue Card No. 78-190379

Cover design by Lynn Campbell

James Lewis & Samuel, Publishers
35 Britain Street
Toronto
Canada

Printed and bound in Canada

Contents

Introduction
Robert Fulford

Robert Fulford is the editor of Saturday Night *magazine and the author of two books,* Crisis at the Victory Burlesk *(1968) and* This Was Expo *(1968).*

We hoped, from the beginning of this project, that *Read Canadian* would be a book you could enjoy browsing through, a book that would reward the curious reader by leading him unexpectedly down new streets of enjoyment and interest. Now that the material is all together we can say with pleasure that it is indeed this kind of book: for those people interested in both Canada and books, these pages will provide a good many interesting and pleasant surprises. Certainly they have already for the editors. But that wasn't, and isn't, the central point. The main purpose of this collection is to serve as a handbook, a guide to a couple of dozen separate fields of expertise that can be approached in a Canadian context.

Most of the people who contributed the articles in *Read Canadian* are experts, people who have in the course of their ordinary work read a large part of the available Canadian material in their fields. But the book is not written for experts. It is a book for the general reader, whether privately or professionally involved. We like to think it will serve equally well for the citizen exploring a subject that has begun to interest him, a student working on his own or a teacher exploring a field new to him. (In some cases he may be a teacher exploring an *old* field, but one in which he knows only foreign material.)

The editors of *Read Canadian*, working as writers, editors and teachers, have all had occasion to realize the need for a collection like this. Lecturing outside our ordinary contexts, or writing articles on the need for more Canadian content in our schools, we are confronted again and again with the demand for some minimal guidance in Canadian studies.

To take only two experiences from many of my own: Last year, lecturing at a high school in a small Ontario city, I was approached by an English teacher. She had heard about Canadian Literature courses, she said, and she had been approached by some students with the suggestion that she begin to teach one. Her principal, for his part, was agreeable. There was only one problem: she didn't know anything about Canadian literature. She had graduated in English from a Canadian university; she had received her specialist's certificate in English, but nowhere along the way had the Canadian novel been so much as mentioned. How does one begin to teach it? What novels do you teach? She had read hardly any.

I wasn't sure what to tell her. A reading list, which I provided, was hardly adequate, but a course in Canadian literature at the nearest university offering one was beyond her means. I couldn't then tell her exactly how to start, but I can now: read William New's essay on modern fiction in this book. Begin there.

Another experience, in an entirely different setting, convinced me again of the need for more attention to Canadian studies. A writer in her twenties, who works with me sometimes, told me recently that she had just discovered the most magnificent and surprising book, *As for Me and My House*, a novel about the prairies by Sinclair Ross. I was delighted that she had found it, but I wondered silently why it had taken her so long. She had, after all, gone through high school in western Canada and taken a degree at a western university; yet she had never even heard the name of perhaps the best novel ever written about the Canadian West, certainly the best novel written about the western experience of the Depression. She discovered it only when someone put it on a reading list in a women's liberation course at the University of Toronto.

It is the belief of this book's editors that Sinclair Ross's novel, and many other Canadian books, should be part of the curricula in our high schools, our community colleges and our universities. To us it is self-evident that in Canadian education, Canadian books should play a major role: without them we cannot begin to understand Canada's situation, values and problems. Yet we know, as anyone who has studied the issues knows, that many courses, particularly in the social sciences and the arts, simply ignore Canadian material. It is not at all uncommon for a course on women's rights to pass over Canada without a mention, for a course on drug use to be developed entirely from American sources, for a course *in a Canadian university* on radicalism to leave out Quebec. In many cases the reason is that the course is taught by someone new to Canada, and we believe that not the least of this book's uses will be to put foreign professors in touch with Canadian material which, in the nature of things, was never mentioned in the undergraduate and graduate schools they attended. But foreign professors are not alone the cause of this neglect. Many Canadian teachers have found it easier to work only from imported books, either because these are more easily available or because they, in turn, came to know them as undergraduates.

The editors of *Read Canadian* differ politically in various ways, but we hold in common a point of view that might generally be called nationalist. In cultural terms this means, among other things, that we believe Canadians should be encouraged to pay a great deal more attention to Canada and the Canadian story than they have in the past.

In choosing contributors to the book we have not set out to construct any coherent philosophy; rather we have tried to find, in each of the twenty-nine fields covered, the person most familiar with the material to be covered and best able to provide an overview of it. In each case the writer has provided a description of the literature and a bibliography; in cases where this approach is suitable, the writer has also organized the books under the arbitrary headings of general, advanced and professional, so that a reader working on his own may be more precisely guided. The choice of books to be covered has been entirely the writer's, and in cases where the writer's own work is essential to an understanding of the subject he has been encouraged to include it.

The reader will also discover three brief sections that we hope will, in their different ways, stimulate an interest in Canadian books and publishing. One is an article by David Godfrey and James Lorimer (Lorimer, incidentally, conceived the idea for this volume) on the issue of ownership in Canadian publishing. Another is a list of Canadian-owned publishing houses, broken down according to the extent of their original Canadian publishing. The third is a playful attempt at the creation of a kind of pantheon of Canadian writing—a list of Ten Best Books (or maybe Ten Golden Oldies) put together by a vote among the contributors and the editors of this book. It is offered in the passionate hope that it will start arguments everywhere Canadian books are read.

The editors and contributors have not aimed at comprehensiveness—in no case do we claim to provide a complete list of important titles. At best we hope to offer an introduction that will be followed later by more extensive reading. In many cases, our writers have omitted important books—one thinks immediately, for instance, of Pierre Berton's and Peter Newman's popular histories—because these are so obviously valuable and so easily available in libraries and elsewhere. Nor have we covered every field that needs covering. We have concentrated heavily on the arts, the social sciences and history, in the belief that these are the fields in which interest in Canadian content is now swiftly growing. Even here we haven't ranged as widely as we might. A few subjects we hoped to cover have been, for various unforseen reasons, omitted (two examples: children's books and the literature of ethnic minorities). One subject I particularly miss, now that the contents list is completed, is Canadian popular fiction, the tradition that includes L. M. Montgomery, Mazo de la Roche and Arthur Hailey.

These omissions, we hope, will be corrected in a later edition. For we plan to make *Read Canadian* an ongoing project, to be revised and published again in new editions at irregular intervals, as circumstances dictate. To this end we invite readers to send us their comments about this first try, and suggestions for other subjects and other Canadian books to be included in the next one.

1 History

Canadian History
Michael Cross

Michael S. Cross is associate professor of history and dean of men at Victoria University, the University of Toronto. He is general editor of the Champlain Society, associate editor of the Canadian Historical Review *and a member of the editorial board of the* Canadian Forum.

Every historian feels the urge to philosophize about his subject, to generalize from his specific area to the history of his nation. And textbooks, every aspiring academic is told by his seniors, are where the money is. These two factors help to account for the plethora of survey histories to be found in every national historiography, including that of Canada. That neither is an entirely convincing reason for writing a book helps account for the distressingly low standards of most of these surveys. Fortunately the law of averages, if nothing else, dictates that at least some will have special merits. The selection below is admittedly subjective and arbitrary. It attempts to deal only with those surveys of particular quality, and excludes high-school texts.

Of the multitude, three one-volume survey histories have received special prominence. Edgar McInnis's *Canada: A Political and Social History,* first published in 1947, has probably been used in more university classrooms than any other. Donald Creighton's *Dominion of the North* and A. R. M. Lower's *Colony to Nation* have been most widely read by the general public.

Dominion of the North is undoubtedly the most readable book of its kind. The finest expression of the "Laurentian" approach to Canadian history, it has an epic sweep, a consistency of interpretation and a passionate commitment unusual in such volumes. Creighton's Laurentianism is a conservative, centralist, economic perspective. It sees Canada developing around the commercial system of the St. Lawrence River, expanding west across the continent through the Montreal fur trade and later the Canadian Pacific Railway, always in defiance of the rival economic system of the United States. In this interpretation, the heroes are those businessmen and politicians who had the vision to advance the interests of Laurentian commerce, to maintain Canada's vital links with Britain and to oppose the destructive influence of the United States. The villains, clearly, are those who retarded these developments— petty provincial politicians, Liberal continentalists, reformers who opposed business progress, French Canadians.

These themes are treated in more detail in two other books by Creighton: his first major work, *Commercial Empire of the St. Lawrence* (1937), which surveys the period from 1760 to 1850; and his latest, *Canada's First Century* (1970), covering the years 1867 to 1967. All are written with the clean, clear style that has made Creighton the most widely read of Canadian historians. This style is both the greatest pleasure of the books, and the greatest danger: it is so entertaining and so compulsively readable that it tends to lull, to make one accept too easily the conservative and controversial nature of the author's views. Yet these remain works of exceptional quality and *Dominion of the North* remains the most satisfactory of all one-volume surveys.

A. R. M. Lower's *Colony to Nation* is an opinionated, well-written and intelligent textbook. It is also a useful antidote to Creighton, for Lower's ideas are as classically liberal as Creighton's are conservative. While sharing Creighton's belief in a strongly centralized confederation, Lower shows greater appreciation of the regional nature of the country and of the contributions of French Canada. Similarly, he indicates his strong support for such liberal movements as the rebellions of 1837 and the drive for autonomy from Britain in the 1920s. While conventionally organized, the book is better balanced than most surveys, giving due weight to economic and social factors in Canadian development. It lacks, however, the consistency of *Dominion of the North*. Lower lays great weight on the role of the frontier, of the backwoods areas, in his treatment of the pre-Confederation era. After 1867, however, he becomes nearly Creightonian in his evaluation of the place of metropolitan centres in Canadian development.

The third of the highly successful textbooks is McInnis's *Canada: A Political and Social History.* Its strengths are clarity and comprehensiveness, obvious virtues in a text, and it is well illustrated. It also has a clear viewpoint, if a somewhat clichéd one: in his introduction to the third edition, McInnis summed up his theme as ". . . a study in political survival." While useful as a textbook, then, McInnis is less interesting and less provocative than either Creighton or Lower. And the title is somewhat misleading, for McInnis has given no more than the usual emphasis to social developments. In many ways, his is a summary of the conventional wisdom, picturing Canada's struggle for survival, a survival achieved by eschewing the extremes and marching down the great middle way: competent but hardly exciting or enlightening.

Among later one-volume texts, W. L. Morton's *The Kingdom of Canada* stands out. Morton adopts a posture somewhere between Creighton and Lower. Conservative, emphasizing the creative role of the British connection—as his title dramatizes—Morton at the same time resists total commitment to the Laurentian-centralist approach, frequently expressing his sympathies with the outlying areas, especially his native West. Written with flair and elegance, the book has a sustained narrative flow that ranks it with *Dominion of the North.* Also worth noting is the *Pelican History of Canada* by Kenneth W. McNaught. Thanks to its low price and to the effective promotion of Penguin Books, it has become a best seller. Unfortunately, its once-over-lightly approach, sloppiness in detail and its lack of any clear viewpoint make it no bargain even at under two dollars.

In a special category is John Bartlet Brebner's *North Atlantic Triangle,* first published in 1945 and reissued in paperback in 1966. The capstone of an extensive series of volumes by major scholars—the Carnegie Endowment for International Peace series, The Relations of Canada and the United States—*North Atlantic Triangle* was an attempt to assess the interplay of Britain, the United States and Canada from the discovery of North America to the Second World War. With his focus very much on Canada and how she was influenced by Britain and the United States, what emerged was a general history of Canada that placed this country firmly in its international context. As a Canadian who taught for many years in New York, Brebner was a strong advocate of Canadian-American co-operation and a firm believer in the truism that Canada could act as an interpreter between Britain and the United States. Nevertheless, his book demonstrated clearly that Canada, all too often, had been the victim in dealings between her more powerful cousins. Reflecting the strengths and weaknesses of the series it completed, *North Atlantic Triangle* was best on diplomatic and economic relations, poorest in its conventional treatment of Canadian domestic politics. Overall, however, it remains a provocative discussion of Canadian development, viewed from a broad and enlightened perspective.

French Canadian historians have been less addicted to the one-volume survey. Their general accounts have tended to be greatly detailed and in many volumes. Among useful, brief studies in French two may be mentioned. The classic statement of traditional French Canadian nationalism is expressed in *Histoire du Canada français depuis la découverte,* written by the cleric and nationalist leader, Lionel Groulx. Here are all the themes of pre-Quiet-Revolution thought: New France as a golden age; the providential mission of Catholic Quebec; the struggle of French Canadians to maintain their culture and religion under British domination. Groulx was among the most passionate exponents of these views. He, more than any other historian, drew a vivid picture of a garrison French Canada, beleaguered by a perfidious enemy, forced to relive the Conquest in the Act of Union of 1841 and in Confederation. There was no objectivity here; history was a weapon in a cultural war. His history was frankly propagandistic, written with force and excitement, in a bombastic rhetorical style. A contrast is represented by Robert Lacour-Gayet's *Histoire du Canada.* Not, like Groulx, a partisan in the struggles he describes, the Frenchman Lacour-Gayet gives a balanced treatment of both French and English Canada, as seen through the eyes of its major historians who Lacour-Gayet summarizes and assesses. Looking at both sides, he is impressed with the over-all unity of the Canadian mosaic rather than by its divisions. His cool and sympathetic study is a counterbalance to Groulx's frenzied partisanship.

An increasingly popular form of text is the documentary collection. A pioneer in this approach, and still one of the most satisfactory of its kind, is *A Source-Book of Canadian History,* edited by J. H. Stewart Reid, Kenneth McNaught and Harry S. Crowe. With minimal introductions to its ten parts, conventional in its organization and choice of documents, it is a workmanlike collection that offers substantial chunks of primary materials on the major themes from Norse exploration to the Massey report of 1951.

More comprehensive is the three-volume Canadian Historical Documents series. Cameron Nish edited and translated the documents in volume one, *The French Régime.* Nish's organization is chronological, in four parts covering the period from 1534 to 1760, with each part subdivided to cover major themes such as military history, religion and the state. Unlike the other two volumes, Nish employs footnotes and appendices, welcome additions. However, while the documents are presented with introductory material more concise and more informative than that found in either later volume, the usefulness of the volume for senior students or more informed laymen is limited by the use of familiar, readily accessible material. Fully half of Nish's documents come from seven sources, mainly old standards. The same criticism applies to Peter Waite's *Pre-Confederation,* easily the weakest of the three. Its quality is very uneven, ranging from well-rounded and consistently interesting sections on the West and the Hudson's Bay Company to dull and truncated sections on Newfoundland and Prince Edward Island. Throughout important subjects are overlooked in favour of trite descriptive passages. By a wide margin, the *Confederation to 1949* volume, edited by R. C. Brown and M. E. Prang, is the strongest. It has serious gaps, notably in the areas of religion and Canadian-American relations, but its more broadly based, more interesting selection of longer and more meaningful excerpts, with much more use of original primary documents, makes it a model of a documentary textbook.

A somewhat different approach is adopted by J. M. Bumsted, editor of the two volumes of *Documentary Problems in Canadian History.* In collaboration with twenty-three other historians, he presents twenty-four topics in Canadian history, equally divided between the pre- and post-Confederation eras. Each topic has a brief introduction setting it in its context and giving a selective bibliography, followed by anywhere from a dozen to thirty documentary excerpts. The novelty of some of the topics makes the collection refreshing: for instance, included are the Indian problem in the seventeenth century, the religious "Great Awakening" in the Maritimes, the triumph and decline of prohibition. But many topics are very narrow—the York South by-election of 1942 and D'Arcy McGee, for example—and the documents are often chopped beyond comprehension. This is not a basic collection, but one for more advanced use or for those interested in some of the minor themes in Canadian history.

The co-operative survey has a long history in Canada. The monumental *Canada and Its Provinces,* edited by Adam Shortt and A. G. Doughty, appeared in twenty-three volumes between 1913 and 1917. Organized into provincial and special theme volumes, it remains a basic source, crammed with information not readily available elsewhere. The most ambitious effort since *Canada and Its Provinces* is the Canadian Centenary Series. Projected to include eighteen volumes, it is organized both chronologically and regionally in a series of books that make up a unified conception but each of which stands on its own. Since 1963, eleven volumes have appeared.

Some have been genuinely excellent. Gerald M. Craig's *Upper Canada, 1784-1841*, is the first general treatment of that province, and is marked by a broad-ranging if conservative viewpoint. In *Canada under Louis XIV, 1663-1701*, W. J. Eccles has altered fundamentally interpretations of New France, which he pictures as a humane and successful society. The volumes on the North—E. E. Rich's *The Fur Trade and the Northwest to 1857* and Morris Zaslow's *The Opening of the Canadian North, 1870-1914*—are not marked by any powerful analytical insights but they open important new ground in Canadian historiography. Others, alas, are much weaker. In *Early Voyages and Northern Approaches, 1000-1632*, the late Tryggvi Oleson presented, in a nearly incomprehensible way, his idiosyncratic views on the North and on the origins of the Eskimos. W. S. MacNutt's *Atlantic Provinces, 1712-1857*, suffers badly from attempting to cover too much ground and George F. G. Stanley's *New France, 1744-1760*, is little more than a description of endless military manoeuvres. The other volumes, listed in the bibliography, are all useful and competent general treatments.

For students and general readers, two recent collaborative efforts, taken together, may make the most satisfactory survey history available. In 1967, J. M. S. Careless and R. C. Brown edited *The Canadians*, a handsome study of post-Confederation Canada. The first section was a decade-by-decade history of the country, each chapter written by a different historian. Part two was made up of nineteen thematic chapters by experts on the fields surveyed, which included such subjects as sports, literature, the armed forces, unions and communications. While the quality was obviously varied, the contributions taken together gave a comprehensive analysis of Canadian development. The first part, the decade-by-decade history, was later issued in paperback. In 1971, this volume received a companion piece for the period 1760 to 1867, *Colonists and Canadiens*, edited by Careless. Again each decade was treated by a different historian. While little unity of approach emerges from such a format, especially when each historian is dealing with a number of disparate colonies, it offers the strength of a variety of viewpoints and analytical techniques. The result is a two-volume survey history as pleasing and interesting as any available.

SUMMARY BIBLIOGRAPHY
All are general.

Brebner, John Bartlet. *North Atlantic Triangle.* Toronto: Ryerson, 1945. Paper ed. Toronto: McClelland and Stewart, Carleton Library, 1966.

Bumsted, J. M., ed. *Documentary Problems in Canadian History.* 2 vols. Georgetown, Ont.: Irwin-Dorsey, 1969.

Canadian Centenary Series. Toronto: McClelland and Stewart.

    Oleson, Tryggvi J. *Early Voyages and Northern Approaches, 1000-1632* (1963).

    Eccles, W. J. *Canada under Louis XIV, 1663-1701* (1964).

    Stanley, George F. G. *New France: The Last Phase, 1744-1760* (1968).

    Neatby, Hilda. *Quebec: The Revolutionary Age, 1760-1791* (1966).

    Craig, Gerald M. *Upper Canada: The Formative Years, 1784-1841* (1963).

    MacNutt, W. S. *The Atlantic Provinces: The Emergence of Colonial Society, 1712-1857* (1965).

    Careless, J. M. S. *The Union of the Canadas: The Growth of Canadian Institutions, 1841-1857* (1967).

    Rich, E. E. *The Fur Trade and the Northwest to 1857* (1967).

    Morton, W. L. *The Critical Years: The Union of British North America, 1857-1873* (1964).

    Waite, P. B. *Canada, 1874-1896: Arduous Destiny* (1971).

Zaslow, Morris. *The Opening of the Canadian North, 1870-1914* (1971).

Canadian Historical Documents. Scarborough: Prentice-Hall, 1965-66.

Nish, Cameron, ed. *The French Régime.*

Waite, P. B., ed. *Pre-Confederation.*

Brown, R. C., and M. E. Prang, eds. *Confederation to 1949.*

Careless, J. M. S., ed. *Colonists and Canadiens, 1760-1867.* Toronto: Macmillan, 1971.

Careless, J. M. S., and R. C. Brown, eds. *The Canadians, 1867-1967.* Toronto: Macmillan, 1967.

Creighton, Donald. *Canada's First Century.* Toronto: Macmillan, 1970.

———. *Dominion of the North: A History of Canada.* 2nd. ed. Toronto: Macmillan, 1957.

———. *The Empire of the St. Lawrence.* New ed. Toronto: Macmillan, 1956. First published as *The Commercial Empire of the St. Lawrence, 1760-1850.* Toronto: Ryerson, 1937.

Groulx, Lionel. *Histoire du Canada français depuis la découverte.* 4 vols. Montreal: L'Action Nationale, 1950-52. 2 vols. 1962.

Lacour-Gayet, Robert. *Histoire du Canada.* Paris: Librarie Arthème Fayard, 1966.

Lower, A. R. M. *Colony to Nation: A History of Canada.* Toronto: Longmans, 1946. 4th ed. 1969.

McInnis, Edgar. *Canada: A Political and Social History.* Toronto: Holt Rinehart and Winston, 1947. 3rd ed. 1969.

McNaught, Kenneth. *The Pelican History of Canada.* Harmondsworth and Don Mills: Penguin, 1969.

Morton, W. L. *The Kingdom of Canada.* Toronto: McClelland and Stewart, 1963.

Reid, J. H. Stewart, Kenneth McNaught and Harry S. Crowe, eds. *A Source-Book of Canadian History.* Toronto: Longmans, 1959. Rev. ed. 1964.

Shortt, Adam, and A. G. Doughty, eds. *Canada and Its Provinces.* 23 vols. Toronto: Glasgow, Brook, 1914-17.

Quebec History
Jean-Pierre Wallot

Jean-Pierre Wallot is professor of history at Sir George Williams University in Montreal, specializing in French Canadian history of the late eighteenth and early nineteenth centuries.

By Quebec history is meant here the birth and development of French Canada during the French régime, its Conquest and its subsequent evolution on the territory of modern Quebec. The difficulty in listing ten English books on that subject stems from the fact that most studies are in French or/and are stamped by one of the two or three "global" interpretations of French Canada's past, themselves fed by the perennial problem of the relationships between the "two founding peoples" or "nations." We have thus compromised, reviewing twelve books besides enumerating at the end a few particular studies. The remaining gaping holes will be filled partly by the chapter on Quebec nationalism.

General Studies
French-Canadian Society, Rioux's and Martin's now-dated effort, remains the only general study combining historical perspective and sociological analysis. Renowned social scientists scrutinize numerous facets of French Canadian society: rural settlement and life; family and parish; socio-cultural structures and change; ideologies. Although some chapters attack the "folk-society" myth, the general tendency is to buttress the popular image of a seventeenth and eighteenth century French Canada that was static, feudal, conservative and rural. The second part of the book, which tries to decipher social structures and change in "contemporary" French Canada (i.e., post-1945), delves much deeper into the material. On the whole, an uneven, unsatisfactory, yet still useful sociological approach to

past and near-present.

Mason Wade's large-scale study, *The French Canadians 1760-1967,* theoretically covers the whole period, including a chapter on the French régime's "heritage." In practice, it does not delve systematically into the whole chronological development. Different chapters, while not entirely neglecting less important problems, emphasize the main crises that explode or fizzle during more than two centuries, for instance: "The Struggle for Survival: 1791-1834"; "Riel, the West and Mercier: 1818-97"; "The Conscription Crisis: 1916-19"; "The Not-so-Quiet Revolution: 'Maîtres chez nous enfin?' 1945-66." The work contains a tremendous amount of documentation, often too much or too specialized for a balanced view and for the analysis. The style flows easily. Political and cultural factors particularly are stressed. Finally, the interpretation is clearly pan-Canadian and, on contemporary Quebec, strongly biased and moralist. Unfortunately, Wade's is the only general study in the field in English, a situation that confers upon his interpretations a definitive character to which they are not entitled.

Two much shorter studies have the advantage of being comparable and of expressing two different theses in French Canadian history. Though short and very compact, Jean Hamelin's "The Historic Development of French Canada" (later published in French as a book) brings together much essential information in an ordered fashion. It also generally follows the Laval or "Quebec" interpretation, with its tendency to mute ethnic conflicts and to stress social and economic difficulties, to downgrade the degree of development of French Canada during the French régime and to enhance its progress after 1760—except for its own stubborn resistance to change. This highly readable summary should be contrasted with a more specialized work which offers a counter-interpretation, that of the "Montreal School": Maurice Séguin's *L'Idée d'indépendance au Québec: Genèse et historique.* For Séguin and his disciples (notably Guy Frégault and Michel Brunet), a nation cannot survive and develop by culture alone.

To really live and evolve harmoniously, it must act by itself in the main areas of collective life: in economics (domination of its economy), politics (self-government) and in culture in the widest sense. Thus the Conquest stopped the natural growth of French Canada and condemned it to economic subordination, minority status, a provincial character and cultural stagnation. *L'Idée d'indépendance* is mostly interesting, however, for its analysis of the different schools of separatism (and, necessarily, of nationalism) in Quebec after 1760. Ouellet and Brunet reproduce this duality in Ramsay Cook's *French-Canadian Nationalism: An Anthology* (see Quebec Nationalism).

The French Régime

For the French régime, one book at least succeeds in grasping the main lines of the story, from 1534 to 1760, while at the same time going into structural problems such as social life, institutions and the like. William J. Eccles's *The Canadian Frontier, 1534-1760* combines solid scholarship, vivid style and general interest and usefulness as a reference book (it contains excellent illustrations, index and bibliography). The chapters are either chronological or thematic: "The Nature of the Canadian Frontier"; "New France, 1534-1629: A Commercial Outpost"; "Commerce and Evangelism, 1632-1662"; "Society and the Frontier"; "The Fur-Trade Frontier, 1663-1700"; "The Imperial Frontier, 1700-1750"; "The Military Frontier, 1748-1760"; "The Closing of the Canadian Fur-Trade Frontier."

Much more specialized, yet cutting through the economic and social fabric of the French Canadian society during the French régime, R. Cole Harris's book on the seigneurial system *(The Seigneurial System in Early Canada: A Geographical Study)* constitutes a major revision in Canadian historiography. Essentially, Harris downgrades the importance attributed by historiography to the seigneurial régime in New France and, in so doing, discredits many of the myths about seigneurs, rural life and lack of dynamism among French Canadians, traces of which are very much sprinkled

through Rioux's and Martin's *French-Canadian Society.*
Harris scrutinizes the land system, the form and distribution of seigneuries and habitant holdings, the characteristics of farms, their spatial organization, the
influence of laws, the distribution of population and its
standard of living. He then concludes that "seigneur and
seigneurie were simply irrelevant" in a society that
would have been much more dynamic had there been
other opportunities than the fur trade. The text is
sometimes technical, although nearly always clearly
written. Moreover, each chapter concludes with a good
summary of the evidence marshalled and of the con-
clusions drawn from it.

Guy Frégault's *Canada: The War of Conquest,* although more than fifteen years old, is still the best work
on the last years of New France, on the high stakes of
the war, on the divisive conflicts between Frenchmen
and Canadians. The preface and conclusion summarize
in absolute and rather too systematic terms the
"Montreal thesis" about the consequences of the Conquest: after 1760, there would remain French Canadians, but no French Canada. A good index and a
bibliography help the reader.

1760-1970

Many good studies concentrate on the years 1760-1850,
nearly none afterwards. Creighton's *Empire of the St.
Lawrence,* because of its poetic style, its trenchant
theses, its apparently solid documentary basis, remains a
classic nearly thirty years after its first edition. But once
the power of the language and style is set aside (and that
is indeed very difficult to do in this case), Creighton's
interpretation of Quebec's development between 1760
and 1850 appears very simple and narrow indeed. The
British colonists, particularly the dynamic merchant-
entrepreneurs, had to struggle during the whole period
against criminal negligence in England, unfair American
competition and, worst of all, a semi-feudal, decadent
French Canadian society that was a dead weight in
Canadian development, except when the French co-
operated with the English as servants with masters.

Many specialized studies have modified or contradicted Creighton's position considerably. The main interest of the book, however, lies in its author's endorsation of the views of the British merchants, thus truly reflecting their consciousness of themselves as a social group and their hatred and suspicions of French Canada. This thesis of a struggle between feudalism and capitalism, between backward farmers and modern merchants, has even marked French Canadian historiography (Fernand Ouellet's *Histoire économique et sociale du Québec, 1760-1850,* for instance, published in 1966). Thus its importance.

Hilda Neatby's *Quebec: The Revolutionary Age 1760-1791* roughly encompasses the first generation after the Conquest. This well-researched study, perhaps a little heavy for general readers, supersedes Burt's *The Old Province of Quebec* in information and interpretations. Instead of falling into the "feudal" outlook dear to Burt and Creighton, Neatby even traces the development of progressive (perhaps radical for their time and place) political ideas among the French Canadian leaders in the 1780s: an understanding of the importance and working of British parliamentary institutions and a desire to use them to gain political power, the better to serve the French Canadian "nation." An excellent index and a select bibliography will guide the general reader who may not want to immerse himself in the fine detail of certain legal and political battles.

Then, an interested reader should pick up the excellent book by Helen Taft Manning, *The Revolt of French Canada 1800-1835: A Chapter in the History of the British Commonwealth.* This standard work covers, although sometimes too quickly, a period still characterized by a dearth of specialized studies. The main qualities of the book, which will appeal to most readers, are the author's concern for social as well as for political conflicts, for individuals as well as for groups, for imperial as well as for colonial matters, for style as well as for conciseness. Manning closes with the years just before the rebellions. About her concluding interpretation, one wonders how the constitutional reform of the

1840s could really have been a victory for French Canada, at least on the scale (a "national" future) dreamt of by its leaders prior to the crushing defeat of the patriot movement in 1837. A bibliography and an index are included.

Jacques Monet's *The Last Cannon Shot: A Study of French-Canadian Nationalism 1837-1850* starts where Manning stops. It picks up the sinuous and tangled threads that made up the changing fabric of French Canadian "public opinion" during the crucial period from the defeat and ruin of 1837 to the necessary association with the English Canadians through the 1840s. Three main crises influenced French Canadian nationalism during this period and brought it to the "open-minded" *bonne entente* which, for the author, characterizes the post-1840 period: the debates over union, the struggle for responsible government and the annexationist crisis in the late 1840s. This book should prove popular: it is well constructed, well written, and it espouses very federalist and monarchist principles. For those who read French, the other side of the coin may be seen in Jean-Paul Bernard's recent (1971) book, *Les Rouges. Libéralisme, nationalisme et anti-cléricalisme au milieu du XIXe siècle*. Both contain an index and a bibliography.

Subsequently, there is a large gap in English historiography on Quebec, except for a few studies on the recent past that lack some historical perspective and are more concerned with Quebec nationalism per se (e.g. Herbert F. Quinn's *The Union Nationale: A Study in Quebec Nationalism)*, and several rather technical and specialized works (e.g. William F. Ryan, *The Clergy and Economic Growth in Quebec 1896-1914*). An exception might be sociologist Marcel Rioux's *Quebec in Question*. The author, a late convert to separatism, tries to reinterpret French Canada's evolution from the beginnings to the present. The book is decidedly strongest in the chapters dealing with twentieth century social and ideological evolution. It sheds interesting light on recent developments. It has no bibliography nor index, although it suggests a cursory chronology.

Because of the paucity of good studies in English on Quebec history, we cannot recommend two series of studies written by renowned scholars too strongly to both students and the general public. First, a number of the inexpensive booklets of the Canadian Historical Association pertain directly or indirectly to Quebec history. The studies in the second series, Issues in Canadian History, deal with specific historical problems. They quote extracts from different authors expounding different hypotheses and usually indicate a large number of sources. The recommended volumes from both series are listed in the bibliography.

Finally, two general books cover the whole of Canadian history after 1760 and include some excellent material on Quebec history: *Colonists and Canadiens*, edited by J. M. S. Careless, and *The Canadians, 1867-1967*, edited by Careless and R. C. Brown.

SUMMARY BIBLIOGRAPHY
General

Canadian Historical Association, Ottawa.

    Stanley, G. F. G. *Louis Riel: Patriot or Rebel?* (1954).

    Frégault, G. *Canadian Society in the French Régime* (1954).

    Burt, A. L. *Guy Carleton, Lord Dorchester, 1724-1808* (1955).

    Trudel, M. *The Seigneurial Régime* (1960).

    Ouellet, F. *Louis-Joseph Papineau: A Divided Soul* (1961).

    Brunet, M. *French Canada and the Early Decades of British Rule, 1760-1791* (1963).

    Eccles, W. J. *The Government of New France* (1965).

    Cornell, P. G. *The Great Coalition* (1966).

    Bonenfant, J.-C. *The French-Canadians and the Birth of Confederation* (1966).

Careless, J. M. S., ed. *Colonists and Canadiens, 1760-1867*. Toronto: Macmillan, 1971.

Careless, J. M. S., and R. C. Brown, eds. *The Canadians, 1867-1967.* Toronto: Macmillan, 1967.

Hamelin, J. "The Historic Development of French Canada." *Quebec Yearbook* (Quebec, 1966-67), pp. 50-79.

Rioux, Marcel. *Quebec in Question.* Toronto: James Lewis & Samuel, 1971.

Séguin, M. *L'Idée d'indépendance au Québec: Genèse et historique.* Trois-Rivières: Boréal Espress, 1968.

Advanced

Burt, A. L. *The Old Province of Quebec.* 2-vol. ed. Toronto: McClelland and Stewart, Carleton Library, 1968.

Cook, Ramsay. *French-Canadian Nationalism: An Anthology.* Toronto: Macmillan, 1969.

Creighton, Donald G. *The Empire of the St. Lawrence.* New ed. Toronto: Macmillan, 1956.

Eccles, W. J. *The Canadian Frontier, 1534-1760.* Toronto: Holt Rinehart and Winston, 1969.

Frégault, G. *Canada: The War of the Conquest.* Toronto: Oxford University Press, 1969.

Issues in Canadian History. Toronto: Copp Clark.

    Clark, L. *The Manitoba School Question: Majority Rule or Minority Rights?* (1968).

    Nish, C. *The French Canadians, 1759-1766: Conquered? Half-Conquered? Liberated?* (1966).

    ———. *Quebec in the Duplessis Era, 1935-1959: Dictatorship or Democracy?* (1970).

    ———. *Racism or Responsible Government: The French-Canadian Dilemma of the 1840s* (1967).

Manning, H. T. *The Revolt of French Canada 1800-1835.* Toronto: Macmillan, 1962.

Monet, J. *The Last Cannon Shot: A Study of French-Canadian Nationalism 1837-1850.* Toronto: University of Toronto Press, 1969.

Quinn, H. F. *The Union Nationale: A Study in Quebec Nationalism.* Toronto: University of Toronto Press, 1963.

Rioux, Marcel, and Y. Martin, eds. *French-Canadian Society.* Toronto: McClelland and Stewart, Carleton

Library, 1964, 1966, 1968.

Wade, M. *The French Canadians 1760-1967*. 2nd ed. 2 vols. Toronto: Macmillan, 1968.

Professional

Bernard, Jean-Paul. *Les Rouges. Libéralisme, nationalisme et anti-cléricalisme au milieu du XIXe siècle.* Montréal: Presses de l'Université du Québec, 1971.

Harris, R. C. *The Seigneurial System in Early Canada: A Geographical Study.* Québec: Presses de l'Université Laval, 1966.

Neatby, Hilda. *Quebec: The Revolutionary Age 1760-1791.* Toronto: McClelland and Stewart, Canadian Centenary Series, 1966.

Ouellet, F. *Histoire économique et sociale du Québec, 1760-1850.* Montréal: Fidès, 1966.

Ryan, W. F. *The Clergy and Economic Growth in Quebec 1896-1914.* Québec: Les Presses de l'Université Laval, 1966.

The West: History and Politics
Hart Bowsfield

Hart Bowsfield is university archivist and lecturer in history at York University in Toronto. He is the author of a biography of Louis Riel, The Rebel and the Hero.

There is no single volume that covers the story of the West and British Columbia from the age of discovery to the present day. There are, however, several general histories dealing with part of that period. A. S. Morton's *A History of the Canadian West to 1870-71,* published in 1939, may be considered now by many libraries as a scarce item and will be difficult to obtain. But it is still the most useful general history of the prairies and the Pacific-coast province to their entry into Confederation.

Morton's work is a long, detailed and scholarly volume based on years of research in original source material—it was one of the first studies to make extensive use of the records of the Hudson's Bay Company. While the fur trade remains at the centre throughout the narrative the author does not neglect the Indian people, geographical influences or the increasing pressure of settlement from Canada and the United States, all of which are used to analyze disparate sections of Canada that at times defy unified treatment.

The prairie interior of the continent and the Pacific coast are dealt with from the viewpoint of approaches to them by England, France, Spain, Russia and the United States, the common purpose of these nations being, at first, the search for fur-bearing animals. The narrative moves from the rivalry between these nations in Hudson Bay and on the Pacific coast to the rivalry between the London-based Hudson's Bay Company and the Montreal fur-trading companies, and the violence between these companies associated with the establishment of an agricultural community at Red River by Lord Selkirk. The final chapters deal with the development of this community, the advance of settlement in British Columbia, the movement towards Confederation with Canada and the Riel rebellion of 1869-70.

Douglas Hill's *The Opening of the Canadian West* is what is usually referred to as popular history. The author's purpose was not to provide evidence of new research or to present new interpretations but to give readers a lively, readable account of events in the West and British Columbia. The "opening" he refers to is not limited, as might be expected, to the story of immigration and the development of agricultural settlement in the nineteenth century. It encompasses rather the history of the two areas from the days of the first explorers to the granting of provincial status to Saskatchewan and Alberta in 1905. This date, says Hill, was a climax and conclusion to the "opening" process. The pioneer period was over and the period of development and utilization began.

British Columbia does not always fit smoothly into his narrative and its history is often dealt with as a separate story. Nevertheless, a unifying theme is found in the account of the penetration and development of the two areas from the age of the fur trader to the age of the railway builder. Each event is seen in epic proportion—the fur trade, the Selkirk Settlement, the Riel rebellions. Whether he is telling the story of the well-known personalities of western history or minor ones such as Jerry Potts, a half-breed guide for the North West Mounted Police, or "Twelve-Foot" Davis, a legendary figure of the Cariboo gold-rush days, Hill's enthusiasm is evident. With the story of the Canadian Pacific Railway and the homesteaders his narrative takes on an exciting pace and he writes vividly and with forthright opinions. The isolation and loneliness of the prairie settler is pointedly depicted and nowhere will a reader find a more sympathetic account of the ethnic groups that make up the mosaic of present-day western Canada. The reader should be warned, however, that there are many minor errors of date and geographical location.

To date no scholarly history of either Saskatchewan

or Alberta has been written. Edward McCourt's *Saskatchewan*, James Wright's *Saskatchewan, the History of a Province* and Robert Kroetsch's *Alberta* will, however, serve as introductions to these provinces. British Columbia and Manitoba, on the other hand, have been the subjects of excellent provincial histories. From the date of its first publication in 1957, W. L. Morton's *Manitoba, a History* has been consistently referred to as the best provincial history produced in Canada. When Margaret Ormsby's *British Columbia: A History* appeared in 1958 it was called "a model of provincial history." Both books are the product of years of careful research. Each reflects the writer's close and personal intimacy with the province.

In many ways the early chapters of these books deal with similar events—exploration, fur trade, settlement and the entry of the two areas into Confederation. Even after 1870-71, though the history of the two provinces diverges topically, the story is basically the same—how they were integrated politically and economically with the nation. This theme enables the two historians to rise above what might have been mere local history, for throughout the narrative both have kept an eye on the national scene. Events in Manitoba lend themselves readily to this treatment. The Red River rebellion of 1869-70, the disallowance by the federal government of provincial railway legislation and the Manitoba schools question were issues of provincial as well as national significance. The two books are similar in another way. Neither is all politics and government. Both historians have included the social, economic and cultural background of the province.

No list of reference books on the history of the West would be complete without a history of the Hudson's Bay Company. The most scholarly of the many histories of the company is *The History of the Hudson's Bay Company 1760-1870* by E. E. Rich, an English historian whose work is based on an extensive use of the company's archives. His knowledge of the company's activities is astounding and his attention to detail meticulous. His history, however, will be a formidable one for the general reader since it is not only the history of the Canadian West and the Pacific coast from the period of exploration to the entry of those areas into Confederation, but also the story of the Hudson's Bay Company as a business—its financial organization and operation, its dividends and its marketing methods. Fortunately these matters do not overpower the narrative and the persistent reader will find that they are treated in a clear and understandable way. Rich covers much of the same ground in the less formidable volume, *The Fur Trade and the Northwest to 1857.*

A more readable and popular account of the company's activities and its place in the history of the West is Douglas MacKay's *The Honourable Company.* MacKay purposely chose to concentrate on men and events rather than business organization and management. His narrative will appeal to those whose interest lies in the epic features of the fur trade and the courage and audacity of the traders and explorers whose careers prove that not all Canadian history lacks colour and excitement. MacKay maintains the emphasis on personalities throughout the story, beginning with the manipulations of Radisson and Groseilliers in the early days of the company's history and continuing with the explorations of the interior by such company men as the young boy Henry Kelsey, the achievements of Alexander Mackenzie and the other "pedlars" from Montreal who explored and mapped the country across the continent to the Pacific coast. Lord Selkirk and George Simpson dominate the story of the first agricultural settlement at Red River, the fierce rivalry between the Hudson's Bay and North West companies and the increasing attack on both the company's monopoly trade position and its role as governing authority. After the death of Simpson in 1860 the story leads quickly to the surrender of the company's territories to Canada in 1869 and the resistance of the Métis under Louis Riel to Canadian rule. A final, anticlimactic chapter deals in a very compressed form with the company in the years after 1870.

In *The Birth of Western Canada*, George Stanley

covers the dramatic events of the Red River and North-west rebellions, and the enigmatic figure of Louis Riel. Stanley has done, in addition, a definitive biography of the Métis leader. Some writers have maintained that the rebellions, particularly that of 1869-70 at Red River, should be interpreted within the context of the racial and religious tension between Ontario and Quebec. Stanley, however, sees the rebellions as the last effort of primitive peoples—Indian and Métis—to withstand the advance of white civilization. The rebellions were thus the result of cultural conflict.

One of the most valuable parts of Stanley's book is the light it sheds on the years between the two rebellions. After dealing with Manitoba's entry into Confederation in 1870, he covers the movement of the Métis people from that province to the Northwest Territories and outlines the growing unrest and discontent in that area from the point of view of the Métis, the Indians and the white settlers. No other writer has examined as carefully the federal government's reactions to the problems in the Northwest and Stanley's conclusion is that the government was guilty of delay, inefficiency and neglect. In the light of later developments in the West it is of interest to note that he places the Métis uprising of 1885 within the framework of the western agrarian protest movement of the 1880s.

Third-party political movements in Canada have attracted the attention of many writers. Three of these parties, representing western regional protest against the political and economic influence of central Canada—the Progressive, Social Credit and CCF parties—have been dealt with in *Democracy and Discontent* by Walter D. Young. This small but useful study will serve as an introduction to the more specialized studies.

W. L. Morton in *The Progressive Party in Canada* traces the origin of the Progressive revolt against the traditional party structure back to the sectional grievances of the 1880s. The aim of the grain growers' associations was to educate the prairie farmer in collective action, and to direct an organized agrarian interest in an attack on national economic policies and party practices. The farmers saw themselves as victims of an economy designed to favour the commercial and industrial centres of eastern Canada and of a political party system that catered to those interests. Out of their protest came political action.

Morton follows the fate of this agrarian revolt first in provincial politics and then at the federal level. In the provinces, Progressives embraced a reform movement—social welfare, temperance, extension of the franchise to women, reform of the civil service, relaxation of partisan politics. At the federal level the prairie farmers attacked the protective tariff and the railway rate structure, sought an end to political patronage, reform of the Senate, public ownership of railways, and promoted a graduated tax on income, inheritance and corporation profits.

In 1921 the Progressive party won sixty-five seats in the House of Commons. Morton analyzes the conduct of this group from the initial victory to its disintegration in the mid-twenties. Its failure, he finds, resulted from its weakness as a regionally based party, its inability to act as a disciplined group in the House of Commons, the manoeuvres of Liberal Prime Minister Mackenzie King in accepting part of its program and attracting some of its members back into the Liberal fold, and the divisions within the party itself. One section, led by Henry Wise Wood of Alberta, refused to consider the Progressive movement as a political party, believing that party government was an evil. The other, led by Thomas Crerar of Manitoba, wished to work within the party system, hoping to modify Liberal party policy.

John Irving's *The Social Credit Movement in Alberta* is an analysis of the period between 1932, when William Aberhart embraced the doctrine of Social Credit, and 1935, when the party won an overwhelming victory in the Alberta provincial election. Irving refers to his work as the story of collective behaviour in a democracy under stress, that is, the depression crisis of the 1930s. In the midst of misery, unemployment and drought the people of Alberta responded to Aberhart's questioning of an economic system that, as was said, produced poverty in the midst of plenty. His simplistic solution, that of providing the community with credit based on the resources of the province, appealed to those who saw themselves victims of a monetary system controlled by eastern banks and the mortgage and loan companies. As Aberhart expressed it, the people had a right to share in the wealth from the natural resources of the province, wealth that was being selfishly manipulated and controlled by the "Fifty Big Shots of Canada." Irving surveys the response of the Alberta electorate both to this economic cure and to Aberhart, its "prophet."

Since Aberhart was the key to the success of the movement, Irving devotes a chapter to Aberhart's background and personality—his fundamentalist theology, his career as a school teacher in Calgary, his organization of the Calgary Prophetic Bible Institute and the significance of his radio sermons, through which he had built up a personal following and by means of which he introduced Social Credit doctrines to a mass audience. Included is a chapter on the secondary leaders who set up local Social Credit study groups and acted as speakers, organizers and campaign managers in the election of 1935. Much of the information on these people was based on personal interviews. Using the same method Irving obtained data on the response of a cross section of the electorate to Aberhart and his theories. His purpose was to investigate the interaction between "the leader and the led" and to understand the "deeper layers" of the movement. In a final chapter he analyzes the strategy and tactics of the 1935 campaign and attempts an interpretation of the movement and the personality of its leader.

A third movement of political protest originating in western Canada is the subject of Seymour Martin Lipset's *Agrarian Socialism*, a study of the CCF party in Saskatchewan. The study, subtitled "A Study in Political Sociology," was first published in 1950. In 1968, an "up-dated" edition was issued which includes not only a new introduction by the author but a series of essays by sociologists who examine the intervening years.

Agrarian Socialism is indispensable to an understanding of the CCF movement. Lipset, a sociologist, places the emphasis in the work on such matters as class, class organization, social and economic status, social change, the relationship between a political party and social structure, and how the CCF involved the people of Saskatchewan in direct political action to an extent unknown elsewhere in North America.

The rise of the CCF is placed within the context of North American agrarian protest—the reaction of farmers to economic ills, the co-operative movement and the shift to political action during the depression of the 1930s. Lipset attributes the success of the party in the provincial election of 1944 to a tradition of co-operation in the agricultural community, the instability of the wheat economy, the homogeneity of the social and economic structure of Saskatchewan society and the failure of the traditional parties to provide leadership during the depression years.

He notes that the doctrinaire socialist position of the party (e.g., the nationalization of land), was qualified as the party approached success and that many compromises were made once it was in office. In a broader context he raises such questions as why Canada has supported a large number of third-party movements as compared to the United States and why a socialist party flourished in Canada and not in the United States.

The general reader may be disturbed by the sociological "language" and the inclusion of sociological statistics, and wish that more attention had been paid to individuals prominent in the movement. But he should keep in mind the author's frame of reference as a sociologist.

SUMMARY BIBLIOGRAPHY
General

Hill, Douglas. *The Opening of the Canadian West.* London: Heinemann, 1967.
Kroetsch, Robert. *Alberta.* Toronto: Macmillan, 1968.

McCourt, Edward A. *Saskatchewan.* Toronto: Macmillan, 1968.

MacKay, Douglas. *The Honourable Company: A History of the Hudson's Bay Company.* Toronto: McClelland and Stewart, 1936. 2nd ed. 1949.

Morton, William Lewis. *Manitoba, a History.* Toronto: University of Toronto Press, 1957. 2nd ed. 1967.

Ormsby, Margaret Anchoretta. *British Columbia: A History.* Toronto: Macmillan, 1958.

Rich, Edwin Ernest. *The Fur Trade and the Northwest to 1857.* Toronto: McClelland and Stewart, 1967.

Stanley, George Francis Gilman. *The Birth of Western Canada: A History of the Riel Rebellions.* Toronto: University of Toronto Press, 1961.

———. *Louis Riel.* Toronto: Ryerson, 1963.

Wright, James Frederick Church. *Saskatchewan, the History of a Province.* Toronto: McClelland and Stewart, 1955.

Young, Walter D. *Democracy and Discontent: Progressivism, Socialism and Social Credit in the Canadian West.* Toronto: Ryerson, 1969.

Advanced

Irving, John A. *The Social Credit Movement in Alberta.* Toronto: University of Toronto Press, 1959.

Morton, Arthur Silver. *A History of the Canadian West to 1870-71, Being a History of Rupert's Land (The Hudson's Bay Company's Territory) and of the North-West Territory (Including the Pacific Slope).* London: Thomas Nelson, 1939.

Morton, William Lewis. *The Progressive Party in Canada.* Toronto: University of Toronto Press, 1950.

Rich, Edwin Ernest. *The History of the Hudson's Bay Company 1670-1870.* New ed. 3 vols. Toronto: McClelland and Stewart, 1960.

Professional

Lipset, Seymour Martin. *Agrarian Socialism. The Cooperative Commonwealth Federation in Saskatchewan: A Study in Political Sociology.* Berkeley:

University of California Press, 1950. Paper ed. New York: Doubleday, Anchor Books, 1968.

Bibliographies

Peel, Bruce Braden. *A Bibliography of the Prairie Provinces to 1953*. Toronto: University of Toronto Press, 1956. *Supplement* (1963).

A Bibliography of British Columbia. Victoria: University of Victoria Social Sciences Research Centre. Vol. 1, *Laying the Foundations 1849-1899*, by Barbara J. Lowther (1968). Vol. 2, *Navigations, Traffiques and Discoveries, 1774-1848*, by G. M. Strathern (1970).

The Atlantic Provinces:
History and Politics
George Rawlyk

*Currently working on a major research project dealing
with Canadian Maritime views of the US, 1763-1896,
George A. Rawlyk is professor of history at Queen's
University in Kingston.*

For many Canadians the Atlantic region remains an
anachronistic backwater of political, social and cultural
despair. Furthermore, according to the high priests of
the so-called Upper Canadian historical and political
tradition, the main thrust of Canadian development has
owed little, if anything, to events or persons in the four
Atlantic provinces. But despite the largely negative contemporary stereotype and the profound impact the
authorized version of the Canadian past has had in textbooks and the classroom, it should be realized that in
terms of scholarly output, the Atlantic area is definitely
not a backwater. The rich, historical heritage of New
Brunswick, Nova Scotia, Prince Edward Island and
Newfoundland has spun off, especially during recent
years, an increasingly assertive and sophisticated written
record.

Dalton Camp's *Gentlemen, Players and Politicians*,
for example, is probably the best piece of autobiographical writing ever published about Canadian politics.
This superb volume deals with Camp's fascinating
political career in the Atlantic region. It is one of those
rare books that is impossible to put down once begun
and one that has as much interest for the ordinary
reader as it does for the academic specialist. Superbly
written, *Gentlemen, Players and Politicians* is also filled
with perceptive insights about the Maritime mind and
the almost bizarre political culture of New Brunswick,
in particular, and the Atlantic provinces in general.
Camp describes his own political conversion and in the
process is devastatingly critical of the Liberals he once

adored. He then goes on to discuss, in often cutting yet humorous fashion, his own crucial role in pumping life and sophistication, especially during the 1950s, into the Progressive Conservative party. Camp's book should be required reading for all those Canadians interested in what really goes on in provincial and federal politics.

There is another fascinating account of contemporary political life in the Atlantic area; it is Richard Gwyn's *Smallwood: The Unlikely Revolutionary.* It is a sympathetic critical biography of a living father of Confederation. Smallwood began his career as an ardent Socialist propagandist. Gradually his ideological commitment, however, was neutralized by the hard, practical realities of Newfoundland existence. His leadership of the Confederation movement in the island catapulted him to provincial political power in 1949 when Newfoundland became Canada's tenth province. In power, he ruled his province like a Byzantine despot. He destroyed his enemies and blatantly used patronage to reward his friends. In a very real sense, Joey Smallwood was Newfoundland personified. Gwyn tries very hard to come to grips with Smallwood's complex personality and the reasons for his amazing political success. Gwyn's biography is gracefully written, well organized and often shrewdly penetrating. It casts a great deal of light on Newfoundland political development in the twentieth century.

Further background material for the political life of New Brunswick and Newfoundland may be found in two somewhat more specialized books. H. G. Thorburn's *Politics in New Brunswick* provides a straightforward description and analysis of what the author calls "the political dynamics of New Brunswick." In S. J. R. Noel's recently published *Politics in Newfoundland,* a noteworthy attempt is made to understand the existing political culture of the island by examining its often turbulent pre-Confederation political past.

The other two Atlantic provinces have also received more than adequate treatment from two leading political scientists. Frank MacKinnon's *The Government of Prince Edward Island* is a detailed study of how the tiny colony-province has conducted its governmental affairs. This book is not easy reading for the non-specialist. Nevertheless, it does have a tremendous volume of valuable material about the island crammed into its three hundred and fifty pages of text. Professor J. M. Beck's *The Government of Nova Scotia* should have a somewhat wider appeal. It is the one available general survey, not only of Nova Scotia politics but also of Nova Scotia political history. Beck is really a political historian. He knows his twentieth century Nova Scotia better than any other political scientist and he certainly knows more about nineteenth century Nova Scotia history than does any Canadian historian. *The Government of Nova Scotia* is an indispensable book for anybody interested in Nova Scotia history or politics. It is written in clear, uncomplicated and economic prose, and is extremely well organized. Beck's book has not received the attention it merits.

In terms of the historiography of the Atlantic provinces, what is most striking is the initial absence of any book-length studies specifically dealing with the post-Confederation period. But for the earlier period, for the golden age of "wooden ships and iron men," there are a number of valuable studies. Without question, the two most important and influential are J. B. Brebner's *New England's Outpost* and his *The Neutral Yankees of Nova Scotia.* In the former, Brebner's major concern was to explain, as he cogently puts it, how and why "New England . . . stimulated and carried out the expulsion of the Acadians in 1755." He carefully traces New England's special relationship with Acadia, a relationship forged over one hundred years of continuous contact. In his *Neutral Yankees,* Brebner carries his study of Nova Scotia's history up to the end of the American Revolution. It is primarily a book about why Nova Scotia did not join the revolution. For Brebner, the "Yankees," those thousands of New Englanders who had emigrated to Nova Scotia in the 1760s to replace the Acadians, were compelled by force of circumstances to walk the knife edge of neutrality during the revolutionary years. Obsessed with his "neutrality thesis,"

Brebner tends to view all events in pre-1755 New England-Nova Scotia (Acadia) relations as pointing inevitably to the expulsion; then he throws the strait-jacket of neutrality forward, from his location in time in 1755, to catch all the Nova Scotia residents during the revolutionary crisis. Some recent research has brought the viability of Brebner's neutrality thesis into question. But, for the vast majority of historians, his brilliant treatment of pre-Loyalist Acadia-Nova Scotia remains what has been called the "classic and satisfactory" interpretation.

Brebner's work has been assiduously carried on by W. S. MacNutt. His *The Atlantic Provinces: The Emergence of Colonial Society, 1712-1857* is an ambitious attempt to present a sophisticated historical synthesis of the entire Atlantic region. What is remarkable is that Professor MacNutt has been able to impose some kind of meaningful overview on the historical development of four quite different and distinctive colonial societies. He was required to cram into one volume what should have been contained in at least three or four. MacNutt's *Atlantic Provinces* is an excellent starting point for anyone wishing to get a general picture of the history of the Atlantic region for the 1712 to 1857 period. For a fuller treatment of the New Brunswick scene, MacNutt's *New Brunswick a History: 1784-1867* should be consulted. Other more specialized and somewhat revisionist studies concerned with the pre-Confederation period are Gordon Stewart and George Rawlyk, *"A People Highly Favoured of God": The Nova Scotia Yankees and the American Revolution;* G. Gunn, *The Political History of Newfoundland, 1832-1864;* J. M. Beck's sympathetic reassessment of Joseph Howe in *Joseph Howe: Voice of Nova Scotia;* P. B. Waite, *The Life and Times of Confederation;* and A. H. Clark, *Acadia: The Geography of Early Nova Scotia to 1760.*

Professor A. H. Clark, a distinguished historical geographer, has also written an ambitious and penetrating analysis of the development of Prince Edward Island. His *Three Centuries and the Island* is a sensitive piece of scholarship blending together the different approaches of the geographer and the historian. His book is beautifully illustrated and is written in such a way as to appeal as much to the layman as to the specialist. About the only other useful study devoted solely to the island is F. W. P. Bolger's well-researched *Prince Edward Island and Confederation 1863-1873*.

In C. W. Dunn, *Highland Settler: A Portrait of the Scottish Gael in Nova Scotia*, imaginative use has been made of literary evidence as well as oral interviews to try to come to grips with the Scots fact in Nova Scotia. It is often forgotten how significant the Celtic influence was on the historical evolution of Nova Scotia. This book is obviously a labour of love and should appeal to more than just the legion of professional Scots who live in various regions of Canada. *Highland Settler* is both a scholarly and a popular piece of writing.

Recently, an attempt was made to bring together in one volume some of the more important articles written about the history of the Atlantic provinces. It was felt that such a collection was necessary because so many of these studies have been buried in periodicals few people, especially non-academics, ever read. In G. A. Rawlyk's *Historical Essays on the Atlantic Provinces* are to be found fourteen key articles in addition to a useful select bibliography on the history of the region. Other more detailed bibliographies are to be found in MacNutt's *The Atlantic Provinces* and Clark's *Acadia*.

In conclusion, a few other books that should be mentioned as being quite useful and rather illuminating have been noted in a supplementary reading list following the bibliography.

SUMMARY BIBLIOGRAPHY
General

Camp, Dalton. *Gentlemen, Players and Politicians.* Toronto: McClelland and Stewart, 1970.

Dunn, C. W. *Highland Settler: A Portrait of the Scottish Gael in Nova Scotia.* Toronto: University of Toronto Press, 1953.

Gwyn, Richard. *Smallwood: The Unlikely Revolutionary.* Toronto: McClelland and Stewart, 1968.

Advanced

Beck, J. M. *The Government of Nova Scotia.* Toronto: University of Toronto Press, 1957.
———. *Joseph Howe: Voice of Nova Scotia.* Toronto: McClelland and Stewart, 1964.
Bolger, F. W. P. *Prince Edward Island and Confederation 1863-1873.* Charlottetown: St. Dunstan's University Press, 1964.
Brebner, J. B. *The Neutral Yankees of Nova Scotia.* Ed. W. S. MacNutt. Toronto: McClelland and Stewart, 1969.
———. *New England's Outpost.* New York: Columbia University Press, 1927.
Clark, A. H. *Acadia: The Geography of Early Nova Scotia to 1760.* Madison: University of Wisconsin Press, 1969.
———. *Three Centuries and the Island.* Toronto: University of Toronto Press, 1959.
Gunn, G. *The Political History of Newfoundland, 1832-1864.* Toronto: University of Toronto Press, 1967.
MacKinnon, F. *The Government of Prince Edward Island.* Toronto: University of Toronto Press, 1951.
MacNutt, W. S. *The Atlantic Provinces: The Emergence of Colonial Society, 1712-1857.* Toronto: McClelland and Stewart, 1965.
———. *New Brunswick a History: 1784-1867.* Toronto: Macmillan, 1963.
Noel, S. J. R. *Politics in Newfoundland.* Toronto: University of Toronto Press, 1971.
Rawlyk, G. A., ed. *Historical Essays on the Atlantic Provinces.* Toronto: McClelland and Stewart, 1967.
Stewart, G., and G. A. Rawlyk. *"A People Highly Favoured of God": The Nova Scotia Yankees and the American Revolution.* Toronto: Macmillan, 1972.
Thorburn, H. *Politics in New Brunswick.* Toronto: University of Toronto Press, 1961.

Waite, P. B. *The Life and Times of Confederation 1864-1867.* Toronto: University of Toronto Press, 1962.

Supplementary Reading List

Armstrong, M. W. *The Great Awakening in Nova Scotia 1776-1809.* Hartford: American Society of Church History, 1948.

Bell, W. *The "Foreign Protestants" and the Settlement of Nova Scotia.* Toronto: University of Toronto Press, 1961.

Bumsted, J. M. *Henry Alline.* Toronto: University of Toronto Press, 1971.

Fingard, J. *The Anglican Design in Loyalist Nova Scotia, 1783-1816.* London: SPCK, 1972.

Harvey, D. C. *The French Régime in Prince Edward Island.* New Haven: Yale University Press, 1926.

MacNaughton, K. F. C. *The Development of the Theory and Practice of Education in New Brunswick 1784-1900.* Fredericton: University of New Brunswick Press, 1947.

Rawlyk, G. A., and Ruth Hafter. *Acadian Education in Nova Scotia: An Historical Survey.* Ottawa, 1971.

Whitelaw, W. M. *The Maritimes and Canada before Confederation.* Toronto: Oxford University Press, 1967.

Wright, E. C. *The Loyalists of New Brunswick.* Fredericton, 1955.

The North
Trevor Lloyd

Trevor Lloyd has travelled widely in Scandinavia, the USSR, Greenland, Alaska and northern Canada, and has served the Canadian government as consul to Greenland and as chief of its Geographical Bureau. He is professor of human geography at McGill University.

From schools and universities, public libraries and business offices, comes a rising demand for information about northern Canada. This is in part because the discovery of oil and gas in the North seems at long last to promise the rich rewards that have been sought there since the voyages of Martin Frobisher four hundred years ago. More important is recognition that Canada now has the manpower, the wealth and the technical capacity to absorb the North as it did the prairies fifty years ago. To books recording how explorers from elsewhere pieced together the map of far northern North America can now be added those recounting the exploits of Canadians. Northern books are increasingly being published in Canada. Equally encouraging is the growing practice of reissuing, usually in facsimile, of classics of the North, until now too high priced to continue in general circulation. Eventually there will be a larger market for books within the North itself, as there now is among the growing number of Canadians who have been there as government officials, school teachers, field scientists or tourists.

There is no readily available listing of works exclusively on northern Canada, but there is the magnificent *Arctic Bibliography* covering the whole of the world's northlands, on all subjects, in all languages. For this we must thank the foresight of the Arctic Institute of North America, which more than twenty years ago assembled a team of librarians and linguists and scratched around for the financial support that has now produced fifteen volumes, with others to appear year by year. The most accessible current listing of books—again not limited to the Canadian Arctic—is the periodical accession list of the Arctic Institute library in Montreal, available through subscription. The library also issues briefer lists of Arctic books suitable for school and other small libraries and for the general reader.

If only because of the preponderant share that government activities take in northern affairs, one would expect a steady flow of good reading from the several departments concerned. Traditionally their publications have tended to be of the blue-book type, written and printed as required by the statutes rather than to meet the needs of a growing reading public. Having for some years published an admirable periodical, *North,* the Department of Indian Affairs and Northern Development could usefully encourage the future publication of books to include the geography (encompassing all aspects of the environment), economic activities, the residents and their daily lives, the social services, transportation and the rest, together with handbooks of the regions into which the enormous area naturally falls. Volumes already exist (and very good too) to enable ships to reach safe harbour there (*The Arctic Pilot),* and for those using aircraft. The government's comprehensive store of information and its broad range of expertise should now be reaching the citizen at large in well-written and attractively published volumes, as is the case in other northern lands, including Greenland and the USSR.

Now as to what is already available. Much Canadian writing on the North is relatively new. Most of the expedition books and many of the earlier historical studies originated in Britain or the United States. Much of the exploration, in the traditional sense, was over before Canadians became active in the North. Among the most prolific of northern explorer-authors during the present century was Vilhjalmur Stefansson who, although born in Canada, and here during the years of his active field work, was a resident of New York and published there. Yet he thought of himself—at least in his Arctic writing—as a Canadian, and so one of his best-known books is described below.

There is a considerable literature about the native peoples of the North—particularly the Eskimos. Some books have been written by formally trained anthropologists, others by residents of the North—missionaries, school teachers or traders—and in recent years, by a few Eskimos themselves. The resurgence of folk art among the Eskimos has also led to several excellent books. Canada is gradually contributing more or less technical works on the North—in specialized fields such as permafrost, geophysics, economics, physical geography, oceanography, surveying and so on. This suggests that there is an increasing need for such works, and that we now have the specialists capable of carrying out not only the original research but also of writing interestingly about it.

The books that are discussed below have been chosen to meet some of the needs mentioned. They are not selected as best sellers or because they have been put together by popular authors, sensitively aware of a rising market for northern material. The list is intentionally short on history, since this is also discussed elsewhere. There are no examples of the memoirs that have been written by former northern residents, be they bush pilots, bishops or administrators. I have also omitted accounts written by instant experts who have looked in on the North hurriedly in the intervals of a busy career in the south. Such are often interesting, but usually ephemeral.

The Land of the Long Day was the title of a memorable film of Eskimo life issued in the nineteen fifties by the National Film Board of Canada. Doug Wilkinson, author of the book of the same name, made that film. To do so he travelled widely in the eastern Arctic. Now, many books, films and photographs later he is a resident of Yellowknife, NWT. *The Land of the Long Day* is illustrated with coloured and black-and-white photographs, and has a serviceable map. Although first issued seventeen years ago, it remains one of the very best accounts of Eskimo life as it existed in the period of transition between the real, nomadic society that passed with the arrival of the trader, and the present-day, post-DEW Line, proto-urban existence that lingers on outside the larger settlements. Wilkinson had been in the Arctic many times in search of material for his films when he became convinced that Canada was failing to devise adequate policies concerning the future of the Eskimos, mainly because of simple ignorance of their way of life, desires and capabilities. So, with a grant from the Arctic Institute, he set off to northern Baffin Island to spend a whole year with a small Eskimo group. Near Pond Inlet he already had a friend, Idlouk, who provided the link he needed with native family life. This book was the outcome. It follows the changing seasons—travel by dogsled, seal hunting, whaling, life in tent and snow house, the soggy misery of break-up and the long bright days of the following summer. Wilkinson weaves into the later chapters his views on the changing needs of the Eskimos, and on policies that could avoid creation of a group of second-class citizens, which he saw as the inevitable outcome of what was going on. Since 1955 there have been dramatic changes, and Doug Wilkinson has been an influence in bringing them about.

Fred Bruemmer's *Seasons of the Eskimo, a Vanishing Way of Life* is, interestingly enough, almost a companion volume to *The Land of the Long Day*, since it is also the work of a professional photographer thoroughly familiar with the Canadian eastern Arctic. It sets out to describe what remained of the traditional Eskimo way of life in 1969. No attempt is made to debate the pros and cons of the rapidly changing Northland, nor to argue for this or that administrative policy. This is a book of photographs with sufficient authoritative text to give the general reader some understanding of how the Eskimo held on to life, not grimly but cheerfully, on the very edge of the liveable world. The four seasons, beginning with winter, are the theme of the photographs, many of them in colour. Bruemmer's large-format, marvellously printed volume will serve as a permanent record of the land of the long day as it drew to its close.

Now that Eskimo children are passing through the northern school system and into adult life, we can hope for Arctic literature from the typewriters of northerners themselves—as has long been the case on the other side of Davis Strait in Greenland. One trouble is that the more facile the young Canadian Eskimo becomes at expressing himself in English, the less he knows and understands about his own people. Fortunately *I, Nuligak* was written before the "uniformitarianism" of the public school system had obliterated the folk recollections of one Eskimo from the western Arctic. Nuligak was born in the Mackenzie Delta area in 1895, so that he was eleven years of age when Stefansson first reached there and Amundsen went through the Northwest Passage. While the San Francisco whalers had already ravaged the north coast of Alaska, the Mackenzie was near the easternmost extremity of their travels and Eskimo life was thus still comparatively unaffected. The original text of *I, Nuligak* was written in Eskimo, largely in pencil. It has been translated with great care by Maurice Metayer, and illustrations have been drawn by the Eskimo Ekootak. The author's recollections begin with his childhood, when he was orphaned and began drifting from family to family. Fortunately he learned to read and write English from an early missionary, but formal schooling was out of the question in those days. Nuligak's memoirs are a mixture of incidents during his long life—hunting at all seasons, long-distance travelling, contacts with traders and others from the outside, together with recollections of tales heard during the long winter nights in the igloo and some incidents about the nineteenth century explorers, passed along by his elders. This is as close to an early Eskimo autobiography as we can expect to get. It also illustrates clearly the problems of translating from Eskimo with its unfamiliar construction and alien manner of thought.

The new North, which still retains some superficial aspects of the old Eskimo ways but is closer to the icebreaker, the skidoo, the radio and aeroplane than to the dog-drawn komatik or the kayak, is well presented in a volume in the Story of Canada series. Written by R.

A. J. Phillips and well illustrated, *The Story of the Yukon and Northwest Territories* provides a summary of the modern Northland in a format well suited to school use. The concluding pages discuss the direction in which northern Canada is likely to evolve, concluding that minerals will provide most of the economic base, that the native peoples will take an increasingly active part in the region's affairs and that the Canadian mosaic of the south will eventually extend throughout the Northland.

Tourism offers, in the opinion of some, a quick and relatively painless route to wealth for the North, and this has not been overlooked by the planners of the series, The Traveller's Canada. Edward McCourt's volume, *The Yukon and Northwest Territories,* is intended for both real and armchair voyagers, and achieves its purpose without becoming a guidebook of the Baedeker sort. Recognizing the geographical distinctiveness of the two territories he covers, the author makes no attempt to merge them. The Yukon is covered in the first one hundred and forty pages and the Northwest Territories in the following seventy-five. There are several appendices on source materials and on the practicalities of northern travel. The section on the Yukon is reasonably comprehensive, but that on the Northwest Territories, no doubt wisely in the light of still-limited facilities for moving around easily or economically, is restricted to the mainland west of Hudson's Bay, the part of the Northland that is reached by way of Edmonton and Yellowknife.

The books mentioned so far have been judged to be within the range of interest of the general reader, without specialized interest in the North. The next group, while still having broad appeal, penetrates rather deeper and should appeal to those with more specialized interests.

In the Royal Ontario Museum is a collection of Eskimo material made by Stefansson during his first eighteen-month visit to the Arctic in 1906. Busy with subsequent and more wide-ranging exploration, he did not complete a book on that first expedition until fifteen years after his return. Less well known than *The Friendly Arctic* and *My Life with the Eskimos, Hunters of the Great North* is nevertheless in some ways his best book because it records his initial contacts with Eskimos who were following their traditional way of life. While being an account of his experiences along the western Arctic coast and in nearby Alaska, unlike the typical expedition account this narrative pauses to introduce detailed and always vivid scenes of Eskimo daily life— hunting caribou, sealing, pursuing polar bears, constructing igloos and getting accustomed to living as an Eskimo on a diet of frozen fish.

The astonishing present-day development of Eskimo art is sometimes thought of as an unusually successful winter-works program devised to occupy the Arctic unemployed. As the Stefansson material demonstrates, traditional handicrafts have long existed among the Eskimos, and this is re-emphasized from the other side of the continent by the Flaherty collection, which is displayed in Carpenter, Varley and Flaherty's *Eskimo.* This is an "art book" but an unusual one. Robert Flaherty travelled widely in Ungava more than fifty years ago, mapping minerals, and along the way collected Eskimo craftwork, much of it carved from walrus ivory. Edmund Carpenter, the anthropologist, has written a text discussing the Flaherty collection and also the paintings and sketches made by Frederick Varley on his visit to the eastern Arctic in the 1930s. The text also enlarges on the unusual manual aptitude of the Eskimos and the space concepts that enabled them to travel over apparently untracked wilderness. The continuity of Eskimo art is well demonstrated by *Inunnit,* a book about the art of the Canadian Eskimos put together by W. T. Larmour for publication by the Department of Indian Affairs and Northern Development. Prepared in both French and English texts, the bulk of the volume is occupied by reproductions of contemporary Eskimo prints and photographs of carvings. While some of the techniques employed (such as printing from stone blocks) are new to the Eskimos, the themes are traditional, and very clearly linked to the collections of

Flaherty and Stefansson.

As with *Inunnit,* the federal government has occasionally published books about the North. Certainly the most successful ones are a pair of colourfully bound handbooks that summarize the results of the many scientific inquiries into the North since the Second World War. *The Unbelievable Land* and *People of Light and Dark* were in a sense thrust on the government by the CBC, which had organized two series of broadcast talks directed to northern residents. From recordings the editors assembled almost fifty sections, each a few pages long, concerning permafrost, butterflies, beetles and the historical, social and human state of affairs in the Arctic. Well illustrated, these two small volumes could serve as patterns for a continuing series on northern Canada, well suited to schools, universities and the public at large.

A most useful device for introducing present-day readers to the reports of early explorers is to combine extracts from the original texts with editorial continuity. Fairley's *Sverdrup's Arctic Adventures* and Paul Nanton's *Arctic Breakthrough* both do this successfully. The first introduces Canadians, perhaps for the first time, to the Norwegian expedition that seventy years ago put on the map many of the far northern islands now being explored for oil and gas. Sverdrup, a former companion of Nansen, carried through a four-year program of exploration with complete success and with none of the tragedy that in those days seemed to accompany Arctic exploration. After reading Fairley's volume many will want to go back to Sverdrup's original book, *New Land.* Nanton, who has employed a similar technique with the three expeditions of Franklin, rightly focuses on the first two, which travelled overland from eastern Canada to the coast of the western Arctic. The book succeeds in retaining the flavour of the original writing without the sometimes tedious and rather heavy-footed naval style of the original. Young Canadians—not least those living in Yellowknife and other modern communities along Franklin's routes—are likely to discover that as history, the Arctic is a good deal more exciting than ploughing through the clauses of the British North America Act!

Canada's Changing North is one of the excellent Carleton Library series of paperbacks. William C. Wonders has assembled about forty short papers which he has grouped together in eight sections. The eleven that deal with history cover everything from the Vinland voyages to Plaisted's trip to the North Pole by skidoo. Other sections cover the northern environment, native peoples, economic resources, transportation and communication, northern settlements and finally, problems of the North. There are excellent maps. All that is missing is an annotated bibliography on northern Canada. This is an admirable little volume, certain to sell very well for use in schools and universities and, if adequately distributed, also to the general public.

Canada had to wait until its Centennial and for the fortunate coincidence of a northern administrator who could also write readable prose, for its first comprehensive book on the North. R. A. J. Phillips's *Canada's North* provides in fifteen chapters, with maps and excellent photographs, a readable, comprehensive and accurate view of the forty per cent of the country that lies north of the sixtieth parallel of latitude. In addition the author draws comparison with similar parts of the Soviet Union, some of which he has visited. Here is geography, history, science, art, literature and social problem solving. The final chapter, "The Still Point," is a realistic appraisal of the successes and failures of Canada's twenty-five-year northern-development programs. On the whole the balance is positive, with the people of the North now in a better position to influence their own destiny.

Canada's North would be an appropriate book with which to end this listing, but there needs to be some mention of more specialized volumes that reflect the intense effort that has gone into northern studies in the past few decades. Four only will be mentioned.

Diamond Jenness first went to the North with Stefansson in 1913. Fifty years later he was still studying and writing, and in his late seventies produced a notable set of five volumes on *Eskimo Administration* in North America, including Greenland. The book on Canada is far more than a discussion of administration, and had it been given a more glamorous title and bound in anything but blue paper, might have become more widely known. It begins more than two thousand years before Christ with the arrival of the Eskimos from Asia and ends with a program for modern Eskimo youth. Here is the depressingly long record of government maladministration and neglect down to the nineteen forties, but also the story of Eskimo education, the transformation of health services and the struggles to provide a viable northern economy. And through it all comes the astringent optimism of one of the few Canadians who has lived with and admired the old Eskimos and yet welcomed the adaptation of Eskimo society to an industrial age.

Professor J. B. Bird of McGill University has been engaged in northern field research in physical geography since the end of the Second World War. In *The Physiography of Arctic Canada* he has brought together the results of his own work, that of many of his students and assistants and contributions from government field scientists. This is probably the first summary of Arctic landscapes ever produced and provides a platform from which to launch new inquiries. Technically comprehensive, it is sufficiently readable to provide a background for those planning the resource development now going on in the North. K. J. Rea has provided the basic study of the economic evolution of the Yukon and Northwest Territories, *The Political Economy of the Canadian North*. It falls into three main sections—the privately sponsored economic activities, the various forms of publicly sponsored activity and the problems of territorial development. There is a useful summary of statistical data. The author concludes by suggesting that there is need in the North for some form of central development agency specially adapted to its regional needs.

Anyone who studies problems of the contemporary North sooner or later inquires about how things are ordered in the Soviet North and Greenland. It is towards the international relationships of northern Canada that *The Arctic Frontier,* edited by Dean R. St. J. Macdonald, is directed. In a dozen chapters, prepared by recognized specialists, most of them Canadians, the book provides a comparative study of northern Canada, the USSR and Alaska, with unfortunately only passing reference to Greenland. The Arctic Institute of North America and the Canadian Institute of International Affairs were jointly responsible for launching the studies that appear here and have succeeded in providing, well in advance, a manual that should be helpful during the current Soviet-Canadian rapprochement in the North and in the attempts being made to protect the northern environment by joint action among the polar powers. Several chapters are outstanding—particularly so Terence Armstrong's "The Administration of the Northern Peoples of the USSR" and Gordon W. Smith's "Sovereignty in the North."

SUMMARY BIBLIOGRAPHY
General

Bruemmer, Fred. *Seasons of the Eskimo, a Vanishing Way of Life.* Toronto: McClelland and Stewart, 1971.

McCourt, Edward. *The Yukon and Northwest Territories.* Toronto: Macmillan, 1969.

Metayer, Maurice, trans. *I, Nuligak.* Toronto: Peter Martin Associates, 1966.

Phillips, R. A. J. *The Story of the Yukon and Northwest Territories.* Toronto: McGraw-Hill, 1966.

Wilkinson, Doug. *The Land of the Long Day.* Toronto: Clarke, Irwin, 1955.

Advanced

Carpenter, E., F. Varley and R. Flaherty. *Eskimo.* Toronto: University of Toronto Press, 1959.

Fairley, T. C. *Sverdrup's Arctic Adventures.* Toronto: Longmans, Green, 1959.

Larmour, W. T. *Inunnit, the Art of the Canadian Eskimo.* Ottawa, 1967.

Nanton, Paul. *Arctic Breakthrough.* Toronto: Clarke, Irwin, 1970.

Phillips, R. A. J. *Canada's North.* Toronto: Macmillan, 1967.

Smith, I. Norman, ed. *The Unbelievable Land.* Ottawa, 1964.

Stefansson, Vilhjalmur. *Hunters of the Great North.* New York: Harcourt, Brace, 1922.

van Steensel, Maja, ed. *People of Light & Dark.* Ottawa, 1966.

Wonders, William C., ed. *Canada's Changing North.* Toronto: McClelland and Stewart, 1971.

Professional

Arctic Institute of North America. *Arctic Bibliography.* Ed. Marie Tremaine. Montreal: McGill University Press, 1953—.

Bird, J. Brian. *The Physiography of Arctic Canada.* Baltimore: Johns Hopkins, 1967.

Jenness, Diamond. *Eskimo Administration, Canada.* Montreal: Arctic Institute of North America, 1964.

Macdonald, R. St. J. *The Arctic Frontier.* Toronto: University of Toronto Press, 1966.

Rea, K. J. *The Political Economy of the Canadian North.* Toronto: University of Toronto Press, 1968.

Rural and Frontier Canada
Clara Thomas

*Clara McCandless Thomas, who has published four
critical and biographical studies of Canadian writers,
is professor of English at York University in Toronto
and president of the Association of Canadian University
Teachers of English, 1971-72.*

The nineteenth century air is full of the sound of voices,
a perfect babel of the records of preachers, teachers,
travellers and settlers in Canada. Before that, we hear
only the towering, lonely voices of the explorers, the fur
traders and the missionaries recording hardship and
endurance, awe, excitement and faith in their experience of a new, vast, uncharted land. *The Jesuit
Relations*, the journals of Samuel Hearne, David
Thompson and Alexander Henry and the *Voyages* of
Alexander Mackenzie are among the most impressive of
their accounts.

Salvation, O the Joyful Sound (1968) was the special
message of the itinerant Methodist ministers in
nineteenth century Canada and is the name of a collection of the writings of John Beulah Carroll, one of the
most eager and articulate among them. But during the
course of a century when even heaven came to seem like
another colony of the British Empire, "salvation" in a
variety of contexts was the tenor of many travellers' and
settlers' accounts of frontier Canada. In England there
was a rapidly increasing reading public, a constant
market for travel literature and a growing demand for
useful information about this land which offered so
much hope to the deprived of England and to the
destitute of Scotland and Ireland.

There were those like Anna Jameson who came to see
and tell, but not to stay in the new country. Mrs.
Jameson was the wife of the attorney general and first
vice-chancellor of the combined provinces. Long before

she came to Toronto in 1836 to visit her husband, she
was an indefatigable traveller and writer: her *Winter
Studies and Summer Rambles in Canada* (1838) combined keen, critical observation of society in Toronto,
"a fourth- or fifth-rate provincial city," with an out-
going enthusiasm for people and places that took her on
tour in the summer months across the province and up
the lakes to Sault Ste. Marie, farther than any white
woman had gone before her. Mrs. Jameson wrote her
experiences in the form of a journal addressed to a
friend at home, a device which gave a kind of narrative
and dramatic unity to her work; its main distinction,
however, is in the range and the authenticity of her
observations, recorded with precision, wit and enthusiasm, and in her evident ease—once she left Toronto—
with all kinds and degrees of people. A considerable
amount of *Summer Rambles* is given over to observations of the Indians, Indian lore and the relative position
of women and men (Mrs. Jameson was an early
feminist), all based in intelligent reading as well as on
her personal experiences. She knew how to make a good
book and she buttressed her own adventures with documentary material from both explorers and missionaries.

Today her analysis of the Upper Canadian political
situation in the months immediately preceding the
rebellion seems particularly apt: she had been in an
excellent post for observation and she had made the
most of her opportunity, her own intelligence and her
own experience. Above all, through all her work, there
runs the thread of a traveller's detachment: she enjoyed
tripping in the wilds, she was a brave woman, a competent writer and a trained observer—and she was not
going to stay!

Comparable in the breadth of his background and in
his literary skill was William "Tiger" Dunlop, warden of
the forests for the Canada Company and master of
Gairbraid, in Goderich. Dunlop had been in Canada
during the War of 1812 as a medical officer; two
decades later he became a settler and administrator in
Upper Canada. In between he had been an army doctor
and journalist in India and one of the distinguished

group of witty, radical literary men who were associated with John Wilson, the "Christopher North" of *Blackwood's* magazine. Dunlop's *Recollections of the American War, 1812-1814* and his *Statistical Sketches of Upper Canada* (1832), his highly idiosyncratic manual for immigrants, are published together in *Tiger Dunlop's Upper Canada* (1967). The former work conveys some of the grim aura of war and the confusion of this particular frontier war, but more of Dunlop's own practicality and zest for adventure. The latter was written under a nom de plume—"A Backwoodsman"— and partly as a corrective to the shockingly misleading information handed out by land speculators to gullible prospective immigrants; but more than that, it combines the experience, the advice, the enthusiasm and the cautionary tales of a highly individualistic adventuring Scot. No aspect of the land was without colour for Dunlop—none was without hardship—but every facet of Canada was to him both challenge and satisfaction. He made legends of the events of his own life, whether it be the taming of the tiger in Bengal, or of the forests of Upper Canada, or the dispensing of hard-drinking hospitality at Gairbraid where his liquor decanters, the "Twelve Apostles," were drained at every sitting of his rousing, all-male dinner parties. He recognized in Canada a hope—often the only hope—for a multitude of men and women, and he had patience with nothing less than the will to work with unremitting common sense and effort towards a goal that he was sure could finally be won. Furthermore, in his robust world, the land was a sportsman's paradise and every man must surely glory in such bounty.

That same feeling is basic to *Forest Scenes and Incidents in the Wilds of North America* (1838), Sir George Head's account of his winter travels from Halifax to Penetang. Head was an army officer and one of the first who wrote down a step-by-step journal of a trek of some twelve hundred miles across the great variety of land and waterway between the coast and Upper Canada. There is a strong Crusoe flavour in Head's account and in this aspect it is particularly fascinating. In fact, from the form and the tone of the work, one would speculate that some time between taking his trip and preparing his journal for publication, Head had taken Defoe for his model. He is the "hero-narrator," a solitary figure, self-sufficient and always alert to his circumstances and his opportunities; others who, from time to time, serve him or share his adventures are distanced and detached, as remote from his familiar companionship as Friday was to Crusoe. There is also in his attitude an amusing tone of calm acceptance of the vast and various land he travelled through as a heaven-ordained game preserve—a kind of hunter's Eden specially preserved and offered by a benign providence for the exercise of his various skills by the British gentleman-officer.

The Crusoe theme runs through much of this literature: Samuel Strickland's *Twenty-seven Years in Canada West* (1853) was written in recollection, a reconstruction of his youth, and published long after Strickland's first experiences as a settler. It is an account of adventure, high spirits and hardship, but more important, of progress and success for a young man with no prospects otherwise, who broke land and founded a family, moving from settling to the establishment of a property in a new land. Anna Jameson and George Head could and did retain the detachment of travellers; they looked upon the land as "Nature"—one with the eye of an artist, as Henry Schoolcraft said of Mrs. Jameson, and the other with the appraisal of a sportsman. But true settlers quickly developed a different and often ambivalent approach to the land. To them it was livelihood; survival was their first and basic challenge and after that they had to learn to make the land productive. Admiration, awe and fear—these were indulgences forbidden to the man or woman engaged in clearing and planting for subsistence.

Susanna Moodie, the sister of Samuel Strickland, would have been happy had she been able to remain detached, but she could not. She rhapsodized over the magnificence of Quebec's Citadel, but she was immediately confronted by the terrifying spectacle of the sober, serious immigrants she had travelled with, transformed into unrestrained "savages." These were the people she had to live among. The land, which she loved to see as romantically sublime or picturesque, became so many acres of bush to be cleared, crops to be planted, potatoes to be hoed. Had Susanna been free, as Anna Jameson was free, her account might very well have been very similar, for the Stricklands were a literary family, and before emigration Susanna had had a modest success in publication. She was an unwilling immigrant and an unremitting, regretful exile, but the experience of settling, of financial distress and social deprivation did enhance, or release, latent creative powers that she had never shown before. Consequently, her *Roughing It in the Bush* (1852), a series of sketches first begun for Mr. Lovell's *Literary Garland* of Montreal, became both financial succour and mental therapy for her. As a result, this work is a strange and haunting combination of observation, experience and dramatization. Susanna shows the fiction writer's impulse in every sketch: she is her own heroine, and while she insisted that she wrote only to warn other gentlefolk from emigrating to a land only fit for the rough, hardy lower classes, she inadvertently produced both far more and far less than such a warning. It is extremely doubtful that her work would have had any deterrent effect at all, but it is certain that it entertained and offended its readers then as much as it appeals now for its highly coloured dramatic reporting of one woman's experience. *Roughing It in the Bush* transcends yet complements Susanna's real life in which, in fact, she did survive, endure and found a family.

On the other hand, her sister, Catharine Parr Traill, who emigrated at the same time as Susanna, was perfectly suited to her life in Canada. Her letters to her mother, edited of intimacies, were published as *The Backwoods of Canada* (1836) at the same time that Susanna was beginning her passionate sketches. Nothing could contrast more basically than their attitudes—while Susanna's pillow was wet with tears at the thought of emigrating, Catharine Traill speaks with calm rationality of coming to Canada with her husband to establish a "landed property" to hand on to their children. While Susanna recorded shock and revulsion at her new compatriots, Catharine Traill gloried in her "Crusoe experience" and, in fact, later wrote a children's book called *Canadian Crusoes* (1852). Her acceptance and her tolerance are particularly demonstrated in this work, where she finally suggests the intermarrying of Scottish and French, English and Indian, as the solution for Canada's best future. "Nature" to her was neither the romantically picturesque and sublime nor the stubborn, unyielding land, but was truly, in its potential, a garden that would yield abundance in return for the knowledge of good husbandry which she proceeded to amass about it. Her *Studies of Plant Life in Cánada* (1885) and *Canadian Wild Flowers* (1869) brought her international recognition in the later nineteenth century, and if there was one of the swarm of manuals for emigrants that was likely to live up to its promise of instruction it must certainly have been her *Canadian Settler's Guide* (1855). This book is the classic of its kind, as distinctive for the style and tone that are all a part of the fabric of Catharine Traill's rational optimism, as for the variety and precision of its information and instruction.

Of the exiled Irish immigrants who so terrified and revolted Susanna Moodie, there are few written records. However, the *Journals of Mary O'Brien, 1828-1838* tell the story of one Irish girl whose high spirits, optimism and good humour speak for the experience of many others whose level of literacy made written records impossible (for the first generation at least).

When this group was recording the experiences of settlers in Upper Canada, the Rev. Thomas McCulloch in *The Stepsure Letters* (1860) and Thomas Chandler Haliburton in *The Clockmaker* (1836) were observing and recording the attitudes of the people of Nova Scotia and were, also, didactically bent on improving the society of the Maritimes. Haliburton is a second-generation Loyalist Tory gentleman who, like his great English eighteenth century forerunners, Addison and Steele, wrote to improve manners, morals and the general tenor of society in his time and place. In the process he created the character of Sam Slick, the Yankee clock peddler, the first and perhaps the most widely known and enduring of all our fictional characters. *The Stepsure Letters,* which first appeared fifteen years before Haliburton's sketches, are a series of shrewd and humorous essays in common sense, their central figure, Mephibosheth Stepsure, a shining example of a Canadian, nineteenth century self-made man. With a great measure of wit and colour they reflect the solid virtues of the Protestant work ethic—and a good deal of its corresponding limitation, its gracelessness and capacity for stifling the imagination and the heart.

The growth of Canada into an urban and business-oriented nation accelerated rapidly after Confederation. Samuel Thompson's *Reminiscences of a Canadian Pioneer for the Last Fifty Years* (1884) is a record of careful planning and financial success in Canada's rapidly growing Toronto, measured by a steady growth in possessions that was having its counterpart in the lives of Canadians in all the older provinces. But there was still the excitement of the western frontier, the immense burgeoning optimism of the immediate post-railway days, when G. M. Grant's *Ocean to Ocean* (1873) recorded his trans-Canada trip with Sandford Fleming in terms of excitement, adventure, opportunity, Canadian nationalism and a sense of a special Christian destiny within the empire for this new Dominion. Such also is the mood of *Lady Dufferin's Journals* (1891), an enthusiastic account of her life and many travels during the tenure of Lord Dufferin as governor general.

The nineteenth century was over before Canadian fiction writers turned from romance and adventure to recording in their novels the experience of life in this country. Then, in the introduction to *The Man from Glengarry* (1901), Ralph Connor wrote: "The solid forests of Glengarry have vanished, and with the forests the men who conquered them. The manner of life and the type of character to be seen in those early days have gone too, and forever. It is part of the purpose of this book to so picture these men and their time that they may not drop out of mind. The men are worth remembering." Connor's novel, Sarah Jeannette Duncan's *The Imperialist* (1904), Louis Hémon's *Maria Chapdelaine* (1914) and Stephen Leacock's *Sunshine Sketches of a Little Town* (1912) are our first great quartet of fictional commemorations, portraits of a young country and of the men and women who are, indeed, abundantly worth remembering.

SUMMARY BIBLIOGRAPHY
All are general.

Canadiana Reprint Series. Toronto: Coles.
> Dufferin and Ava, Harriet G. *My Canadian Journal* (1971).
> Grant, George M. *Ocean to Ocean* (1970).
> Head, George. *Forest Scenes and Incidents in the Wilds of North America* (1970).

Canadiana Reprint Series. Edmonton: Hurtig.
> Grant, George M. *Ocean to Ocean*. Introduction by Lewis H. Thomas. 1967.
> Hearne, Samuel. *A Journey from Prince of Wales' Fort in Hudson's Bay to the Northern Ocean*. Introduction by L. H. Neatby. 1970.
> Henry, Alexander. *Travels and Adventures*. Introduction by L. G. Thomas. 1969.
> Mackenzie, Alexander. *Voyages from Montreal . . . to the Frozen and Pacific Oceans in the years 1789 and 1793*. Introduction by Roy Daniells. 1971.
> Strickland, Samuel. *Twenty-seven Years in Canada West*. Introduction by Carl F. Klinck. 1970.

Carroll, John. *Salvation! O the Joyful Sound*. Ed. John W. Grant. Toronto: Oxford University Press, 1967.

Connor, Ralph. *The Man from Glengarry*. Introduction by S. Ross Beharriell. Toronto: McClelland and Stewart, New Canadian Library, 1960.

Duncan, Sarah Jeannette. *The Imperialist*. Introduction by Claude Bissell. Toronto: McClelland and Stewart, New Canadian Library, 1961.

Dunlop, William. *Tiger Dunlop's Upper Canada:* comprising *Recollections of the American War, 1812-1814* and *Statistical Sketches of Upper Canada for the uses of emigrants, by a Backwoodsman.* Introduction by Carl F. Klinck. Toronto: McClelland and Stewart, New Canadian Library, 1967.

Haliburton, Thomas Chandler. *The Clockmaker.* Introduction by Robert L. McDougall. Toronto: McClelland and Stewart, New Canadian Library, 1958.

———. *The Sam Slick Anthology.* Toronto: Clarke, Irwin, 1959.

Hearne, Samuel. *A Journey to the Northern Ocean.* Ed. Richard Glover. Toronto: Macmillan, Pioneer Books, 1958.

Hémon, Louis. *Maria Chapdelaine.* Trans. W. H. Blake. Toronto: Macmillan, 1969.

Jameson, Anna B. *Winter Studies and Summer Rambles in Canada.* Introduction by Clara Thomas. Toronto: McClelland and Stewart, New Canadian Library, 1965.

Leacock, Stephen. *Sunshine Sketches of a Little Town.* Introduction by Malcolm Ross. Toronto: McClelland and Stewart, New Canadian Library, 1960.

McCulloch, Thomas. *The Stepsure Letters.* Introduction by Northrop Frye. Toronto: McClelland and Stewart, New Canadian Library, 1960.

Mealing, Stanley R., ed. *The Jesuit Relations and Allied Documents.* Toronto: McClelland and Stewart, Carleton Library, 1963.

Moodie, Susanna. *Roughing It in the Bush.* Introduction by Carl F. Klinck. Toronto: McClelland and Stewart, New Canadian Library, 1962.

———. *Life in the Clearings.* Ed. Robert L. McDougall. Toronto: Macmillan, Pioneer Books, 1959.

O'Brien, Mary. *The Journals of Mary O'Brien, 1828-1838.* Ed. Audrey Saunders Miller. Toronto: Macmillan, 1968.

Thompson, David. *Travels in Western North America 1784-1812.* Ed. Victor G. Hopwood. Toronto: Macmillan, 1971.

———. *History of the Late War between Great Britain and the United States of America.* New York: Johnson Reprint, 1966.

Thompson, Samuel. *Reminiscences of a Canadian Pioneer.* Toronto: McClelland and Stewart, 1968.

Traill, Catharine Parr. *The Backwoods of Canada.* Introduction by Clara Thomas. Toronto: McClelland and Stewart, New Canadian Library, 1969.

———. *A Canadian Settler's Guide.* Introduction by Clara Thomas. Toronto: McClelland and Stewart, New Canadian Library, 1969.

Supplementary Reading

Grove, Frederick Philip. *Fruits of the Earth.* Introduction by Malcolm Ross. Toronto: McClelland and Stewart, New Canadian Library, 1965.

———. *Settlers of the Marsh.* Introduction by Thomas Saunders. Toronto: McClelland and Stewart, New Canadian Library, 1965.

Thomas, Clara. *Love and Work Enough: The Life of Anna Jameson.* Toronto: University of Toronto Press, 1967.

———. *Margaret Laurence.* Toronto: McClelland and Stewart, Canadian Writers Series, 1969.

———. *Ryerson of Upper Canada.* Toronto: Ryerson, 1969.

2 Economics and Politics

Economic History
Mel Watkins

Melville H. Watkins is a member of the National Council of the New Democratic party and professor of political economy at the University of Toronto. He was chairman of the Pearson government's task force on the structure of Canadian industry and principal author of its 1968 report, Foreign Ownership and the Structure of Canadian Industry.

Economic history, meaning simply the history of the economy, has long been alive and well in Canada. As a recognized field of study, economic history emerged in Germany and England in the late nineteenth century in some part as a way to counter the abstractions of laissez-faire economics, and particularly the doctrine of free trade, with actual historical experience. With Canada committed from 1879 to a National Policy of high tariffs, economic history was more acceptable to the ruling establishment than economics proper. So it was that the first appointment to the chair in Political Economy at the University of Toronto was an economic historian, and that the habit caught on.

The bias paid off handsomely in the 1920s and 1930s in the powerful and prolific writings in Canadian economic history of Harold Innis. While his encyclopedic knowledge and cryptic style hardly make for easy reading, the serious student of Canadian economic history can begin nowhere else.

His two great classics are *The Cod Fisheries: The History of an International Economy* and *The Fur Trade in Canada: An Introduction to Canadian Economic History.* The titles reflect the focus on the commodity, or staple, as a unifying theme; the subtitles suggest the ambitiousness of the task that Innis set himself. In effect, these two books are the standard reference works for the pre-industrial history—maritime and continental—of what is now Canada.

Massive though these books are, they do not exhaust the essential Innis. Hardly an aspect of Canada's history escaped his pen, and after his death in 1952 his important essays in Canadian economic history were collected together in the one-volume *Essays in Canadian Economic History*. They sum to a persistent emphasis on Canada as a hinterland economy serving external metropoles and on the limitations of Canadian governments in alleviating this condition.

Innis's influence was pervasive and he cast a long shadow. As cases in point, take first textbooks and readers in Canadian economic history. The standard college textbook is *Canadian Economic History* by W. T. Easterbrook and Hugh G. J. Aitken. The alternating chapters on continental (fur) and maritime (cod) developments down through square timber to wheat are strictly in the Innisian tradition. Both authors have made important independent contributions to Canadian economic history and their combined effort is a mine of information that pulls together and synthesizes a large literature. In the nature of a text, however, the limitations of that literature are also unavoidably exposed, particularly in a generally unsatisfactory discussion of the post-World War I period when wheat loses its power to unify the economy on an east-west basis and no single staple dominates.

The only reader, again widely used in college courses, is the Carleton Library paperback *Approaches to Canadian Economic History* edited by W. T. Easterbrook and M. H. Watkins. Pride of place is given to the staples approach, with two excerpts from Innis. W. A. Mackintosh, a contemporary of Innis's at Queen's University and a co-founder of the staples approach, is represented by his path-breaking 1923 essay "Economic Factors in Canadian History." Economic analysis loomed larger in Mackintosh's writing than Innis's and this bias is reflected in two essays that appeared simultaneously in 1963 by M. H. Watkins and Gordon W. Bertram. Watkins rewrites the staples approach in the language of contemporary theory in international economics and economic development, while Bertram relates industrial development to the impact of the staples trades and provides thereby an important essay in the relatively neglected field of industrial history. Both conclude that the staples approach remains highly relevant to understanding past and present developments in the Canadian economy. Of the many studies done of the great staple trades, the editors reprint a monograph by the distinguished Queen's University historian, A. R. M. Lower, on "The Trade in Square Timber."

The remaining two-thirds of the reader includes essays on diverse themes: by Donald Creighton on merchant capitalism in the St. Lawrence in the 1830s, with particular reference to the rebellions; by Bray Hammond on pre-Confederation banking; by Hugh G. J. Aitken on the role of the state in Canada as a hinterland of successive empires; and by Vernon C. Fowke on the National Policy.

It is the view of at least one of the editors that the book needs revising by dropping some of the essays not cited here and adding such writings referred to below, as: Alfred Dubuc on the nature of Confederation and its consequences for Quebec; Bruce Archibald on the underdevelopment of the Atlantic provinces; W. T. Easterbrook's comparative analysis of Canadian and American economic development; H. C. Pentland on the origins of the Canadian working class; Stanley Ryerson's explicitly class analysis of St. Lawrence merchant capitalism; and excerpts from an unpublished manuscript, "Metropolis and Hinterland: Dialectics of Canadian Economic History," by R. T. Naylor.

The Canadian historian whose contribution to Canadian economic history ranks second only to Innis, and closely complements the latter, is Donald Creighton. The staple-producing economy is, in the nature of the case, characterized by the dominance of the export-import trade or by merchant capitalism. In *The Empire of the St. Lawrence*—first published in 1937 as *The Commercial Empire of the St. Lawrence 1760-1850*—Creighton shifts the focus from the commodity as unifying theme to the merchants as the dominant class. The approach risks lionizing the businessman, and the tendency is not always successfully resisted, but the book nevertheless provides an overview of economic development from the late eighteenth to mid-nineteenth century that is invaluable; one's major regret must be that it stops at 1850 and no other historian has been able to carry Creighton's theme forward in time.

Appearing since Creighton's book, and closely complementing the emphasis on merchant capitalism with an emphasis on finance capitalism, is a long chapter on British North America in the American Bray Hammond's masterful book *Banks and Politics in America from the Revolution to the Civil War;* the chapter is reprinted in full in Easterbrook and Watkins.

Like Innis, Creighton is also highly prolific. Though best known among historians and the general public as the biographer of Sir John A. Macdonald, economic historians would insist on the importance of his 1939 study for the Rowell-Sirois Commission on Dominion-Provincial Relations, *British North America at Confederation.* Creighton delineates a major but complicated issue, the role of the state or of government. He demonstrates that the BNA Act was fundamentally a document in public finance, and further enables us to see Confederation as a response to US aggressiveness and the emulation of the US frontier experience. The former theme is explicitly developed by Alfred Dubuc in the context of an insightful essay on the economic history of Quebec in Peter Russell's *Nationalism in Canada.* The latter theme is skillfully characterized as "defensive expansionism" in an excellent précis on the role of the state in Canadian economic growth by Hugh G. J. Aitken, reprinted in Easterbrook and Watkins.

Ranking high on any list of the founding fathers of Canadian economic history is W. A. Mackintosh. After his initial somewhat theoretical work on the nature of a pioneer or staple economy, Mackintosh joined Creighton as a researcher for the Rowell-Sirois commission, the last royal commission to generate fundamental work in economic history. His *The Economic Background of Dominion-Provincial Relations*, now available in Carleton Library paperback, is a comprehensive application of economic analysis to the period from Confederation to the Great Depression of the 1930s, and is particularly good on the spread effects of the wheat economy and the impact of the tariff.

No single issue in Canadian economic history has received more attention than the tariff. The best single monograph, putting the tariff in the broad context of the overall strategy of economic development and having the additional merit of offering a perspective from western Canada where the tariff's contributions are not so automatically assumed as in central Canada, is Vernon C. Fowke's *The National Policy and the Wheat Economy*. Fowke supplements Mackintosh's analysis on the nature of a pioneer economy, while providing an excellent introduction to the large literature on wheat marketing and an economic background for the equally large literature on agrarian protest movements. The concern with the National Policy leads Fowke into broader considerations of the role of the state in Canada, a theme made explicit in a 1952 essay, "The National Policy—Old and New," reprinted in Easterbrook and Watkins.

On the tariff proper, a stimulating and controversial book by John Dales, *The Protective Tariff in Canada's Development*, applies economic theory to the National Policy of 1879 and concludes that its result has been to create a poorer but larger Canada.

The Atlantic provinces, the other hinterland of Montreal-Toronto-Ottawa, have yet to produce a Fowke, but the recently issued paperback *Essays on the Left* contains a provocative essay by Bruce Archibald on the underdevelopment of the Atlantic provinces, consequent on their historic external domination.

The emphasis on Canada as the hinterland of empire has led, in spite of a relative neglect by Innis, to a concern with its most conspicuous dimension in the last century, the extent of foreign ownership and control.

The only comprehensive historical work is the 1936 volume *Canadian-American Industry: A Study in International Investment* by Herbert Marshall, Frank A. Southand and Kenneth W. Taylor. It stays close to the facts and figures and contains a wealth of information on individual industries and firms. Hugh G. J. Aitken offers a good and very readable statement of American investment in Canada, concentrating mostly on the resource industries in the 1950s, in his *American Capital and Canadian Resources.* Of a spate of contemporary literature, only Kari Levitt's *Silent Surrender,* with its focus on the multinational corporation and its impact on hinterland areas, sufficiently transcends narrow economic analysis to be useful to the economic historian, though her view of the historic tendency of the Canadian business class increasingly to emasculate itself awaits firm historical testing.

A focus on Canada in this century as the hinterland of the United States has resulted over the years in a vast outpouring of writing, little of it memorable, on Canadian-American relations. An exception is *Canadian-American Industry;* so too is Marcus L. Hansen and J. Bartlet Brebner, *The Mingling of the Canadian and American Peoples.* The titles suggest a continental bias that has more recently given way, particularly among younger scholars, to a focus on the Americanization of Canada. In a 1970 collection of essays edited by Ian Lumsden, *Close the 49th Parallel, etc.,* the emphasis is mostly contemporary, but there is a significant historical essay by Michael Bliss on the tariff and foreign ownership and a substantive historical dimension to a number of the essays, notably C. W. Gonick on foreign ownership, Daniel Drache on the Canadian bourgeoisie and Mel Watkins on Canadian economic thought.

The Canada-US dimension includes as well the possibility of comparative studies of the two countries. To the usual difficulties of writing good comparative history is added the particular problem posed in this case, at least for this century, of comparing a metropole with one of its own satellites. A serious attempt to work in this area has been made by W. T. Easterbrook in a number of essays in scholarly American journals.

Reference has already been made to the absence of any comprehensive overview of the history of the Canadian capitalist class since 1850, and particularly since 1867. For contemporary Canada, there is the pioneering sociological research of John Porter in *The Vertical Mosaic*, and the student of economic history will find many useful insights. Between Creighton and Porter lies a large historical gap only partially illuminated by a number of specialized monographs by economists on selected industries and the usual business histories by public-relations types. A neglected contribution to Canadian business history, about to be reissued, that corrects the latter bias, is the 1914 *History of Canadian Wealth* by the famous American muckraker, Gustavus Myers. As Myers makes clear, sophisticated discussions of the interrelationships of business and the state may merely mystify us by distracting our attention away from the straightforward day-in-and-day-out realities of corruption and the rip-off.

The staple trades, the business class, the state—what is missing so far is the working class. There are two comprehensive histories of Canadian trade unions, H. A. Logan's *Trade Unions in Canada* and Charles Lipton's *The Trade Union Movement of Canada;* the latter is the more lively and controversial. The broader and more complex history of the working class mostly awaits serious historical study; an important exception, though virtually inaccessible, is an unpublished doctoral thesis by Pentland précised in "The Development of a Capitalistic Labour Market in Canada" in the *Canadian Journal of Economics and Political Science,* November 1959.

A discussion of working-class history leads directly into a consideration of that small, but at this moment very vital, literature on Canadian economic history consciously written from a radical or class perspective. Pentland writes on the origins of the Canadian working class from a Marxist perspective. The historian who has done the most comprehensive writing within such a framework is Stanley Ryerson; his *Unequal Union* offers an alternative evaluation of Creighton's merchant capitalists and is essential reading on the economic basis of the relationship between English Canada and Quebec.

There is currently a new, indeed historically unparalleled, interest in Marxist studies among younger scholars. A book now in progress under the editorship of Gary Teeple will contain original essays on class and the national question in Canada. In particular, it will include an excerpt from an unpublished monograph by R. T. Naylor (which should eventually be issued as a book in its own right) which is a brilliant new overview of the nature of the hinterland bourgeoisie and the state in the context of changing varieties of imperialism. It decisively corrects the recent bias of the staples approach towards narrow economic analysis and gives a fresh dimension to Innis's work on the nature of a staple-producing economy and Creighton's on the nature of the Canadian business class. It promises, by distinguishing between merchant capitalism, finance capitalism and industrial capitalism, to initiate much-needed research on the fundamental question of the nature of Canadian capitalism, and thereby to permit of a new synthesis of the diverse existing literature on the triad of Canadian history—staples, the tariff and foreign ownership.

There is yet another dimension to radical history that is also just beginning to surface, and that is popular history. The most spectacular example is Léandre Bergeron's *Petit Manuel d'Histoire du Québec,* available in English translation as *The History of Quebec: A Patriote's Handbook.* English Canada has yet to find its Bergeron, but two short popular histories deal with the struggles of working people and are increasingly being used in high schools and colleges—*She Named It Canada (Because That's What It Was Called)* and *The People's History of Cape Breton.*

Economic history, particularly in the hands of Innis, has constituted the indigenous Canadian contribution to economics. Orthodox economic analysis, being narrow, conservative and Americanized, is today becoming irrelevant in Canada. The economic historians of a hinterland area, like Canada, are likely to be the salvation of economics in hinterland areas. Intellectual liberation and creativity contribute to liberation generally. That, plus their inherent interest, is sufficient reason to master these writings and create new ones.

SUMMARY BIBLIOGRAPHY
All are general.

Aitken, Hugh G. J. *American Capital and Canadian Resources.* Cambridge, Mass.: Harvard University Press, 1961.

Archibald, Bruce. "Atlantic Regional Underdevelopment and Socialism," in *Essays on the Left: Essays in Honour of T. C. Douglas,* ed. Laurier LaPierre et al. Toronto: McClelland and Stewart, 1971.

Bergeron, Léandre. *The History of Quebec: A Patriote's Handbook.* Toronto: New Canada Press, 1971.

Corrective Collective. *She Named It Canada (Because That's What It Was Called).* Vancouver, 1971.

Creighton, Donald G. *The Empire of the St. Lawrence.* Toronto: Macmillan, 1956.

———. *British North America at Confederation.* A study prepared for the Royal Commission on Dominion-Provincial Relations. Ottawa, 1939.

Dales, J. H. *The Protective Tariff in Canada's Development.* Toronto: University of Toronto Press, 1966.

Dubuc, Alfred. "The Decline of Confederation and the New Nationalism," in *Nationalism in Canada,* ed. Peter H. Russell. Toronto: McGraw-Hill, 1966.

Easterbrook, W. T., and Hugh G. J. Aitken. *Canadian Economic History.* Toronto: Macmillan, 1956.

Easterbrook, W. T., and M. H. Watkins, eds. *Approaches to Canadian Economic History.* Toronto: McClelland and Stewart, Carleton Library, 1967.

Fowke, Vernon C. *The National Policy and the Wheat Economy.* Toronto: University of Toronto Press, 1957.

Hansen, Marcus L., and J. Bartlet Brebner. *The Mingling of the Canadian and American Peoples.* Toronto: Ryerson, 1940. Vol. 1, *Historical.*

Innis, Harold A. *The Cod Fisheries: The History of an International Economy* (1940). 2nd ed. Toronto: University of Toronto Press, 1954.

———. *The Fur Trade in Canada: An Introduction to Canadian Economic History* (1930). 2nd ed. Toronto: University of Toronto Press, 1956.

———. *Essays in Canadian Economic History.* Edited by Mary Q. Innis. Toronto: University of Toronto Press, 1957.

Levitt, Kari. *Silent Surrender: The Multinational Corporation in Canada.* Toronto: Macmillan, 1970.

Lipton, Charles. *The Trade Union Movement of Canada, 1827-1959.* 2nd ed. Montreal: Canadian Social Publications, 1968.

Logan, H. A. *Trade Unions in Canada: Their Development and Functioning.* Toronto: Macmillan, 1948.

Lumsden, Ian, ed. *Close the 49th Parallel, etc.: The Americanization of Canada.* Toronto: University of Toronto Press, 1970.

   Bliss, Michael. "Canadianizing American Business: The Roots of the Branch Plant."

   Drache, Daniel. "The Canadian Bourgeoisie and Its National Consciousness."

   Gonick, C. W. "Foreign Ownership and Political Decay."

   Watkins, M. H. "The Dismal State of Economics in Canada."

Mackintosh, W. A. *The Economic Background of Dominion-Provincial Relations: A Study Prepared for the Royal Commission on Dominion-Provincial Relations.* Ottawa, 1939; Toronto: McClelland and Stewart, Carleton Library, 1964.

Marshall, Herbert, Frank A. Southard and Kenneth W. Taylor. *Canadian-American Industry: A Study in International Investment.* New Haven and Toronto: Yale University Press and Ryerson, 1936.

Myers, Gustavus. *History of Canadian Wealth.* Chicago, 1914. Reprinted as *A History of Canadian Wealth.* Toronto: James Lewis & Samuel, 1972.

Pentland, H. C. "The Development of a Capitalistic Labour Market in Canada." *Canadian Journal of*

Economics and Political Science 25 (Nov. 1959): 450-462.

People's History of Cape Breton. Halifax (P. O. Box 1282, North Postal Zone), 1971.

Porter, John. *The Vertical Mosaic: An Analysis of Social Class and Power in Canada.* Toronto: University of Toronto Press, 1965.

Ryerson, Stanley. *Unequal Union.* Toronto: Progress Books, 1968.

Teeple, Gary, ed. Essays on class and the national question in Canada. Forthcoming.

Labour History
Irving Abella

Irving Abella is an assistant professor of Canadian history at Glendon College, York University, in Toronto. He is chairman of the Committee on Canadian Labour History and has recently completed a book on international unionism, Communism and the Canadian labour movement from 1930 to 1956.

A distressing aspect of the trade-union movement in Canada is that few people seem to care enough to write about it. There are well over two million Canadians who are, or at one time were members of a trade union—many times the number who have ever belonged to a Canadian political party. Yet, while there are scores of books on Canadian political parties and politicians, there is but a mere handful dealing with Canadian unions and labour leaders. Not only have academics consciously ignored the labour movement, but the actual participants themselves, the union leaders and organizers, have been inordinately reluctant to write about their experiences. Not one Canadian labour leader of note has ever published his recollections. This stands in stark contrast to the American and European experience where there exists a vast union literature made up almost equally of books from the academic community and from the labour movement itself.

Students of Canadian labour are thus faced with the seemingly insurmountable task of learning about their union movement from books that are not only in short supply but often quite inadequate. Fortunately, though few in number, there are several outstanding books that are essential for an understanding of the Canadian labour movement. Perhaps more important, in the past few years academics have begun paying increasing attention to Canadian unions with the predictable result that more—and better—books on Canadian unions are now being published.

To the present time, however, no first-rate history of the Canadian labour movement has yet appeared. There are two general histories of trade unionism in Canada, both of them informative and valuable but neither definitive nor even completely satisfactory.

The first history of Canadian labour, Harold Logan's *Trade Unions in Canada*, was published in 1948. This pioneering effort provides a vast store of information on almost every aspect of Canadian trade-union development. In fact, this book is so congested with data that it is very difficult to read. It abounds with names, statistics, dates and abbreviations; even the most committed students find the book confusing, and the general reader, confronted with such a constant barrage of facts, may find it difficult to retain the thread of Logan's story. Nevertheless, despite its organizational defects, *Trade Unions in Canada* is still the most comprehensive study of the Canadian labour movement available. Logan devotes each of his chapters to a description of the growth and development of unionism in a specific industry. In addition, he also describes and analyzes the activities and philosophies of the major Canadian labour organizations since 1900. In a dispassionate, impartial manner he examines the role and significance in the Canadian labour movement of such radical groups as the One Big Union and the Communists. Though it is now badly dated, *Trade Unions in Canada* is the one indispensable reference book for all students of Canadian labour.

The other history, *The Trade Union Movement in Canada 1827-1959* by Charles Lipton, is a more readable though less valuable book. For many years an active member of a left-wing union, Lipton presents an extremely partisan account of the Canadian labour movement from a quasi-Marxist perspective. His book is much less informative than Logan's and his analyses and interpretations are often superficial and biased.

The real strength of the book lies in Lipton's description of the early period of Canadian labour, the period up to 1920. In these early chapters Lipton is at his best.

His research is thorough, his analysis lucid and his approach straightforward. It is only when Lipton writes about Canadian labour since the 1920s that his partisanship interferes with his perspective, perhaps because he was involved in many of the events he describes.

Strangely, the best history of Canadian labour was not meant to be a history at all. In 1966, Stuart Jamieson was commissioned by the federal task force on labour relations to study labour unrest in Canada since 1900. The result, *Times of Trouble,* though limited in its scope, is perhaps the most useful of the histories of the trade-union movement in Canada.

It must be recognized that Jamieson's basic concern is the study of labour unrest and strikes in Canada since 1900, so many of the significant aspects of Canadian unionism are scarcely mentioned. But Jamieson did expand the work to cover other areas of Canadian union development. He presents a chronological history of labour discontent in Canada that is both enlightening and analytical. The book describes in detail most of the important events in Canadian labour history and brings to them a new perspective.

John Crispo's *International Unionism* is an excellent study of the nature and impact of international unionism in Canada. Each of the book's ten chapters deals with a different facet of the presence of American unions in Canada. There are chapters devoted to their origin and history, to the response of employers and governments to their existence, and to their effect on the development and structure of the Canadian labour movement. The best and most timely chapters are those in which Crispo analyzes the advantages and drawbacks to Canada of the international union presence. Unquestionably this book is required reading for anyone interested in the organization and development of the union movement in Canada.

The one aspect of the Canadian labour movement that has received some attention from academics is its relationship with political parties. The two books that discuss the role of unions in the political process are Martin Robin's thorough *Radical Politics and Labour in*

Canada, covering the period from 1880 to 1930, and Gad Horowitz's *Canadian Labour in Politics,* which takes Robin's story up to 1966. Of the two, the latter is the more important. Not only does Horowitz examine the relationship between unions and political parties, but in the deservedly famous first chapter of the book he presents a brilliant explanation for the relative success socialist parties have had in Canada compared to their abject failure in the United States. He also describes why organized labour in Canada decided to support a socialist party rather than follow the American example of working within the major political parties. In the remaining seven chapters of the book Horowitz shows how the Canadian union movement became involved with the CCF, and how in 1961 the unions and the CCF combined political forces to create the New Democratic party.

A truly disgraceful feature of the literature of the Canadian union movement is that, aside from Paul Phillips's superb study of labour in British Columbia, *No Power Greater,* there are no books on the union movements in the various provinces and regions of Canada. This is especially shocking for the province of Quebec, whose labour history differs markedly from the rest of Canada.

Perhaps the most interesting book on labour in Quebec, given the recent prominence of its author-editor, is *La Grève de l'amiante* by Pierre Elliott Trudeau. The book, which for some reason has not been translated into English, consists of a series of essays dealing with the famous Asbestos strike in Quebec in 1949, a strike which helped undermine the corrupt Duplessis régime and marked the beginnings of the Quiet Revolution in Quebec. Asbestos first brought into the public eye several previously unknown men whose names are now quite familiar to most Canadians—Jean Marchand, Gerard Pelletier and, of course, Pierre Trudeau.

The one event in our labour past of which most Canadians seem aware is the Winnipeg General Strike of 1919, the only successful general strike in North

American history. D. C. Masters's book, *The Winnipeg General Strike,* is the most comprehensive study of the event, though the best short description and analysis of the strike can be found in K. W. McNaught's biography of J. S. Woodsworth, *A Prophet in Politics.*

For more advanced students of Canadian labour there are three other invaluable books that should be consulted. *Canadian Labour in Transition,* edited by Fraser Isbester and Richard Millar, consists of eight instructive essays on such timely topics as labour and politics, unions in Quebec since 1949, the philosophy of Canadian trade unionism and the future of Canadian labour. Senator Eugene Forsey's *History of Canadian Trade Unionism 1812-1902* is the definitive work on the formative period of Canadian labour. This is a masterful study and without doubt the most thoroughly researched work on the history of trade unions in Canada. Irving Abella's *Struggle for Industrial Unionism in Canada* covers the period from the depression to 1957. He examines the important role played by the Communists and other radicals in building the modern Canadian labour movement and describes how, in the key years between 1940 and 1956, American unions were able to gain ultimate control of the trade-union movement in Canada.

Quite clearly then, there are still serious gaps in the literature dealing with the Canadian labour movement. However, what should be equally apparent is that there is now a sufficient number of good books on Canadian unionism to provide anyone interested in our trade unions with a deeper insight into their history, development and problems.

SUMMARY BIBLIOGRAPHY
General

Crispo, John. *International Unionism: A Study in Canadian-American Relations.* Toronto: McGraw-Hill, 1967.

Jamieson, Stuart. *Times of Trouble: Labour Unrest and Industrial Conflict in Canada, 1900-1966.* Task Force on Labour Relations, study no. 22. Ottawa, 1968.

Lipton, Charles. *The Trade Union Movement in Canada 1827-1959*. Montreal: Canadian Social Publications, 1966.

Logan, Harold. *Trade Unions in Canada*. Toronto: Macmillan, 1948.

Advanced

Abella, Irving. *The Struggle for Industrial Unionism in Canada 1930-1956*. Toronto: University of Toronto Press, 1972.

Forsey, Eugene. *The History of Canadian Trade Unionism 1812-1902*. Montreal: McGill-Queen's University Press, forthcoming.

Horowitz, Gad. *Canadian Labour in Politics*. Toronto: University of Toronto Press, 1968.

Isbester, Fraser, and Richard Miller, eds. *Canadian Labour in Transition*. Toronto: Prentice-Hall, 1971.

Masters, D. C. *The Winnipeg General Strike*. Toronto: University of Toronto Press, 1950.

McNaught, Kenneth. *A Prophet in Politics*. Toronto: University of Toronto Press, 1959.

Phillips, Paul. *No Power Greater—A Century of Labour in BC*. Vancouver: British Columbia Federation of Labour, 1967.

Robin, Martin. *Radical Politics and Canadian Labour*. Kingston: Queen's University Industrial Relations Centre, 1968.

Trudeau, Pierre, ed. *La Grève de l'amiante*. Montreal: Cité Libre, 1956.

The Economy
Ian Drummond

Ian M. Drummond is a member of the Department of Political Economy at the University of Toronto, specializing in Soviet affairs and twentieth century British economic history.

There is a difficulty with respect to the literature on Canadian economic policy. Most of the serious studies make sense only to those who already know some economics, while other, more accessible material is often deficient in analysis, presentation or objectivity. In this list I have tried to avoid items that are excessively professional, journalistic or trivial.

The basic accounting framework for Canadian economic studies is to be found in Statistics Canada's System of National Accounts, which includes quarterly and annual *National Income and Expenditure Accounts* and the *Balance of International Payments,* which also prints our *Balance of International Indebtedness.* Details with respect to the operation of foreign-owned corporations are to be found annually in the report published by the Department of Industry, Trade and Commerce under the Corporations and Labour Unions Returns Act (CALURA). These accounting schemes are discussed in Ian M. Drummond's *The Canadian Economy: Structure and Development,* which also presents recent basic information on Canadian finance, labour markets and competitive conditions, discussing policy problems in these areas and in the area of foreign ownership. Similar but more detailed information is in André Raynauld, *The Canadian Economic System.* A dated but still very useful compendium of policy-oriented essays is T. N. Brewis's collection, *Canadian Economic Policy.* For an assessment of the sources of Canadian economic growth, consult *Economic Growth in Canada: A Quantitative Analysis,* by N. H. Lithwick. For a somewhat more up-to-date but considerably more difficult collection of policy-oriented essays, see L. A. Officer and L. B. Smith, *Canadian Economic Problems and Policies*. The essays in J. J. Deutsch and others, *The Canadian Economy: Selected Readings*, are somewhat shorter and a good deal easier.

On cities and poverty the literature is still thin. For data-packed polemic, see the special Senate committee's report, *Poverty in Canada*. For a collection of useful papers, see N. H. Lithwick and G. Paquet, *Urban Studies: A Canadian Perspective*. The account in L. O. Stone's *Urban Development in Canada* is more statistical and historical. More sociological perspectives, with some economic relevance, are found in *Poverty in Canada*, edited by John Harp, and in *Poverty and Social Policy in Canada*, edited by W. E. Mann.

Much of Canadian economic research is buried more or less deeply in the works of our recent royal commissions. The wave begins with the 1957 Gordon commission on Canada's economic prospects. Its report is still of interest—not least because it marks the beginning of the worries about foreign ownership that have burgeoned so strikingly since 1957. Among the commission's many studies, only John Young's *Canadian Commercial Policy* was disowned by the commissioners; partly for this reason, and partly for its high quality, it commands respect and study. D. H. Fullerton's work on *Canadian Secondary Manufacturing*, though obviously dated, is still valuable.

In 1964 came the Porter commission on banking and finance. Its report is almost a textbook on Canadian financial institutions. Though the 1967 revisions of banking legislation changed the picture in some important respects, the Porter conspectus is still of great value. It can be supplemented and updated by Binhammer's excellent textbook, *Money, Banking and the Canadian Financial System*.

Next was the Carter royal commission on taxation. Its report is of little value to the general reader, but there is much meat in five of its staff studies: R. M. Will on *The Budget as an Economic Document;* W. E.

Gillespie on *The Incidence of Taxes and Public Expenditures in Canada;* R. M. Will again on *Canadian Fiscal Policy, 1945-1963;* J. H. Lynn on *Federal-Provincial Fiscal Relations;* and finally, N. H. Lithwick and T. Wilson on *The Sources of Economic Growth.*

Beside these and other royal commission reports lies the bulky output of the Economic Council of Canada, which was established in December 1963. It grinds out annual reports that are brief, vacuous, formal and empty. Most of its staff studies can also be ignored. There are two exceptions: F. T. Denton's and Sylvia Ostry's work on *An Analysis of Postwar Unemployment,* and Gordon Bertram's measurement of *The Contribution of Education to Economic Growth.* There is also Walter Hettich's gallant attempt to measure *Expenditure, Output and Productivity in Canadian University Education.* However, the council's annual reviews are often extremely interesting. Their contents are far less vacuous than their titles. And they reflect, from year to year, the obsessions of a segment of our academic, official and business élite. The reader should not assume that council pronouncements are revealed truth. They are the product of a semipolitical process within the council, which involves the chairman, vice-chairman, director, twenty-five lay members and sixty professional staff people.

The council also commissions special studies. Among the best are Melvin and Wilkinson on the tariff *(Effective Protection in the Canadian Economy),* David C. Smith on income policy *(Incomes Policies: Some Foreign Experiences and Their Relevance to Canada),* Bodkin's team report on the trade-off between inflation and unemployment *(Price Stability and High Employment)* and Reuber and Roseman on foreign takeovers *(The Takeover of Canadian Firms 1945-1961).*

Finally, we must mention the council's *Interim Report on Competition Policy*—a document that we must presume to have influenced the Trudeau government in its overhaul of our anticombines statutes.

Perhaps because so many Canadian economists have spent so much time working for royal commissions, councils and the like, we have few industry studies. There is, for instance, no recent book on the steel industry, the textile industry or the motor car industry. Regional studies, too, are few. However, one must mention André Raynauld's distinguished treatise, *Croissance et Structures économiques de la Province de Québec.* More historical and all-enveloping is Alan Green's *Regional Aspects of Canada's Economic Growth.* Policy problems are treated in T. N. Brewis, *Regional Economic Policies in Canada.*

On the traditional topics taught in university economics courses the literature is richer—though often far from easy. On labour, the standard treatment is still *Labour Policy and Labour Economics in Canada* by H. D. Woods and S. Ostry. The publishers tell us that Mrs. Ostry will shortly publish an updated treatment of labour economics, and that Dean Wood will, rather later, report anew on labour policy. On central banking, see E. P. Neufeld, *Bank of Canada Operations and Policy.* L. A. Skeoch has assembled readings on *Restrictive Trade Practices in Canada.* H. C. Eastman and S. Stykolt have analyzed *The Tariff and Competition in Canada.* A. E. Safarian has provided the only proper scholarly study of *Foreign Ownership of Canadian Industry.* In the report of the Watkins task force— *Foreign Ownership and the Structure of Canadian Industry*—the coverage is somewhat broader and the treatment more impressionistic. In *The Protective Tariff in Canada's Development,* J. H. Dales has treated some of the same matters in a more historical context. Dales has also written illuminatingly on *Pollution, Property and Prices.* And A. D. Scott has written a scholarly but rather difficult study of *The Economics of Conservation.*

Through its Canadian Trade Committee and its Canadian-American Committee, the Private Planning Association has sponsored a series of studies that explore trade and planning questions. Among the most interesting are L. A. Skeoch and David C. Smith, *Economic Planning: The Relevance of West European Experience for Canada;* R. J. and T. H. Wonnacott, *Free*

Trade between the U. S. and Canada; and Bruce W. Wilkinson, *Canada's International Trade: An Analysis of Recent Trends and Patterns.* The association's trade studies have included Kari Levitt's work on our trade with the West Indies and Ian M. Drummond's account of our trade with eastern Europe.

Among semiofficial publications, much can be gleaned from the annual reports of the Bank of Canada and the Central Mortgage and Housing Corporation. Their periodicals—the Bank of Canada *Statistical Summary* and *Canadian Housing Statistics*—are also invaluable.

There is no current bibliography of Canadian economic affairs as such. However, the National Library's *Canadiana* captures the book-length materials, while the useful periodical literature is virtually confined to the *Journal of Canadian Studies*, the *Queen's Quarterly* and the *Canadian Journal of Economics*—formerly the *Canadian Journal of Economics and Political Science.* The CJE tries to review all scholarly contributions to Canadian economic studies. Current developments in the labour field are reported in the monthly *Labour Gazette.* Major institutional changes are reported annually in the *Canada Year Book.* Every year the *Canadian Annual Review of Public Affairs* contains a great deal of material on recent economic events and policies. For more detail, there are many leads in the monthly and annual *Catalogue of Canadian Government Publications.*

SUMMARY BIBLIOGRAPHY
All are advanced.

Binhammer, J. *Money, Banking and the Canadian Financial System.* Toronto: Methuen, 1968.

Brewis, T. N. *Canadian Economic Policy.* Rev. ed. Toronto: Macmillan, 1965.

———. *Regional Economic Policies in Canada.* Toronto: Macmillan, 1969.

Canada. Bank of Canada. *Annual Report.* Ottawa, annual.

———. Bank of Canada. *Statistical Summary.* Ottawa, monthly, with annual supplement.

———. CMHC. *Annual Report.* Ottawa, annual.

———. CMHC. *Canadian Housing Statistics.* Ottawa, annual.

———. Privy Council. *Foreign Ownership and the Structure of Canadian Industry: Report of the Task Force on the Structure of Canadian Industry.* Ottawa, 1968. (The Watkins Report)

———. Royal Commission on Banking and Finance. *Report.* Ottawa, 1964. (The Porter Commission)

———. Royal Commission on Canada's Economic Prospects. *Report.* Ottawa, 1957. (The Gordon Commission)

———. Royal Commission on Canada's Economic Prospects. Studies.

    Fullerton, D. H. *Canadian Secondary Manufacturing Industry* (1957).

    Young, J. H. *Canadian Commercial Policy* (1957).

———. Royal Commission on Taxation. *Report.* Ottawa, 1966.

———. Royal Commission on Taxation. Studies.

    Gillespie, W. E. *The Incidence of Taxes and Public Expenditure in the Canadian Economy* (1968).

    Lithwick, N. H., and T. Wilson. *The Sources of Economic Growth* (1968).

    Lynn, J. H. *Federal-Provincial Fiscal Relations* (1968).

    Will, R. M. *The Budget as an Economic Document* (1966).

    Will, R. M. *Canadian Fiscal Policy 1945-1963* (1968).

———. Special Senate Committee on Poverty. *Poverty in Canada.* Ottawa, 1971.

———. Statistics Canada. *The Canada Year Book.* Ottawa, annual.

———. Statistics Canada. *National Income and Expenditure Accounts.* Ottawa, quarterly and annual.

———. Statistics Canada. *Balance of International Payments.* Ottawa, quarterly and annual.

Dales, J. H. *Pollution, Property and Prices.* Toronto:

University of Toronto Press, 1971.

———. *The Protective Tariff in Canada's Development.* Toronto: University of Toronto Press, 1966.

Deutsch, J. J., et al. *The Canadian Economy: Selected Readings.* Rev. ed. Toronto: Macmillan, 1965.

Drummond, Ian M. *The Canadian Economy: Structure and Development.* 2nd ed. Georgetown: Irwin-Dorsey, 1972.

———. *Canada's Trade with the Communist Countries of Eastern Europe.* Montreal: Private Planning Association, 1966.

Eastman, H. C., and S. Stykolt. *The Tariff and Competition in Canada.* Toronto: Macmillan, 1967.

Economic Council of Canada. *Annual Review.* Ottawa, 1964-1970.

Economic Goals for Canada (1964).
Towards Sustained and Balanced Growth (1965).
Prices, Productivity and Employment (1966).
The Canadian Economy from the Sixties to the Seventies (1967).
The Challenge of Growth and Change (1968).
Perspectives 1975 (1969).
Patterns of Growth (1970).

———. *Interim Report on Competition Policy.* Ottawa, 1969.

———. *Performance and Potential: Mid-1950s to Mid-1970s.* Ottawa, 1971.

———. Special Studies.

Bodkin, Ronald G., et al. *Price Stability and High Employment: The Options for Canadian Policy.* Ottawa, 1966.

Melvin, J. R., and B. W. Wilkinson. *Effective Protection in the Canadian Economy.* Ottawa, 1968.

Reuber, Grant, and Frank Roseman. *The Takeover of Canadians Firms 1945-1961.* Ottawa, 1969.

Smith, David C. *Incomes Policies: Some Foreign Experiences and Their Relevance to Canada.* Ottawa, 1966.

———. Staff Studies.

Bertram, G. *The Contribution of Education to Economic Growth.* Ottawa, 1966.

Denton, F. T., and Sylvia Ostry. *An Analysis of Postwar Unemployment.* Ottawa, 1965.

Hettich, Walter. *Expenditure, Output and Productivity in Canadian University Education.* Ottawa, 1971.

Green, Alan. *Regional Aspects of Canada's Economic Growth.* Toronto: University of Toronto Press, 1971.

Harp, John, ed. *Poverty in Canada.* Toronto: Prentice-Hall, 1971.

Levitt, Kari. *Canada's Trade with the West Indies.* Montreal: Private Planning Association, 1967.

Lithwick, N. H. *Economic Growth in Canada—A Quantitative Analysis.* Toronto: University of Toronto Press, 1969.

Lithwick, N. H., and G. Paquet. *Urban Studies: A Canadian Perspective.* Toronto: Methuen, 1968.

Mann, W. E., ed. *Poverty and Social Policy in Canada.* Toronto: Prentice-Hall, 1971.

Neufeld, E. P. *Bank of Canada Operations and Policy.* Toronto: University of Toronto Press, 1958.

Officer, L. A., and L. B. Smith. *Canadian Economic Problems and Policies.* Toronto: McGraw-Hill, 1970.

Raynauld, André. *The Canadian Economic System.* Toronto: Macmillan, 1967.

———. *Croissance et Structures économiques de la Province de Québec.* Québec: Ministère de l'Industrie et du Commerce, 1961.

Safarian, A. E. *Foreign Ownership of Canadian Industry.* Toronto: McGraw-Hill, 1966.

Saywell, J. T., ed. *The Canadian Annual Review of Public Affairs.* Toronto: University of Toronto Press, annual.

Scott, A. D. *The Economics of Conservation.* Toronto: University of Toronto Press, 1954.

Skeoch, L. A. *Restrictive Trade Practices in Canada.* Toronto: McClelland and Stewart, 1966.

Skeoch, L. A., and David C. Smith. *Economic Planning: The Relevance of West European Experience for Canada.* Montreal: Private Planning Association, 1963.

Stone, L. O. *Urban Development in Canada.* Ottawa: DBS, 1967.

Wilkinson, Bruce W. *Canada's International Trade: An Analysis of Recent Trends and Patterns.* Toronto: University of Toronto Press, 1968.

Wonnacott, R. J. and T. H. *Free Trade between the US and Canada.* Toronto: University of Toronto Press, 1968.

Foreign Control of the Economy
Abraham Rotstein

*Abraham Rotstein is an associate professor in the
Department of Political Economy at the University of
Toronto. He is the managing editor of the* Canadian
Forum, *and a founding member of the Committee for
an Independent Canada and the University League
for Social Reform.*

The recent and widespread concern for Canadian
independence is not altogether new in Canada. It may
even be argued that little has been added to the discussion since the debates surrounding Confederation over
one hundred years ago; among Canadian historians and
political leaders, some have never ceased to be concerned with the dilemmas of nation building and the
related problems of containing an ever-present tide to
the south. Others have tended to view the process of
North American integration as both inevitable and
desirable.

On the economic side, this debate has centred traditionally on the role of the tariff as the major plank in
Sir John A. Macdonald's National Policy. The fledgling
Canadian manufacturing sector, under this scheme,
would be protected against the influx of cheaper
American goods. The CPR would carry these Canadian
goods across the country and would bring back wheat
from the newly settled Canadian West for export
abroad. These east-west ties would ostensibly hold the
country together around a common economic "belt
line."

While some anticipated that American capital might
find it attractive to leap the tariff wall and establish
branches and subsidiaries in Canada in a protected
market, no one foresaw the magnitude of the
inundation.

These earlier themes of Canadian economic history

are reviewed in Professor Watkins's essay in this volume. My own discussion will be confined to the past decade, when a growing awareness and concern led to a substantial debate on the question of foreign control of the economy.

The alert was first sounded by Walter Gordon in 1958 in the final report of the Royal Commission on Canada's Economic Prospects. It was a mild and limited statement of concern. Early warnings were also issued in the little-known books by L. C. and F. W. Park, *The Anatomy of Big Business* (1962), and R. S. Rodgers, *Canada Can Thrive* (1962). The first of these was a survey of major corporate links in Canada with American capital. It argued for "a degree of nationalization of US-controlled enterprises in Canada" in order to break out of the growing monopoly control of the Canadian economy. The second volume (which is really a long essay) touched on several different policy approaches to foster "Canadianization" of the economy, including subsidies and rationalization of industry.

A major volume concentrating on the resources question which stands up very well more than a decade later is H. G. J. Aitken, *American Capital and Canadian Resources* (1961). No major policy prescriptions are offered but the basic economic and political issues are clearly stated.

Walter Gordon has two books on this question, *Troubled Canada* (1961) and the more recent and better-articulated position in *A Choice for Canada* (1966). Here Gordon put the case for several measures to restore Canadian ownership of the economy, including the special use of tax policy and making shares in subsidiary companies available to Canadians.

The major opponent of what was termed "economic nationalism" is a well-known economist, Harry Johnson, a Canadian teaching at the University of Chicago and at the London School of Economics. His collection of essays, *The Canadian Quandary* (1963), argues that nationalism "has been diverting Canada into a narrow and garbage-cluttered cul-de-sac." Johnson set the tone for most of the professional economists in Canada by arguing for a laissez-faire position: remove the tariff wall and allow free trade to operate; remove all restrictions against foreign investment in Canada and allow unlimited foreign ownership of any and all industries and natural resources. This, Johnson argues, will bring maximum incomes and employment to Canadians, and indeed, greater independence as well, since "nobody is as independent as a man who can afford to pick up his own cheques." Johnson's was a doctrinaire position that closed off the possibility of giving any expression to the inarticulate but mounting concern slowly beginning to pervade Canadian public opinion as the takeover of the Canadian economy grew.

The other side of the case was put forward by a small group of economists who had to search for an alternative framework for their ideas, since traditional economic theory allowed little room for questions centred on economic independence.

In a collection of essays put out by the University League for Social Reform (ULSR) entitled *Nationalism in Canada* (1966), Stephen Hymer raised the question of whether too high a price was being paid for foreign direct investment, particularly when large (oligopolistic) firms were involved. Detrimental effects to the Canadian economy may include the stifling of local entrepreneurship, the reduction of competition and the avoidance of taxes. A direct role for government intervention was set out which became of great importance in the subsequent debate.

In another essay in the same volume, a second issue was raised by Abraham Rotstein, namely the shift of decision-making power out of the country that occurs with foreign investment. Independence, being the ability to take decisions in our own interest, was thereby diminished as foreign control increased. This was the nub of the political issue surrounding the growth of the foreign sector of the economy.

While the debate was being broadened at the theoretical level, an empirical investigation into the behaviour of foreign firms was launched by A. E. Safarian. His book *Foreign Ownership of Canadian Industry* (1966) was based on questionnaires and voluntary interviews with the managers of both foreign-owned and domestic firms. Safarian concluded that there was no cause for alarm and that the economic advantages brought by foreign investment far exceeded the disadvantages.

Safarian, Hymer and Rotstein all participated in the task force headed by M. H. Watkins whose report, published in 1968, was entitled *Foreign Ownership and the Structure of Canadian Industry*. This report reflected some of the ideas of the three authors mentioned earlier and its major recommendation included a special government agency to supervise the activities of foreign firms. The report is a landmark in the debate on foreign control.

A similar recommendation for a government bureau was put forward by a subsequent parliamentary committee in 1970 headed by Ian Wahn, in the eleventh report of the Standing Committee Respecting Canada-US Relations. This committee also advocated a longer-term goal of fifty-one per cent Canadian ownership of all foreign firms.

The third and most important in this series of government-sponsored reports was the Gray report. Once again a "screening agency" was the main recommendation, reminiscent of the proposals of both the Watkins and Wahn reports.

Two important contributions in 1970 include a volume of essays by the ULSR, *Close the 49th Parallel, etc.*, edited by Ian Lumsden, and *Silent Surrender* by Kari Levitt. The first has contributions in the area of foreign investment and related questions by Michael Bliss, C. W. Gonick, Mel Watkins, Larratt Higgins and Abraham Rotstein. Kari Levitt's book is perhaps the classic statement of the case against the multinational corporation in Canada and deserves to be widely read.

Also published in 1970, the "documentary" *Gordon to Watkins to You* offers a combination of anecdote, document and analysis by Mel Watkins and Dave Godfrey of Watkins's intellectual and political journey to the Watkins Manifesto and the formation of the Waffle group of the NDP. It offers the strongest case for the nationalization of foreign-owned companies.

Reclaiming the Canadian Economy is the Canadian edition of a Swedish book by Gunnar Adler-Karlsson originally entitled *Functional Socialism: A Swedish Theory for Democratic Socialization.* In an introduction to the Canadian edition, Abraham Rotstein points out that this Swedish approach offers a theoretical basis for a government role in the economy centred on subsuming the "rights" or "functions" of foreign-owned firms rather than outright nationalization of titles or an attempt to "buy back" these companies. It will be recalled that "control" rather than "ownership" is the main thrust of the three government reports noted above, although fifty-one per cent Canadian ownership is also included among the recommendations of the Wahn report.

A series of articles on the experience of foreign investment in fourteen countries is brought together in the volume entitled *Foreign Investment: The Experience of Host Countries* edited by Isaiah A. Litvak and Christopher J. Maule. The above authors in conjunction with R. D. Robinson have published a second volume entitled *Dual Loyalty, Canadian-US Business Arrangements,* containing some useful case studies in the relations of parent and subsidiary in Canada.

Two books with useful background information are D. W. Carr, *Recovering Canada's Nationhood,* emphasizing the importance and possibility of Canadian entrepreneurship, and W. H. Pope, *The Elephant and the Mouse,* calling for the abolition of the tariff and the fostering of effective competition in order to reduce foreign control.

For one of the most topical current issues, that of natural resources, the best and virtually only book in the field is James Laxer's slim volume *The Energy Poker Game,* which warns sharply against a continental resources agreement with the United States.

Forced Growth by Philip Mathias offers five case studies of major attempts of our "have-not" provinces to sponsor economic development in co-operation with foreign companies or individuals. Almost all were disasters, and in the introduction to the book Abraham Rotstein raises the question of why it has been difficult to mobilize Canadian firms instead of foreign firms in the task of regional development, particularly when they had substantial expertise in a particular field such as the pulp-and-paper projects in Manitoba (Churchill Forest Industries) and in Saskatchewan (Parsons and Whittemore).

Finally, a broad selection of background articles on foreign ownership and related issues is assembled in the book edited by Abraham Rotstein and Gary Lax entitled *Independence: The Canadian Challenge,* published by the Committee for an Independent Canada (1972).

All the foregoing books are listed in the accompanying bibliography. Some supplementary items not mentioned in the text are listed in a second group ("advanced") for more specialized reading.

SUMMARY BIBLIOGRAPHY
General

Adler-Karlsson, Gunnar. *Reclaiming the Canadian Economy: A Swedish Approach through Functional Socialism.* Toronto: House of Anansi, 1970.

Aitken, Hugh G. J. *American Capital and Canadian Resources.* Cambridge, Mass.: Harvard University Press, 1961.

Canada. Privy Council. *Foreign Ownership and the Structure of Canadian Industry: Report of the Task Force on the Structure of Canadian Industry.* Ottawa, 1968. (The Watkins Report)

———. Royal Commission on Canada's Economic Prospects. *Report.* Ottawa, 1956-1958. (The Gordon Commission)

———. Standing Committee on External Affairs and National Defence. *Report (11th) of the Committee Respecting Canada-US Relations.* Ottawa, 1970. (The Wahn Report)

Canadian Forum Editorial Board. *A Citizen's Guide to the Herb Gray Report.* Toronto: New Press, 1971.

Carr, D. W. *Recovering Canada's Nationhood.* Ottawa: Canada Publishing Co., 1971.

Godfrey, David, and Mel Watkins. *Gordon to Watkins to You, A Documentary: The Battle for Control of Our Economy.* Toronto: New Press, 1970.

Gordon, Walter L. *Troubled Canada: The Need for New Domestic Policies.* Toronto: McClelland and Stewart, 1961.

———. *A Choice for Canada.* Toronto: McClelland and Stewart, 1966.

Johnson, Harry G. *The Canadian Quandary: Economic Problems and Policies.* Toronto: McGraw-Hill, 1963.

Laxer, James. *The Energy Poker Game: The Politics of the Continental Resources Deal.* Toronto: New Press, 1970.

Levitt, Kari. *Silent Surrender: The Multinational Corporation in Canada.* Toronto: Macmillan, 1970.

Litvak, Isaiah A., and Christopher J. Maule, eds. *Foreign Investment: The Experience of Host Countries.* New York: Praeger, 1970.

Litvak, I. A., C. J. Maule and R. D. Robinson.*Dual Loyalty: Canadian-US Business Arrangements.* Toronto: McGraw-Hill, 1971.

Lumsden, Ian, ed. *Close the 49th Parallel, etc.: The Americanization of Canada.* Toronto: University of Toronto Press, 1970.

Mathias, Philip. *Forced Growth.* Toronto: James Lewis & Samuel, 1971.

Park, L. C. and R. W. *Anatomy of Big Business.* Toronto: Progress Books, 1962.

Pope, W. H. *The Elephant and the Mouse.* Toronto: McClelland and Stewart, 1971.

Rodgers, R. S. *Canada Can Thrive.* Toronto: Peter Martin Associates, 1962.

Rotstein, Abraham, and Gary Lax, eds. *Independence: The Canadian Challenge.* Toronto: Committee for an Independent Canada, 1972.

Russell, Peter, ed. *Nationalism in Canada.* Toronto: McGraw-Hill, 1966.

Safarian, A. E. *Foreign Ownership of Canadian Industry.* Toronto: McGraw-Hill, 1966.

———. *The Performance of Foreign-owned Firms in Canada.* Montreal: Canadian-American Committee for the Private Planning Association of Canada, 1969.

Advanced

Behrman, Jack. *National Interests and the Multinational Enterprise.* Englewood Cliffs, N. J.: Prentice-Hall, 1970.

Brecher, Irving. *Capital Flows between Canada and the United States.* Montreal: Canadian-American Committee, 1965.

Brecher, Irving, and S. S. Reismann. *Canada-United States Economic Relations.* In Documents of the Royal Commission on Canada's Economic Prospects. Ottawa, 1957.

Kindelberger, C. P., ed. *The International Corporation: A Symposium.* Cambridge, Mass.: MIT Press, 1970.

Vernon, Raymond. *Sovereignty at Bay: The Multinational Spread of US Enterprises.* New York: Basic Books, 1971.

Federalism and the Constitution
Richard Simeon

Richard Simeon is an associate professor of political studies at Queen's University in Kingston. He is the author of Federal-Provincial Diplomacy, *and is currently working on a study of policy making in Canada.*

One of the first things anyone learns about Canadian government is that it is made up not of one central authority, but of federal, provincial and local units, each of these units possessing differing powers, responsibilities, resources, interests and constituencies. Their activities are closely intertwined, but at the same time they maintain considerable independence of each other. Together they make policy through a complex process of conflict and co-operation. This federalism is a vital element in the institutional framework of Canadian politics. It has profoundly influenced—and been influenced by—the wider political process.

Canada was born as a federal system largely in an attempt to reconcile the desire for a strong national state with the pull of regional and cultural diversity. This tension between centrifugal and centripetal forces is the central thread running through Canadian history and through any discussion of Canadian federalism. At root, federalism involves often competing definitions of the nature of the Canadian political community, and fundamental questions about the relations between French Canadians and English Canadians, Easterners and Westerners, rich regions and poor.

The balance between these forces is constantly shifting, in response to contemporary social, political and economic movements. In the postwar period, for example, many writers talked of the "nationalization" of Canadian life, and the inevitable centralization and federal dominance that implied. But by the sixties assertive provincial governments, led by Quebec, successfully challenged Ottawa. Writers like D. V. Smiley began to talk of the "attenuation of federal power." In fact, governments at both levels have expanded their roles. But more important, we have evolved a pattern of policy making in which governments share responsibility for many of the most pressing policy areas, and must develop programs through a complex process of bargaining, negotiation and mutual influence. The "watertight-compartments" view of federalism no longer applies to Canadian federalism, if indeed, it ever did.

Not surprisingly, federalism has been one of the chief preoccupations of students of Canadian politics. Constitutional lawyers have debated the real meaning of the British North America Act and examined modifications to the constitutional structure stemming from constitutional amendment, judicial interpretation and political bargaining. Economists have studied the complexities of federal-provincial finance, the problems of economic management in a federal state and the perennial issue of regional economic disparities. French Canadian scholars have asked if the federal system can adequately safeguard the rights and aspirations of French Canadians. Students of public administration have examined the tangled relationships between federal and provincial governments, asking how effective policy is to be made when responsibilities are shared. The literature on federalism is both varied and voluminous. Much of it is highly specialized, and unfortunately very few basic overall analyses or assessments have been published.

Therefore the best introduction to the subject is probably found in a collection of readings, *Canadian Federalism: Myth or Reality?* edited by J. Peter Meekison. The generally well-chosen articles touch on most of the major issues confronting Canadian federalism. Separate sections deal with federalism as a general concept, the overall character of Canadian federalism, regionalism in Canada, the constitution, intergovernmental relations and the role of Quebec in the federation. There is a fine bibliography. The book includes several of the most important recent academic assessments of the federal system, as well as a variety of statements by federal and provincial leaders. It is an essential starting point.

Another collection that touches on most of the major issues is the two volumes of essays published by the Ontario Advisory Committee on Confederation in 1967 and 1970. Several of these essays deal directly with the issues faced in the constitutional negotiations that began in 1967. *The Future of Canadian Federalism/L'Avenir du fédéralisme canadien,* edited by P. A. Crépeau and C. B. Macpherson, is a bilingual collection viewing the problems of confederation from the perspective of Quebec's "Quiet Revolution" of the early nineteen-sixties. Especially useful are the articles by Jacques Parizeau (now with the Parti Québécois) and William Hood on problems of economic policy in a federal state, and by Jacques-Yvan Morin and Edward McWhinney on constitutional change. *Concepts of Canadian Federalism,* edited by Gordon Hawkins, is another useful collection with a similar theme. None of the collections, however, have the breadth or quality of the Meekison volume.

By far the best overall analysis of Canadian federalism has been provided by D. V. Smiley of the University of Toronto in his brief but provocative study, *The Canadian Political Nationality.* The book traces the interplay between centripetal and centrifugal forces from 1867 to the present. Smiley is especially effective in describing the rise and decline of federal dominance in the wartime and postwar years, and in assessing Quebec's recent challenge to national unity. His argument is deeply pessimistic. The co-operative federalism that emerged in the fifties and sixties no longer satisfies either major language group. But none of the major alternatives before us—such as rewriting the constitution, or achieving special status for Quebec, or returning to the original 1867 settlement—offers a solution. Smiley suggests a new "national policy" to unite both groups in a great common enterprise, but it seems more a hope than an expectation. The book is essential reading.

Readers should also consult Smiley's other writings, several of which are found in Meekison. A very valuable recent article in which he expresses strong doubts about the ability of our present federal-provincial relations to regulate intergovernmental conflicts is found in another useful reader, *Contemporary Issues in Canadian Politics* by Frederick Vaughan, Patrick Kyba and O. P. Dwivedi. The remaining literature deals with more specific problems of federal systems.

The fundamental defence of a federal political order is that only such a decentralized system can adequately serve the interests of a society as geographically, ethnically, historically, economically and socially diverse as our own. Federal institutions, in this view, are rooted in federal society. To understand federalism, then, one should really understand the dimensions of regional differences in the country. Unfortunately, social scientists have only just begun to map the nature and extent of regionalism. E. R. Black and Alan Cairns, in an article entitled "A Different Perspective on Canadian Federalism" (reprinted in Meekison), provide the best single analysis of the interplay between regional forces and the federal system. The articles by Hodgetts and Conway in Meekison also address this point. The reader might also consult Paul Fox's "Regionalism and Confederation," in volume two of the Ontario Advisory Committee on Confederation papers.

A very useful way to get a feel for the way regional differences are expressed in day-to-day political debate is to read some of the statements of provincial premiers at recent federal-provincial conferences. The *Proceedings* of the first or second constitutional conferences, in 1968 and 1969, are good sources. (An effective classroom exercise might be to have students read the statements of one provincial delegation, then to stage a mock conference at which students play the role of different governments: they will soon find that the long debates reflect real and persisting policy differences.)

Quebec, of course, is the most distinctive region. And of all the problems facing the federation, only the question of Quebec's place in it has the potential to destroy it. Quebec has been the leading instigator of change in the federal system since the early nineteen-sixties. It was Quebec's dissatisfaction with the operation of the existing system and its desire to achieve major constitutional changes that would give the province substantially greater powers which led to the constitutional negotiations. By 1971, the negotiations had reached an impasse, and the dissatisfaction remained.

The literature on Quebec and Confederation is vast, and much of it is summarized elsewhere in this book. Again, the reader should begin with the section on Quebec in Meekison. He should then read Pierre Trudeau's *Federalism and the French Canadians,* a collection of essays written over several years. In it Trudeau makes the case *for* federalism as the only reasonable institutional framework for Canadian society. He attacks both French and English Canadian nationalism. He rejects proposals either for a special status for the province or for a highly centralized federal system. The book is essential for anyone who would understand the present government's view of Quebec and Canadian federalism.

But immediately after reading Trudeau, one should read the contrary view, persuasively argued by René Lévesque in *An Option for Quebec.* He argues that the federal solution is unworkable in a country where French Canadians look more and more towards Quebec for political leadership and English Canadians look more and more to Ottawa. The result can only be mutual deadlock and frustration. The solution is independence for Quebec, after which co-operative arrangements with Canada could be worked out on the basis of equality. This too is essential reading.

Quebec governments have argued for some variant of the special-status solution, maintaining the federal system but in a more decentralized form which would give Quebec much wider powers. Prime ministers Johnson and Bourassa give their views in Meekison and in the proceedings of the constitutional conferences. A succinct statement of the case for special status is made by Claude Ryan, editor of *Le Devoir,* in *Contemporary Issues in Canadian Politics.* John Meisel expresses the point of view of a sensitive English Canadian confronted with difficult alternatives in his "Cancel Out and Pass On: A View of Canada's Present Options," in *One Country or Two?* edited by R. M. Burns. Several other articles in this book examine attitudes to Quebec and Confederation in other sections of the country, and R. L. Watts seeks lessons for Canada by examining the failure of some other federations.

Federal systems are shaped not only by the society in which they are rooted, but also by their constitutional framework. The constitution, by allocating powers and resources, helps shape some of the basic rules of the game between provinces and federal government, although in Canada a great deal of change in the federal system—including, for example, the development of co-operative federalism and the structure of federal-provincial conferences—has occurred with amazingly little change in the formal constitution. English Canadians have tended to feel that major constitutional change is unnecessary and even dangerous (see, for example, Alan Cairns's "The Living Canadian Constitution" in Meekison); French Canadians, on the other hand, have argued that the constitution itself must be altered to reflect changed relationships.

The best introduction to the Canadian constitution is R. I. Cheffins's *The Constitutional Process in Canada,* which is brief, nontechnical and thorough. It is the essential starting point for those interested in the subject. Another excellent discussion of the nature of the constitution is found in R. MacGregor Dawson's classic text, *The Government of Canada.* Those interested in the constitutional role of the courts, especially the much-maligned Judicial Committee of the Privy Council, will find some of the essays in W. R. Lederman's *The Courts and the Canadian Constitution* helpful. More recent is Peter Russell's superb study, *The Supreme Court of Canada as a Bilingual and Bicultural Institution.* A major issue in the constitutional negotiations was the federal proposal to entrench in the constitution a charter of human rights guaranteeing specific civil, political and linguistic rights. The federal position is stated clearly in *A Canadian Charter of Human Rights*. The articles by Peter Russell and Kenneth Kernaghan in *Contemporary Issues in Canadian Politics* elaborate the issues involved quite effectively.

Unfortunately, little in the way of scholarly analysis of the constitutional review which began in 1967 has yet appeared. The great bulk of the articles that have appeared in English have argued that the exercise was ill advised, and that the previous pattern of piecemeal change through political bargaining was preferable to wholesale attempts at constitutional engineering, which were likely to fail. Summaries of the negotiating process up to 1971 are found in Peter Meekison, "Constitutional Reform in Canada," in his book, and in Richard Simeon, *Federal-Provincial Diplomacy*. Again, it is useful to look at the views of the governments themselves. The federal government stated its positions clearly in a series of working papers, of which the most important are *Federalism for the Future, The Constitution and the People of Canada* and *Income Security and Social Services*. Quebec's objectives (as of 1968) are stated in *The Government of Quebec and the Constitution*. Other provincial views are more scattered (though some are found in Meekison). They can be gleaned from the proceedings of the constitutional conferences. The debate touched on virtually all the major issues confronting Canadian federalism: the results to date show how far we are from a national consensus.

The society and the constitutional framework only provide the setting within which contemporary political issues are worked out as political leaders bargain and negotiate with each other. Few policy questions fail to involve both levels of government and a complex structure of federal-provincial committees, from technical officials' conferences up to the federal-provincial conference of first ministers, has developed. Though unmentioned in the constitution, the federal-provincial conference is in some ways Canada's most important legislative body. "Co-operative federalism" was the phrase most commonly used to describe this pattern of joint policy making; "executive federalism" and "federal-provincial diplomacy" are other terms. Again, Meekison provides a very useful introduction to these complex relationships. See especially Black and Cairns, A. W. Johnson's "The Dynamics of Federalism in Canada" and the section on intergovernmental relations.

For a more detailed examination of co-operative federalism, see Smiley's *Constitutional Adaptation and Canadian Federalism since 1945*. *Intergovernmental Liaison on Fiscal and Economic Matters,* a report prepared by the Institute of Intergovernmental Relations, gives a very complete picture of the machinery of negotiation that has emerged.

Three recent examples of joint policy making are examined in my *Federal-Provincial Diplomacy,* which looks at the political dynamics of the bargaining process and tries to assess its implications for the policies that result.

Among the central questions confronting the federal-provincial bargainers, and traditionally the source of acrimonious conflict is, of course, how the financial pie should be divided up. What shares of the most lucrative sources of revenue should go to each government? How much should Ottawa transfer wealth from the rich sections to the poorer through equalization payments? And what rules should govern federal involvement in areas of provincial jurisdiction through the use of conditional grants? It is not an easy or exciting subject but it has very important implications. By far the simplest comprehensive treatment of fiscal relations is a report prepared by an American agency, the Advisory Commission on Intergovernmental Relations, for an American audience. *In Search of Balance: Canada's Intergovernmental Experience* states the issues and results clearly and succinctly, and concludes that the Canadian pattern of intergovernmental finance is far superior to the American. I examine the politics of one round in the recurring fiscal negotiations between the governments in *Federal-Provincial Diplomacy.* For more

detail, those not satisfied with Meekison might look at
A. M. Moore, J. Harvey Perry and Donald I. Beach, *The
Financing of Canadian Federation: The First Hundred
Years.* An intensive analysis of the use of conditional
grants is found in George Carter's *Canadian Conditional
Grants since World War II,* and in Smiley's earlier but
excellent analysis, *Conditional Grants and Canadian
Federalism.* The problem of regional economic dis-
parities is well summarized in T. N. Brewis's *Regional
Economic Policies in Canada.*

Assessments of the effectiveness of the federal-
provincial policy process vary widely. Many writers,
especially on the left, argue that federalism is basically a
conservative force and have blamed what A. H. Birch
called the "complications of federalism" for the late
development of the Canadian welfare state. The view is
argued recently in John Porter's *The Vertical Mosaic.*
There are others, like Trudeau, who argues in "The
Practice and Theory of Federalism" in *Federalism and
the French Canadians* that federalism allows provincial
governments to experiment with social policies in ways
a central government might be reluctant to (as Saskatchewan did with medicare). Others have argued that the
flexible give and take of intergovernmental relations has
permitted escape from constitutional rigidities and
ensured national policies sensitive to regional interests.
Still others have said that preoccupation with petty
competition between governments diverts attention
from the real issues. The answers remain to be found.

Despite recurring strains Canadian federalism has
proven an adaptable and flexible arrangement in the
first century of Confederation. It has provided mech-
anisms for the accommodation of central and regional
interests in Canada. What was initially a highly centralized system has developed into a relatively decentralized
one. Whether it will remain the framework within which
the Canadian communities can satisfy their goals remains unclear. The strains on the federal arrangement
are perhaps greater than ever before, and it is clear from
the outcome of the constitutional debate that we are far
from agreement on some of the most basic features of

the Canadian system. The books and articles I have mentioned do not resolve the dilemma. Nor do they give us many persuasive predictions of the future. But they do illustrate where we have come from and what some of the basic issues to be dealt with are. The reader who returns to the report of the Rowell-Sirois Commission on Dominion-Provincial Relationships submitted in 1940 will find many familiar themes. We can be certain that the system will continue to change. And in understanding that change we must remember that the future of Canadian federalism is ultimately dependent on the political, social, economic and cultural changes in Canada as a whole. So much of the material mentioned elsewhere in this book, especially in the sections dealing with French-English relations, is as vital to understanding the future of federalism as anything I have mentioned.

SUMMARY BIBLIOGRAPHY
General

Burns, R. M., ed. *One Country or Two?* Montreal and London: McGill-Queen's University Press, 1971.

Brewis, T. N. *Regional Economic Policies in Canada.* Toronto: Macmillan, 1969

Cheffins, R. I. *The Constitutional Process in Canada.* Toronto: McGraw-Hill, 1969.

Canada. *The Constitution and the People of Canada.* Ottawa: 1969.

———. Constitutional Conference, First Meeting, February 1968. *Proceedings.* Ottawa, 1968.

———. Constitutional Conference, Second Meeting, February 1969. *Proceedings.* Ottawa, 1969.

———. Constitutional Conference, Third Meeting, December 1969. *Proceedings.* Ottawa, 1970.

———. Department of Justice. *A Canadian Charter of Human Rights.* Ottawa, 1968.

———. *Federalism for Canadians.* Ottawa, 1968.

———. *Income Security and Social Services.* Ottawa, 1969.

Crépeau, P. A., and C. B. Macpherson, eds. *The Future of Canadian Federalism/ L'Avenir du fédéralisme canadien.* Toronto: University of Toronto Press, 1965.

Dawson, R. MacGregor, and Norman Ward. *The Government of Canada.* 5th ed. Toronto: University of Toronto Press, 1970.

Hawkins, Gordon, ed. *Concepts of Federalism.* Toronto: Canadian Institute of Public Affairs, 1965.

Lévesque, René. *An Option for Quebec.* Toronto: McClelland and Stewart, 1968.

Meekison, J. Peter, ed. *Canadian Federalism: Myth or Reality?* 2nd ed. Toronto: Methuen, 1971.

Ontario Advisory Committee on Confederation. *Background Papers and Reports.* Toronto, 1967, 1970. Vols. 1 and 2.

Porter, John. *The Vertical Mosaic.* Toronto: University of Toronto Press, 1965.

Simeon, Richard. *Federal-Provincial Diplomacy: The Making of Recent Policy in Canada.* Toronto: University of Toronto Press, 1972.

Smiley, D. V. *The Canadian Political Nationality.* Toronto and London: Methuen, 1967.

Trudeau, Pierre Elliott. *Federalism and the French Canadians.* Toronto: Macmillan, 1968.

USA. Advisory Commission on Intergovernmental Relations. *In Search of Balance—Canada's Intergovernmental Experience.* Washington, 1971.

Vaughan, Frederick, Patrick Kyba and O. P. Dwivedi. *Contemporary Issues in Canadian Politics.* Scarborough: Prentice-Hall, 1970.

Advanced

Canada. Institute of Intergovernmental Relations. *Intergovernmental Liaison on Fiscal and Economic Matters.* Ottawa, 1969.

———. Royal Commission on Bilingualism and Biculturalism. Documents.

Russell, Peter H. *The Supreme Court of Canada as a Bilingual and Bicultural Institution.* Ottawa, 1969.

Smiley, Donald V. *Constitutional Adaptation and Canadian Federalism since 1945.* Ottawa, 1970.

Carter, George E. *Canadian Conditional Grants since World War II.* Toronto: Canadian Tax Foundation, 1971.

Lederman, W. R., ed. *The Courts and the Canadian Constitution.* Toronto: McClelland and Stewart, 1964.

Moore, A. Milton, J. Harvey Perry and Donald I. Beach. *The Financing of Canadian Federation: The First Hundred Years.* Toronto: Canadian Tax Foundation, 1966.

Smiley, D. V. *Conditional Grants and Canadian Federalism.* Toronto: Canadian Tax Foundation, 1963.

———, ed. *The Rowell-Sirois Report, Book One.* Toronto: McClelland and Stewart, 1963.

Quebec Nationalism
René Durocher

René Durocher has taught Quebec history at the Université de Montréal and is now a member of the Department of History at York University. He has published with P. A. Linteau a bibliography on Quebec history and a book of readings on the economic problems of French Canada, as well as articles on Henri Bourassa and Maurice Duplessis.

Nationalism is certainly one of the most important ideologies in our world. While it is important to understand this phenomenon as a system of ideas or as a political philosophy, it is of the utmost importance to study each particular nationalism in its historical context. As Hans Kohn, in his book *Nationalism,* put it: "Nationalism is not the same in all countries and at all times. It is a historical phenomenon and thus determined by the political ideas and the social structure of the various lands where it takes roots."

Perhaps a Canadian who wishes to understand Quebec nationalism should begin by looking at his own nationalism. His own reactions against American imperialism may be a key for understanding the attitudes of the Québécois vis-à-vis Canada. A reading of *Nationalism in Canada* edited by Peter Russell or the series of essays on that subject published by the review *Canadian Dimension* (kit no. 3) would be a good starting point.

In the selection that follows, I have tried to list books representing different theses, and I hope that readers will use this as an opportunity to look at more than one point of view.

In 1945, Mason Wade published a short book entitled *The French-Canadian Outlook* which was reprinted in 1964 in the Carleton Library collection. In this attempt to explain French Canadian nationalism by tracing the history of French Canada from New France to 1945, Wade's deep sympathy for the French Canadians and his effort to be impartial in the study of French-English relations are clearly evident. Nevertheless, his psychological approach is rather superficial. It is unfortunate that this book has been reprinted without any revision since there is a continuing need for a short account such as this in English. The reader may be well advised to read instead Wade's major two-volume study, *The French Canadians,* which my colleague Wallot mentions in his article on Quebec history. This is a very interesting chronicle of French Canadian nationalism from 1760 to 1967.

Ramsay Cook in recent years has established a reputation as one of the best historians of French Canada. Since 1966 he has published two remarkable series of essays, *Canada and the French-Canadian Question* and *The Maple Leaf Forever.* Cook is extremely critical of all nationalisms. He sees in the ideology a great danger for Canada. If his conception of nationalism seems to me very questionable, as does his "trudeauist" view of the constitutional future of Canada, there is no doubt that he very ably represents an important trend of thought that nobody can neglect in the study of nationalism in Canada. In these two books the reader will find some fine historical essays on both nationalisms in Canada; they discuss such themes as the Conquest, Quebec-Ontario relations and the historiography of French and English Canada, and all of them are extremely good pieces of historical writing.

Cook has also edited an important anthology entitled *French-Canadian Nationalism.* This book reproduces many important nationalist texts that were previously difficult to find even in French, let alone in an English translation. As a documentary source it is of exceptional value. But it is unfortunate that Cook, who knows his subject so well, did not write a short introduction to each document.

Before turning to politics, Prime Minister Pierre Elliott Trudeau, who is certainly the most widely known political thinker in Canada, was a distinguished scholar and an active social reformer. The essays in his book *Federalism and the French Canadians* were written between 1954 and 1964, most of them for his review *Cité Libre,* which had been of some importance in the intellectual and political history of Quebec in the Duplessis era. Trudeau is, in the best meaning of the word, a political philosopher. Not only does he reflect on man and society in general terms but he applies his philosophical premises to the Canadian question. His favourite topics are federalism and nationalism.

Trudeau has acquired the image of the truly modern man but his political philosophy—even if he occasionally called it functionalism—is good old nineteenth century liberalism with its strong emphasis on legalism and individualism. Some English-speaking Canadians may find that they take comfort from the harsh attacks of Trudeau on French Canadian nationalism, but I would urge them to apply Trudeau's thought to their own nationalism and to ask themselves where his utopian federalism would lead Canada. Still, Trudeau's book, if read in a critical manner, certainly remains one of the most brilliant and stimulating on the question.

Wade, Cook and Trudeau share a refusal to see the positive side of nationalism. They all agree on a federalist Canada based on bilingualism and bicul-turalism in the Henri Bourassa tradition.

Opposed to that group are men like Lévesque, Rioux, Vallières and Bergeron who consider that nationalism can be progressive and that Canadian federalism is unworkable. For them the real problem that confronts Canada is not French Canada but Quebec.

René Lévesque, one of the leading figures of the Quiet Revolution, has become, with the creation of the Parti Québécois in 1968, the main spokesman for the independence of Quebec. In his book *An Option for Quebec,* Lévesque presents his blueprint for the inde-pendence of Quebec. In spite of what has happened over the past few months, he continues to adhere to his double proposal of independence combined with a Canada-Quebec economic association. The most important part of the book is the introduction, in which

Lévesque—speaking for thousands of Québécois—explains why independence is necessary for Quebec and why Québécois and Canadians would both benefit from it. It is a detailed statement of Lévesque's position, and a major document to look at carefully.

The sociologist Marcel Rioux in his *Quebec in Question* presents, from my point of view, the best introduction to modern Quebec nationalism. As the publisher of the book put it: "*Quebec in Question* takes the events of October-November 1970 and puts them into the context of Quebec's three-hundred-year history and the re-emergence of separatism since 1960. Marcel Rioux—himself a separatist—takes English Canadians inside the minds of Quebeckers who see independence as a necessity." This book is essential reading for all Canadians.

Pierre Vallières's *White Niggers of America* and *The History of Quebec* by Léandre Bergeron represent what can be called the radical-left point of view, which holds that a full-fledged socialist revolution should coincide with the independence of Quebec.

Vallières, whose name has been associated with the terrorist FLQ, wrote his book in prison. When he writes about history he should be read with caution; when he is talking philosophy he is sometimes obscure; but when he narrates his life as a young Québécois born into a poor family in the Montreal region just before the Second World War, he is clear-sighted, and this becomes an extremely moving and revealing book.

Léandre Bergeron, who has sold over seventy-five thousand copies of his book in Quebec, tries to reinterpret the history of Quebec from a Marxist point of view. "This handbook," writes Bergeron, "simply re-examines the outstanding events in our history, and places them in the struggle between oppressor and oppressed, colonizer and colonized, exploiter and exploited." If, from a historical point of view, his information is sometimes inaccurate and extremely biased, even if his conception of history and of Marxism is rather unsophisticated not to say simplistic, *The History of Quebec: A Patriote's Handbook* is an important document. It represents the feelings of many Québécois who consider themselves colonized and exploited.

Finally, I would like to mention the excellent series *Issues in Canadian History* published by Copp Clark under the general editorship of J. L. Granatstein. This problem-approach series for students of high schools and colleges contains many books related directly or indirectly to specific aspects of Quebec nationalism. In each book prepared by a specialist, the reader will find an introduction, a set of integrated readings stating the opposing points of view taken from contemporary sources and from historians on the problem under study, plus suggestions for further readings. The relevant titles are listed in the summary bibliography.

SUMMARY BIBLIOGRAPHY
General

Bergeron, Léandre. *The History of Quebec: A Patriote's Handbook.* Toronto: New Canada Press, 1971.

Canadian Nationalism and Independence. Canadian Dimension kit no. 3. Winnipeg.

Cook, Ramsay. *Canada and the French-Canadian Question.* Toronto: Macmillan, 1966.

———. *The Maple Leaf Forever: Essays on Nationalism and Politics in Canada.* Toronto: Macmillan, 1971.

———, ed. *French-Canadian Nationalism: An Anthology.* Toronto: Macmillan, 1969.

Granatstein, J. L., ed. *Issues in Canadian History.* Toronto: Copp Clark.

> Bowsfield, Hart, ed. *Louis Riel* (1969).
>
> Clark, L. C., ed. *The Manitoba School Question* (1968).
>
> Levitt, J., ed. *Bourassa on Imperialism and Biculturalism* (1970).
>
> Nish, C., ed. *The French Canadians, 1759-1766* (1966).
>
> ———, ed. *Quebec in the Duplessis Era, 1935-1959* (1970).
>
> Robertson, Susan Mann, ed. *L'Abbé Groulx* (1971).

Lévesque, René. *An Option for Quebec.* Toronto: McClelland and Stewart, 1968.

Rioux, Marcel. *Quebec in Question.* Toronto: James Lewis & Samuel, 1971.

Russell, Peter, ed. *Nationalism in Canada.* Toronto: McGraw-Hill, 1966.

Trudeau, Pierre Elliott. *Federalism and the French Canadians.* Toronto: Macmillan, 1968.

Vallières, Pierre. *White Niggers of America.* Toronto: McClelland and Stewart, 1971.

Wade, Mason. *The French-Canadian Outlook.* Toronto: McClelland and Stewart, Carleton Library, 1964.

———. *The French Canadians, 1760-1967.* 2 vols. Toronto: Macmillan, 1968.

Bibliographies

Boily, Robert. *Québec 1940-1969. Bibliographie: le système politique québécois et son environnement.* Montréal: Les Presses de l'Université de Montréal, 1971.

Durocher, René, et P. A. Linteau. *Histoire du Québec: bibliographie sélective (1867-1970).* Trois-Rivières: Boreal Express, 1970.

Garigue, Philippe. *A Bibliographical Introduction to the Study of French Canada.* Montreal: McGill University Press, 1956.

Party Politics, Pressure Groups and Social Movements

Walter Young

Walter D. Young teaches political science at the University of British Columbia, and his main interest is in Canadian politics. He has been an active member of the New Democratic party since its founding in 1961.

Someday, somewhere, somebody will sit down and write a book about all of Canada's political parties; until that happens we will have to make do with a number of books and chapters in books about particular parties and movements. There is nothing particularly wrong with a lot of books each covering some part of the whole area—after all, what is more Canadian than a mosaic—but when you are beginning a subject it is nice to have one book that puts the whole thing in some perspective.

About the only book that does that for this subject area is not really a book at all; it is a booklet written by Frank Underhill and published as part of the Canadian Historical Association Historical Booklets series. Underhill's *Canadian Political Parties* provides a splendid introduction to the beginnings and development of Canada's political parties, including Social Credit and the CCF, which was the forerunner of the NDP. While the approach is clearly historical, Underhill does provide an indication of the nature of each party's ideology, relating it to the development of the party over time. In this respect it is a particularly useful introduction for it provides a context for subsequent reading in the field. An added bonus is Underhill's wit and crisp prose.

Another book that is a useful introduction, but over a more narrow field, is *Democracy and Discontent* by Walter Young. Beginning with the Winnipeg General Strike of 1919, Young traces the development of the agrarian protest movements and the parties they helped spawn in the West: the Progressive party, the CCF and the Social Credit party. The book ends with a short chapter on the British Columbia Social Credit party. It includes a time chart linking events on the prairies with national and international events. Part of the theme is an explanation of the interrelationship of parties and movements in a parliamentary democracy. It is a readable book and straightforward in its approach.

The last of the three books that could properly be described as introductory and, to some extent, general, is *Party Politics in Canada* edited by Hugh Thorburn. *Party Politics* is a collection of articles by various people dealing with different aspects of parties, the party system and party politics, so while it's not quite the same kind of book as the others, it helps fill a number of gaps and some of the articles are themselves useful introductions to the field, especially the first three articles by Hougham, Reid and Mallory. These are perhaps a shade more difficult than the books by Underhill and Young. Some of the other articles may be a trifle specialized for someone just beginning to sail this particular sea, but they may whet the appetite.

And it is at this point that the general must be abandoned for the particular. Curiously, scholars in Canada have devoted relatively little attention to the two major parties, the Liberals and the Conservatives. Instead they have studied and written about the parties that grew up outside the traditional two-party system and eventually invaded it and converted it to a multiparty system. Of the few books about the Liberals and Conservatives, some are written by politicians in the parties themselves; consequently their pages are suffused with that warm glow of affection that only a politician could have for his own party. Two such are Jack Pickersgill's *The Liberal Party* and Heath McQuarrie's *The Conservative Party*. McQuarrie is the more scholarly of the two and hence his book the more valuable. Neither are particularly exciting books to read and they should be read with some scepticism.

Among the more objective studies of the major parties is J. L. Granatstein's book about the Conservative party, *The Politics of Survival*. His examination of the inner crises of the party as it moved with agony from leader to leader during the period of 1939 to 1945 is scholarship of a high order. Coupled with a gift for writing clearly, his analysis provides a splendid insight into the Tory party that will stand the test of time. But this is no book for the raw beginner—some inkling of the history and personalities of the period would be an advantage.

For the Liberals one must either rely on the Pickersgill potboiler already mentioned or draw sustenance from biography and autobiography. A readable and quite useful biography of Mackenzie King is Bruce Hutchison's *Mackenzie King: The Incredible Canadian,* while the memoirs of Chubby Power edited by Norman Ward, *A Party Politician,* provide some interesting inside views of the Liberal party. These are not formal studies of the party itself although, obviously, Mackenzie King gave the party its shape and style for nearly thirty years.

Hutchison's book is written for the general reader. The prose is a little florid, and it has the style and structure of a novel. Ward's edition of Powers's memoirs, on the other hand, demands a little higher level of sophistication, but is probably more rewarding as a window on the Liberal party.

The minor parties in Canada have been examined by scholars with great energy, particularly so the Social Credit party. Its sudden efflorescence in 1935 created such interest—and its somewhat bizarre philosophy generated such fascination—that eventually a whole series of books was written about its birth and development. Two of those books, taken together, provide a basic introduction. One is W. L. Morton's *The Progressive Party in Canada* and the other John Irving's *The Social Credit Movement in Alberta.* Morton's, as one would expect of a historian, traces the development of the Progressive party from its roots in the farmers' movements of the 1890s through to the constitutional crisis of 1926, which marked the last gasp of the party at the federal level. His last chapter on the progressive tradition in Canadian politics is a particularly useful analysis of subsequent events and of the reverberations of progressivism throughout the party system in Canada. Not a book for the beginner, this is probably the best of the books on the background of Social Credit and certainly the broadest in scope.

John Irving was a social psychologist; hence, his approach to Social Credit places more emphasis on the people involved than on the background and history of the movement. He devotes some space to William Aberhart, the founder and leader of the movement in Canada, and dissects the rise of the party to power in Alberta and the response of the people to this phenomenon. The interviews he quotes provide a striking picture of human response in times of crisis to political movements of the character of Social Credit. Because of this, the study has an immediacy that is stimulating. This is really more a book for the specialist, or at least someone with some grasp of the period and of the terminology of social science. There is no book that deals with Social Credit as a national phenomenon, largely because it has never been a national party in any useful sense of that word.

There is a book about the national CCF, and it is Walter Young's *The Anatomy of a Party.* It examines the party at the national level from start to finish—or to the creation of the NDP. Little has been written about political movements in Canada and one of the useful aspects of this book is that it deals with the CCF as a movement and as a party and that it has something to say about the nature and relationship of movements and parties. Although the approach taken is fairly sophisticated, the prose is clear enough, and sufficiently free from jargon that an advanced general reader would probably find it worthwhile. A useful adjunct to Young's book is one by Leo Zakuta, *A Protest Movement Becalmed.* Zakuta looks at the party from the perspective of its Ontario wing and offers a systematic analysis of its rise and decline. Zakuta's book is more technical.

With all of these books there should be mixed some judicious reading of biography and autobiography. In addition to the two already mentioned, two more could be read profitably by the student of Canadian political parties. One is Kenneth McNaught's biography of J. S. Woodsworth, the first leader of the CCF, *A Prophet in Politics,* and the second is Dalton Camp's autobiography, or at least the first volume of it, *Gentlemen, Players and Politicians.* Both add colour and depth to any investigation of the subject. McNaught's study of Woodsworth illuminates the career of a unique Canadian politician and, in the process, sheds light on the nature of the party system and Parliament. It is a beautifully clear book and, given an interest in political history, most readers would find it fascinating. In addition to the early years of Woodsworth's life, it covers the period from the Winnipeg Strike to the declaration of war in 1939. Camp's book reads like a TV shooting script—it has a great deal of movement and excitement. Its value lies in the flavour of "politics from the inside" that it provides as Camp's early association with the Liberal party, and later with the Conservatives, is crisply explored. Few will find the book tedious.

And as for pressure groups in Canada, well we know that we have them, and we know what they do, but only one book has been written about them and that is S. D. Clark's study, *The Canadian Manufacturers Association.* It was published in 1939 and, in many ways, has only an antiquarian interest. It is a book for the specialist—especially one keen about prewar pressure groups.

Since political parties are mainly concerned with elections it is not a bad idea to read something about the elections held in Canada since Confederation. Murray Beck has written a book, *Pendulum of Power,* that is very useful. It provides an eight-to-ten-page essay on each election from 1867 to 1968; each is compact and highly readable. It lends a good perspective to reading about party politics.

SUMMARY BIBLIOGRAPHY
General

Camp, Dalton. *Gentlemen, Players and Politicians.* Toronto: McClelland and Stewart, 1970.

Hutchison, Bruce. *Mackenzie King: The Incredible Canadian.* Toronto: Longmans, 1952.

Pickersgill, Jack. *The Liberal Party.* Toronto: McClelland and Stewart, 1962.

Underhill, Frank H. *Canadian Political Parties.* Ottawa: Canadian Historical Association, 1957.

Young, Walter D. *Democracy and Discontent.* Toronto: Ryerson, Frontenac Library, 1968.

Advanced

Beck, James Murray. *Pendulum of Power.* Toronto: Prentice-Hall, 1968.

Clark, S. D. *The Canadian Manufacturers Association.* Toronto: University of Toronto Press, 1939.

Granatstein, J. L. *The Politics of Survival.* Toronto: University of Toronto Press, 1967.

Irving, John. *The Social Credit Movement in Alberta.* Toronto: University of Toronto Press, 1959.

McNaught, Kenneth. *A Prophet in Politics.* Toronto: University of Toronto Press, 1959.

McQuarrie, Heath. *The Conservative Party.* Toronto: McClelland and Stewart, 1965.

Morton, W. L. *The Progressive Party in Canada.* Toronto: University of Toronto Press, 1950.

Thorburn, Hugh, ed. *Party Politics in Canada.* 2nd ed. Toronto: Prentice-Hall, 1967.

Ward, Norman, ed. *A Party Politician: The Memoirs of Chubby Power.* Toronto: Macmillan, 1966.

Young, Walter. *The Anatomy of a Party.* Toronto: University of Toronto Press, 1969.

Zakuta, Leo. *A Protest Movement Becalmed.* Toronto: University of Toronto Press, 1964.

Foreign Policy
Thomas Hockin

Thomas A. Hockin is an associate professor of political science at York University in Toronto. His scholarly work is concerned with parliamentary reform, Canadian foreign policy and the theory of public policy.

Over three decades ago a former Canadian prime minister could assert that the "foreign policy" of Canada was "so obvious as to need no discussion" (R. B. Bennett in the House of Commons, February 9, 1937). Since World War II the thrust of Canadian foreign policy has not been so obvious. During the 1970s, as Canada moves towards a new foreign policy based more explicitly on "national interests," it is clear that both past and present policy deserve more attention than ever before if we are to understand the significance of this shift.

Until the last few decades Canadians did not produce many analytical books or scholarly articles on foreign policy per se. Most of the literature discussed Canadian foreign policy primarily within the context of diplomatic history. Within that genre the overarching concerns were (as R. B. Bennett was no doubt emphasizing in 1937) Canada's role in the British Empire (now the British Commonwealth) and Canada's place in the so-called North Atlantic Triangle. Perhaps the classic summation and exhortation of the importance of the North Atlantic Triangle is found in a book by the same name by J. B. Brebner. The most thorough analysis of the Canadian position in the Empire up to 1939 is contained in the two volumes of G. P. deT. Glazebrook's *A History of Canadian External Relations—The Formative Years to 1914* and *The Empire and the World 1914-1939*. Both of these are careful scholarly works. Both, however, may fail to spark the interest of contemporary readers because neither is linked historically or analytically to questions students of Canadian foreign policy might ask today.

I would recommend James Eayrs's first two volumes of *In Defence of Canada* as of far more interest on these two subjects and on other subjects such as Canada's role in the League of Nations. The first volume covers from 1918 to 1935, the second from 1935 to 1945. Mr. Eayrs's impressive and pertinent research is deployed with clarity, irony and originality. His style is lively and immensely readable. Although the focus of both volumes is primarily on military questions, those questions are always closely related to the broader context of foreign policy.

Immediately after World War II until perhaps 1949, Canada was the fourth or fifth most powerful industrial nation in the world and, under the direction of Louis St. Laurent and Lester Pearson, it immersed itself in an unprecedented amount of diplomatic, political and military activity in world affairs. The definitive work on this first busy postwar half-decade has yet to be attempted, let alone written. Yet the wide-ranging comprehension, balanced tone and lucid exposition in John Holmes's collection of essays, *The Better Part of Valour*, puts this period into its diplomatic and political context very well. This collection of essays also serves effectively as an introduction to contemporary issues of Canadian foreign policy. As a one-time top diplomat in the Department of External Affairs and as director-general of the Canadian Institute of International Affairs, Holmes more than any other Canadian has encouraged, through meetings and publications of the institute, countless numbers of Canadians to study and discuss their country's foreign policy. There are few people in Canada who can always say something fresh and useful on such familiar foreign-policy themes as the United Nations, the Commonwealth, US-Canadian relations and the Atlantic Alliance, but John Holmes has consistently done so. Especially compelling and unique in their comprehensive sense of the relevant are his discussions of Canada as a middle power, nationalism in foreign policy, the public in foreign policy, the functional route to international co-operation in the UN, the historical discipline of the Commonwealth and Canada's role in Indo-China. It should be said, however, that this book is for those concerned with the diplomatic dimension more than the economic in Canadian foreign policy. Also useful as a history of Canadian external policy up to 1960, but scholarly and not introductory in their emphasis, are the essays in Hugh L. Keenleyside et al, *The Growth of Canadian Policies in External Affairs.*

The Holmes volume is alert to most of the controversies and differences of opinion that have energized debate on the major issues of Canadian foreign policy since 1945. Yet there will be those who wish to sample the strong wine of these opinions in the original. Let me suggest three books that provide a sampling of the controversies on various sides of the major issues of Canadian foreign policy in the last two decades. *Canadian Foreign Policy since 1945: Middle Power or Satellite?* edited by J. L. Granatstein, contains a number of articles, transcripts of press conferences, House of Commons debates, etc., that reflect the differing arguments on such issues as US-Canadian relations, NATO, nuclear weapons, peacekeeping and Canadian diplomacy. This book does not interpret these "documents." It tries instead to give the reader a brief introduction to the issues by collecting together in one volume snippets of the arguments on most of the issues of Canadian foreign policy from 1945 to 1969: John Holmes defending and Dean Acheson dismissing Canadian diplomatic tendencies; Dale Thomson acerbic, and Lester Pearson concerned, over the Suez crisis. The official flip flops on nuclear weapons for Canada's NORAD forces are here to read again; the arguments for scrapping, revising or supporting NATO; academics quarrelling with politicians over peacekeeping; and finally, Pierre Trudeau, Escott Reid, John Holmes, Dalton Camp and George Ball suggesting wildly different futures for Canadian foreign policy. However this volume does not centre on the economic concerns in Canadian foreign policy. It focuses instead on the question of whether Canada is a "satellite" or a "middle power" at the political, diplomatic and military levels. Also useful for sampling the controversy on these issues is James Eayrs's collection of his predominantly non-scholarly writings—on events of the latter part of the 1950s in *Northern Approaches: Canada and the Search for Peace,* and on events up to the mid-1960s in *Minutes of the Sixties.* Both books are loosely organized compilations of his opinions and comments on other people's opinions and government policies. Most of the selections were written for journalistic audiences (e.g., the readers of the *Family Herald*). Yet parts of both books are worth reading today, especially the latter. Neither book sits safely on the fence but instead wanders into the fray and enlivens the debate on many issues of Canadian foreign policy. Although these two books stimulate more than nourish the inquiring Canadian initiate to international affairs, they are therefore especially useful for provoking, not foreclosing discussions.

The latter part of the 1960s and the early 1970s have witnessed a number of book-length studies and polemics on various emerging issues of Canadian foreign policy. Perhaps the most significant is the volume produced by the University League for Social Reform entitled *An Independent Foreign Policy for Canada?* edited by Stephen Clarkson, which appeared in 1968. It contains twenty articles, most of them critical of particular features of Canadian foreign policy. Although some of the concerns in this book have been replaced by new ones, most of them remain surprisingly relevant in the 1970s. Stephen Clarkson's discussion of "independence" and "quiet diplomacy" is a useful starting point for understanding these notions. For anyone interested in American-Canadian relations, David Baldwin's article remains essential reading and the other articles on the American relationship, such as Charles Hanley's on "the ethics of independence," Peyton Lyon on "Quiet Diplomacy Revisited," Denis Stairs's two case studies and the discussion of "Retaliation: The Price of Independence" are all suggestive. The essays on the domestic environment that influences Canada's foreign policy reflect concerns that have not emerged in the early 1970s but could easily emerge again (i.e., diplomatic biculturalism, special international status for Quebec, the federalist "helpful fixer" role in Canadian foreign policy). Except for Kenneth McNaught's contribution, the essays on the western alliance are not so relevant today, but most of the chapters on Canada's effectiveness in the underdeveloped world are. This book also captures something of the emerging debate on American economic influence on Canada.

For a further taste of the relevance and irrelevance of NATO and NORAD to Canada, it is useful to read Lewis Hertzman's impatience with NATO and his call for less Canadian military spending in *Alliances and Illusions: Canada and the NATO-NORAD Question,* by Lewis Hertzman, John Warnock and Thomas Hockin. This slim volume also gives the reader a taste—in John Warnock's chapter on NORAD—of a firm anti-American position that argues the lack of any need for American-Canadian co-operation in the air defence of North America. The section by Thomas Hockin tries to explain the declining relevance of NATO for Canadian foreign policy, given Canada's "voluntarist" view of the world. It also discusses some of the reasons why the Department of External Affairs and Parliament did not generate a convincing reinterpretation of the role of NATO before Prime Minister Trudeau's decision to cut back Canada's contribution to that alliance.

All these military, political and diplomatic issues remain vital to Canada's foreign policy, but a new concern—Canada's economic independence—has emerged as an increasingly visible part of Canadian foreign policy. A comprehensive and introductory look at this issue has yet to be produced, but a relentless and lucid argument about the erosion of Canadian independence through the penetration of the multinational corporation can be found in Kari Levitt's *Silent Surrender: The Multinational Corporation in Canada.* Here the now-familiar analysis that employs the ideas of the "new mercantilist" school of foreign investment (e.g., the domination of the "hinterland" by the "metropolis" and the dependency of the hinterland) is first introduced in popular but serious form to Canadians.

For a gentle antidote to some of the excessive emphasis on multinational corporations as the key form of US penetration of Canada and, more usefully, for an introductory set of comments on the Trudeau government's 1970 white paper on foreign policy, the reader will be wise to read D. C. Thomson and R. F. Swanson, *Canadian Foreign Policy: Options and Perspectives.* This book appeared in late 1971 and will emerge as an extremely useful introduction to perspectives on Canadian foreign policy for the general reader as well as the beginning student. It discusses Canadian foreign policy under rubrics similar to the government's white paper (e.g., "Canada and Europe," "The Third World and the Pacific"). Yet it gives far more historical background to these issues and provides (as the white paper did not) an introduction to "Domestic Sources of Canadian Foreign Policy," "Canada and East-West Tension" and the "Canadian-United States Relationship." This book is not a polemic. It endeavours instead to "edify the average intelligent Canadian," by going beyond the white paper and, in spots, by gently questioning it. It will not drive any reader to man the barricades but it will help him to locate many of the major forces and issues in Canadian foreign policy in the 1970s. It also is the clearest introduction in the literature to date to the obvious and significant forces that are pushing Canada to emphasize its "national interests" in its foreign policy more than ever before. This volume also includes a helpful and quite complete bibliography of the major books that discuss Canadian foreign policy as well as a brief guide to the journals and documents on this subject.

SUMMARY BIBLIOGRAPHY
General

Clarkson, Stephen, ed. *An Independent Foreign Policy for Canada?* Toronto: McClelland and Stewart, 1968.

Eayrs, James. *Northern Approaches: Canada and the Search for Peace.* Toronto: Macmillan, 1961.

———. *Minutes of the Sixties.* Toronto: Macmillan, 1961.

Granatstein, J. L. *Canadian Foreign Policy since 1945: Middle Power or Satellite?* Toronto: Copp Clark, 1969.

Thomson, D. C., and R. F. Swanson. *Canadian Foreign Policy: Options and Perspectives.* Toronto: McGraw-Hill, 1971.

Advanced

Hertzman, Lewis, John Warnock and Thomas Hockin. *Alliances and Illusions: Canada and the NATO-NORAD Question.* Edmonton: Hurtig, 1969.

Holmes, John. *The Better Part of Valour.* Toronto: McClelland and Stewart, 1970.

Levitt, Kari. *Silent Surrender: The Multinational Corporation in Canada.* Toronto: Macmillan, 1970.

Professional

Brebner, J. B. *North Atlantic Triangle: The Interplay of Canada, the United States and Great Britain.* Toronto: McClelland and Stewart, 1966, 1968.

Eayrs, James. *In Defence of Canada.* Toronto: University of Toronto Press, 1964, 1967. Vol. 1, *From the Great War to the Great Depression.* Vol. 2, *Appeasement and Rearmament.*

Glazebrook, G. P. deT. *A History of Canadian External Relations.* Toronto: McClelland and Stewart, 1966. Vol. 1, *The Formative Years to 1914.* Vol. 2, *In the Empire and the World 1914-1939.*

Keenleyside, Hugh L., et al. *The Growth of Canadian Policies in External Affairs.* Durham, N.C.: Duke University Press, 1960.

3 Society

Canadian Society
Kathleen Herman

Kathleen Herman is assistant professor in the Department of Sociology at Queen's University in Kingston. She has worked for many years in public and private agencies in Canada at the local, provincial and federal levels, and is the co-editor, with D. I. Davies, of Social Space: Canadian Perspectives.

I began thinking about this essay while I was attending a meeting of sociologists from various universities across Canada. I decided it would be interesting and informative to do a small (and most unscientific!) survey. I asked several people there to give me their choices for the five best books about Canadian society. Most, without hesitation, named first John Porter's *Vertical Mosaic*. Many gave as their second choice S. D. Clark's *The Developing Canadian Community*. The third choice did not come quite so easily, though the study of *Crestwood Heights* by John Seeley and his associates was mentioned probably more often than any other. After that there was hesitation, groping, embarrassment. Might edited collections of essays be included? Did they have to be about Canada as a whole or were microscopic studies that focused on some particular facet of Canadian life or some local area admissible choices as well? I recount this anecdote not only because I need an introduction to this essay but because it says something about sociology—and sociologists—in Canada today. Though the sample was small and the settings in which the question was put not always conducive to sober reflection, yet the results are worthy of comment.

First, there are not very many good studies of Canadian society* readily available in book form. This does

*There are some who argue that it makes no sense to speak of *a* Canadian society; at the very least there are two within the one nation. I do not agree. However, I do not think this is the place to enter that debate.

not mean that Canadian society has not been studied by social scientists. To the contrary, a good deal of work has been done, especially by economists, largely under the sponsorship of government departments and agencies or for the numerous royal commissions that have been such a characteristic part of our political process. For the most part these reports are atheoretical, technical, highly specialized and noncumulative. They contain a wealth of information but most of it lies buried in government documents, valuable for scholarly research but not of much interest to the general reader or the beginning student.

Second, sociologists in Canada are divided along linguistic lines. English-speaking sociologists are not very familiar with work done in Quebec by French-speaking sociologists and, though to a lesser extent at least until fairly recently, the reverse holds true as well. This duality parallels the division that exists in most parts of Canadian life which in itself, and to our shame, has not been much studied by sociologists. But linguistic barriers are not the only—perhaps not even the principal—reason for this division. Widely divergent theoretical and methodological orientations have divided sociologists as well. While genuine theoretical introspection and debate is essential for the development of social sciences worthy of the name, yet polemic as a kind of one-upmanship is enervating, self-indulgent and unproductive.

Third, the paucity of good sociological analyses of Canadian society says something about the people who are doing sociology in Canada today or have done it in the past. In his superb study of Canadian social structure, *The Vertical Mosaic*, John Porter has provided abundant evidence of the extent to which Canada has been a way-station for persons passing through on their way to, or back to, the United States. This has been very much the case with sociologists. Until quite recently, most sociologists teaching in Canadian universities had received their graduate education in the United States and many of them were, in fact, natives of that country. These persons came to teach in Canada for a few years, always planning to go back to the States as soon as an opportunity was presented. Their orientation, then, was to American sociology and to research that would start them on the American occupational ladder. Canadian society or Canadian issues were not their central concerns.

Of course there were exceptions. Most notable, perhaps, is Everett C. Hughes, whose 1943 study *French Canada in Transition*, which explored French-English relations in one industrial community in Quebec, became a very good starting point for further sociological inquiry into the extent to which the ethnic structure of Quebec society was a class structure as well. This classic study, now thirty years old, is still well worth reading, for more recent research, particularly that done for the Royal Commission on Bilingualism and Biculturalism, provides plenty of evidence that many of the same structural relations still pertain. Further, Hughes's study demonstrates, poignantly and forcefully, that the wide gulf that kept French and English apart in the working world was not exclusively or even primarily a cultural division. Generated by the social structure of Quebec industry, it became self-reinforcing. A careful reading of this study provides a base line from which to view developments in Quebec today. This study is illuminating in another way as well. It provides a case study of the extent to which structures, while a product of history, generate consequences that reinforce and entrench them ever more deeply. The parallel with Canadian-American relations is striking.

Hughes's pioneering work spawned a host of studies over the next two decades, many of them by French Canadian sociologists who, like Hughes, had been trained at the University of Chicago. As these studies accumulated (for the most part they were not reported in English journals), French Canadian consciousness deepened. It was only a matter of time before the hierarchical division along ethnic lines would come to be seen in Marxian terms as a class division. This is the transition that many Quebec sociologists have now made.

Marcel Rioux's *Quebec in Question* (1971) is just such an analysis. "A century of Confederation," he says, "shows that the State has mystified only the colonized people. The colonial masters have received the dividends of this abstract universalism in staggering quantities of hard cash. What about the proletariat of the dominated nation?" Later he answers his own question. "If the people's awareness of their servile and inferior condition continues to grow, all is not lost." Towards the end of his book Rioux asserts, "Since 1960, ethnic consciousness and class consciousness have developed along parallel lines." I would go further and say that his whole book is eloquent testimony that ethnic consciousness has *become* class consciousness. Rioux is a separatist, and his book is an earnest attempt to get the reader to view the world through his eyes. It is essential for a real understanding of Quebec today.

Rioux is the co-editor, with Yves Martin, of an earlier book, *French-Canadian Society* (1964), which brings together an exceptional collection of twenty-five essays written over a period of thirty years, all but five of them by French Canadians. Each of these essays analyzes changes in Quebec society from the time of settlement up to the Quiet Revolution of the early sixties. A second volume is intended to deal with changes since that time.

(For a more elaborate discussion of Quebec sociology the reader is referred to the essay by Philippe Garigue, "French Canada: A Case Study in Sociological Analysis," which appears in *Canada: A Sociological Profile*, edited by W. E. Mann.)

French-English relations, which have come to dominate much of the political stage in Canada in recent years, were not the principal focus of sociologists outside Quebec. Reflecting the interests of economic historians and political economists (their academic sponsors in Canadian universities), early sociologists directed their attention towards developments on the Canadian frontier. Noteworthy in this regard (but more for reference purposes and scholarly research than for popular reading) is the nine-volume series edited by economists W. A. Mackintosh and W. L. G. Joerg, *Canadian Frontiers of Settlement* (1934-40). The three volumes in this series by Carl Dawson, the first sociologist in this country (with co-authors for two of them), *The Settlement of the Peace River Country; Group Settlement: Ethnic Communities in Western Canada;* and *Pioneering in the Prairie Provinces*, are useful references for students seeking to understand present-day Canadian society and present-day Canadians. The extent to which the experience of isolation combined with the challenge of a harsh physical environment has shaped Canadian attitudes and values (particularly those of western Canadians) is vividly documented in these studies. Canada's ethnic pluralism, which has been noted by most students of Canadian society, can be better understood perhaps as a practical consequence of these early settlement patterns rather than the self-conscious expression of a liberal ethic.

No serious student of Canadian society should be ignorant of the "staples theory of economic development" so richly elaborated by Harold A. Innis, economic historian at the University of Toronto for more than a quarter of a century. Whether he focuses on the fur trade, the fisheries on the Atlantic seaboard, the lumbering industry or wheat farming on the western prairies, Innis develops his thesis that the exploitation (originally through the fur trade) of the vast, open and relatively empty space that was later to become Canada required extensive organization which led to the formation of economic monopolies. To protect these monopolies a military policy was needed, and that meant centralized political control, manifest in the activities of the government, the church and the seigneurial system. In his *The Fur Trade in Canada,* he makes this claim: "No such tendency toward unity of structure in institutions and toward centralized control as found in Canada can be observed in the United States. The diversity of institutions has made possible the combination of government ownership and private enterprise which has been a further characteristic of Canadian development." By the time western Canada was opened up this pattern was well established. The introduction of a single-crop economy (wheat) was necessitated largely through external economic needs and technological resources, principally those of Britain and the United States. The fact that rural settlement patterns in Canada (particularly in the West) occurred during and not prior to modern industrialism and, further, that they were shaped by external and not indigenous needs, Innis argues, seriously handicapped the development of a strong sense of community, whether at the local or national level. Very early, people in the hinterland came to perceive themselves as objects of exploitation from the industrial heartland. Innis elaborates on these ideas in his *Problems of Staple Production in Canada* (1933) and *Essays in Canadian Economic History* (1956).

In a recent essay, "Canadian Society and History as Hinterland Versus Metropolis" (in *Canadian Society*, edited by R. Ossenberg), Arthur K. Davis develops the hinterland-metropolis framework further. Essentially this is a dialectical model that rests heavily on Marx's analysis of class conflict. Davis argues that such a model is appropriate to the analysis of Canadian society at any level. In looking at French-English relations, for example, Quebec would be hinterland, English Canada metropolis; or, in our contemporary cities, the urban poor become hinterland to the remainder of the city's metropolis. In the larger context of Canadian-American relations, all Canada is seen as hinterland to the US metropolis. The essential point is that such a theoretical perspective directs our attention to oppositions rather than similarities. While open conflict is not necessary to the resolution of these oppositions (though it certainly cannot be ruled out), the point is that they will be resolved only through major structural change. Mere accommodation at the periphery will, in the long run, accentuate rather than relax the conflict. Davis takes issue with the complacent explanation, so characteristically Canadian, that what distinguishes us from Americans is our lack of a revolutionary tradition or, as some argue, our counter-revolutionary tradition. It might be more fruitful, Davis suggests, to look at Canada as being in a prerevolutionary stage.

I have mentioned the pioneering works of Dawson and Innis because I am convinced one cannot understand Canadian society today without knowing something about how our institutional structures have developed. A shorter book, and easier to read, is S. D. Clark's *The Developing Canadian Community*, which brings together the work of three decades. In his early work Clark views the development of the Canadian frontiers as a continuous cycle of disintegration-reorganization. The frontier, he shows, was not left to develop unchecked, as has been claimed for the American frontier. Rather, it was a controlled development with control remaining in the hands of the central authorities—first the imperial government in England, and later, the central government in Canada. Such control, rather than being resented, was expected and welcomed. Most of Canada was settled by persons who were not rejecting traditional ways of life but who wanted them transplanted and preserved in the New World. Our conservatism and élitism, which so many observers have remarked on, were built in from the beginning.

Clark's discussion of the role of religion in the political development of Canada is particularly intriguing. Much political protest, inhibited from full expression because of the central control exerted on the hinterland, was deflected to religious protest through sectarian movements. Sometimes, as in the case of the Social Credit movement in Alberta, these religious sects became the nucleus for innovative political movements, though not losing their fundamentalist flavour. Canada has not lacked revolutionary sentiments, Clark suggests; but these have never been allowed to coalesce to the point where they could become successful revolutionary movements. Always the central power has moved in to crush, frequently in a violent way, any incipient threat to that power.

The rise of Social Credit in Alberta in the 1930s has stimulated more studies by social scientists than any other single phenomenon in our history. (To explain why this is so, and why other landmark events—the Winnipeg General Strike, for example—have been neglected is in itself an interesting study in the sociology of sociology!) John Irving in his *The Social Credit Movement in Alberta* (1959)—one of a ten-volume series—documents the extent to which Social Credit was a reactionary (and not a revolutionary) movement of protest directed against the exploitative eastern banking and financial interests. Alberta farmers, suffering severe deprivation as a consequence of the depression, embraced it with a religious fervour. Though conditions have changed considerably in the ensuing thirty years, western hostility towards the industrial heartland remains.

Seymour Martin Lipset's *Agrarian Socialism* is a much-quoted study that deals with the CCF rise to power in Saskatchewan in 1944. Although it has been much criticized for its uncritical application of an inappropriate American functionalist model without taking into consideration the unique Canadian settlement patterns and political structures (an error the author acknowledges in the revised edition), the book is still worth reading for what it has to say about underlying structures that facilitate the mobilization of a politically self-conscious "class." Because of the special nature of wheat farming on the western prairies, farmers had organized themselves into various self-help collectives, some of which took on the character of study groups. Here, their antagonisms towards eastern banking interests were nurtured and, when the time came, the groups provided a ready-made organization for an effective populist protest. With the wisdom of twenty-five years of hindsight it now seems plain that what Lipset took to be the expression of a genuinely socialist consciousness was but another protest of hinterland against centre. In the revised and updated 1968 edition of the book there are five essays on subsequent developments (including two on the 1962 medicare fight that led to the first doctors' strike on the continent). These essays do indeed suggest that Lipset's interpretation was more sanguine than accurate.

A quite different methodological and theoretical approach is taken by John Porter in his monumental structural analysis of Canadian society, *The Vertical Mosaic* (1965). Despite its subtitle—*An Analysis of Social Class and Power in Canada*—this is not, strictly speaking, a study of either *class* or *power.* Class, as defined by Marx, refers to opposing groups of individuals self-consciously aware of their objective position in the social structure and of their affinity of interests with others in the same position. Conflict is inevitable. Power, as defined by Weber, refers to the capacity to have others do your bidding even against their will. This implies having recourse to force if necessary. What Porter is dealing with is *stratification*, a much milder and less radical concept than class. Stratification refers to the layering of society according to certain attributes that the society as a whole values. In Canada, he shows, the principal ranking systems are along ethnic, economic and religious lines with all of them underscored and reinforced by the educational ranking system. For a full six hundred pages he documents the awesome extent to which the fact of birth is still the most important determinant of one's ambitions and opportunities in this country. This flies in the face of "one of the most important images that Canadians have of their society . . . that it has no classes." But, Porter tells us, "social images are one thing and social realities another." At the apex of each ranking system is a small, tightly knit élite, access into which is carefully controlled from the inside. It is these élites, Porter claims, that make most of the major decisions affecting all aspects of Canadian life. Hence, the power. Though not denying there are men of power in Canada (after the 1970 War Measures Act I am sure there are!), yet Porter's evidence does not prove this to be so. To do that it would be necessary to examine actual acts and decisions, tracing them to their sources and examining their implementation. To document structural rigidities is necessary—and most suggestive—but not sufficient. I do not wish to diminish in any way the immense importance of this study. It has probably done more than any other book to raise the level of consciousness of Canadians (and hence, perhaps, to the formation of classes in the Marxian sense of that term?). Yet it too exhibits some of the same parochial miasma that I have noted of Lipset and others. It may be that without considering Canada's economic bondage to the US, Porter imputes more power to the men at the top than they in fact possess. Also, there is his neglect of women. Apparently he does not see, or did not see at the time he wrote the book, that sex is still the most invidious ranking in our society. (In all fairness it must be said that no one else was thinking much about these matters in 1965 either!)

Since Porter we have become increasingly aware of how little we know about our own society. For the reasons stated at the outset of this essay, social scientists (particularly sociologists) have uncritically assumed—and quite incorrectly—that Canadian society was a pale counterpart of American society. We were just not as far along the continuum of development. Ergo! Learn about Canada by studying America! Or, apply American models to the analysis of Canadian problems. Now, as we are coming to free ourselves from this bondage, new books are appearing that reflect our growing self-awareness.

On the subject of poverty there is *The Real Poverty Report* (1971) by Ian Adams et al, who resigned from the staff of the Senate poverty committee because of fundamental disagreements over the direction that report ought to take. The dissident authors present a forceful case that radical structural change is needed if Canadians are serious about wanting to eradicate poverty. They argue that, by focusing on the plight of the victims rather than on the economic structures that create poverty, meaningful change is unlikely to occur. The book needs to be read. Yet I would argue that we do not arrive at truth by substituting one ideological analysis for another. We cannot focus only on structures; we have to get inside poverty, as it were, in order to see how it shapes the attitudes of its victims. People act on the basis of their subjective perceptions of reality. "If people define situations as real they are real in their consequences." It was said by W. I. Thomas long ago. We need studies then with that quality of empathy that will help us to see how persons variously placed in the social structure define *their* reality.

One such study is *Working People* by James Lorimer and Myfanwy Phillips. Subtitled *Life in a Downtown City Neighbourhood*, the book examines in considerable detail the daily life of four families living east of Parliament in downtown Toronto. The authors lived with these people for about a year and a half and came to know them very well. (This is the methodology of the anthropologist who endeavours to become a part of the community he is studying.) The book tells us a lot. It is a sociological maxim that "identity is socially bestowed," by which we mean that it is through the assessments of others that we come to perceive ourselves. Lorimer has shown how working people, defined by others as inferior, come to accept that judgment of themselves and then act in such ways that it becomes real. Similarly, defined as politically apathetic, they become so—resigned to their powerlessness. Thus the "self-fulfilling prophecy," which is made so plain throughout the book but in a jargon-free way. In two chapters, Lorimer, an economist, adopts a more strictly analytical and theoretical stance. He tells us:

> East of Parliament residents are not different because they live in old houses, because they often have lower-than-average incomes, or because their neighbours are low income. They are different fundamentally because of the basic conditions of their economic and political life—the blue-collar work they do, their experience with political institutions and agencies, and so on. These conditions produce a pattern of life which in most respects, economically and politically as well as socially, is quite different from the pattern of middle-class people.

He argues that working people must end their isolation and work to change the world. "Either they will do it themselves or it will not be done."

One last book on the subject of poverty is the collection of essays, most of them written since 1965, edited by Harp and Hofley and entitled *Poverty in Canada* (1971). There is a nice balance between essays that are theoretical and those that are empirical. Most of these, I suspect, would be criticized by Ian Adams for neglecting the fundamental social, political and economic structures that create poverty. Instead they focus on consequences and make suggestions for the alleviation of some of the more dire ones. I recommend, in particular, Alan Borovoy on Indians, John Harp on the rural poor and Gosselin's "The Third Solitude." Also, the classic statement from George Simmel, written in 1908, which is included in this volume should be read. It is still the best sociological analysis of what it means to be poor. "What makes one poor," Simmel says, "is not the lack of means. The poor person, sociologically speaking, is the individual who receives assistance because of this lack of means." For the reader who wishes to delve further into this most persistent and perplexing problem there is an excellent bibliography.

I have already commented that stratification in Canadian society, whether racial, ethnic, economic or sexual, has not been much studied by Canadian sociologists, whose models have led them to assume all too easily that Canadian society is white, male, English speaking and middle class. We have, for example, practically nothing on Indians and Eskimos (except reports prepared for government departments and agencies) or on blacks. The excellence of the anthropological studies prepared for the purpose of shaping government policy has been muted because of their assumption of white superiority and their belief that assimilation is not only inevitable, but what the native people themselves want. This assumption has been challenged, most dramatically in the case of Indian reaction to the federal white paper (which had been influenced considerably by the two-volume Hawthorn Report).

Once again we have to admit that we have not done our job very well; we must turn to others if we want to understand Indian-white relations. Harold Cardinal's outcry, *The Unjust Society* (1969), Heather Robertson's *Reservations Are for Indians* (1970), and Waubageshig's *The Only Good Indian* (1970) are needed to redress the imbalance. J. L. Elliott has brought together in *Native Peoples* (1971) ten essays that sketch the lineaments of Indians' and Eskimos' situations today, though these too are not completely free of the biases I have referred to.

The Blacks in Canada (1971) by Robin Winks is a mammoth (546 pages) history that spans three hundred and fifty years. Not many of us know, I suspect, that there was slavery in this country for two hundred years (from 1620 to 1833). Not many of us know either, I would guess, that there are an estimated one hundred thousand Negroes in Canada today. In this denial of the black tile in our mosaic, as Winks so colourfully puts it, we give validity to his claim that Canadians publicly accept blacks while rejecting them in private. This is the most invidious kind of discrimination, for it allows us to engage in the charade of denial and to avoid facing up to our real sentiments. Most interesting is Winks's revelation that the blacks themselves—at least until fairly recently—have engaged in the same techniques of denial and reality avoidance. I wonder whether we have something here that tells us more about the Canadian character than the host of speculative analyses that try to place us somewhere (always lower!) on the same continuum as the Americans.

Stanley Lieberson's *Language and Ethnic Relations in Canada* (1970) is an ecological analysis of bilingualism in this country. Using data from censuses as well as from his own research for the B&B commission, he sorts out the social factors affecting bilingualism and its maintenance. Whether a person will learn to speak one or the other or both of Canada's official languages and whether he will continue to speak them and to pass them on to his children is to a considerable extent a function of where he lives and his place in the social structure. It would be unfair to accuse Lieberson of ecological determinism because he does not incorporate social-psychological and cultural factors into his analysis, or because he does not take into account larger questions of political process and social structure. Of course he knows these are important, perhaps even more important than the demographic factors. But it is these latter he has set out to uncover and he does this very well. We learn, for example, that even though bilingualism among the French has remained more or less stable for the past several decades, there has been at the same time a steady and rapid increase of assimilation of French Canadians. These are persons who report French as their ethnic group, but English as their first language. To understand how this comes about we would need to study, by more direct methods, patterns of interaction between French and English in various parts of Canada and throughout the social structure. In this connection it is worth noting that other social scientists have pointed to the role of the ethnic church in perpetuating linguistic and cultural divisions. Though language is not the only basis on which ethnic groups maintain their boundaries, and hence their purity, it is still a very powerful one.

Crestwood Heights (1956) by John Seeley and others is a splendid "study of the culture of suburban life." It is premised on the assumption (which I have contended is erroneous) that Canada's development pattern will be the same as the US. (We are just a little backward!) The authors write: "North Americans may know its [Crestwood Heights's] features well, for some community like it is to be seen in and around almost any great city on this continent from New York to San Francisco, from Halifax to Vancouver." It may well be that the upper-middle-class Forest Hill Village in mid-town Toronto resembles a US suburb more closely than others in Canada. It is easy to find similarities when that is what one is looking for. But if one starts with a model that would require putting Crestwood Heights into the total context of Canadian society, attention might well be directed to differences. Even with these reservations, we can still learn a lot about this kind of community.

We must be careful, though, not to generalize to other Canadian communities or to set up Crestwood Heights as a prototype towards which all Canadian communities are evolving.

Just how much Crestwood Heights is in no way the typical or prototypical Canadian community is well illustrated by Rex Lucas's study of "life in Canadian communities of single industry," *Minetown, Milltown, Railtown* (1971). About a million Canadians live in the more than six hundred communities of less than thirty thousand population that are dominated by a single industry. Lucas challenges the myth that Canada is an urban country, census data notwithstanding. In the first place, Statistics Canada classifies as urban all communities of one thousand and over. This is a definition that has no sociological meaning whatsoever. It is obvious that life in a community of one thousand is qualitatively as well as quantitatively different from life in one of ten thousand, just as life there is different from that in a city of one hundred thousand, and so on. Urbanism as a way of life is not taken into account in census data. But it is "way of life" that Lucas is trying to get at in the three company towns he studied intensively. He gathered indirect data on numerous others. While possibly his sample was skewed so that he depends too heavily on information from the top (whether of union or management), yet still he is able to provide us with a good account of life in these communities. This is a life that Canadians from both our principal ethnic groups share. Their preoccupation with isolation, fatalism, their conservatism and authoritarianism, their dislike of overt display whether of hostility or pleasure or pride, their self-effacement, their resignation to scaled-down ambitions—in a word their colourlessness—is all there. It is just such hinterland communities that have shaped the consciousness and world view of many of us. Though we no longer live in them we probably have more in common with them than with the inhabitants of Crestwood Heights.

For the student looking for a concise overview of the Canadian population structure there is *The Demographic*

Bases of Canadian Society (1971) by Kalbach and McVey. While this is hardly a book that the general reader will curl up with and be unable to put down until he has finished, yet it is a valuable source of reference. "It provides as simply as possible," the authors tell us, "the basic information about Canada's population; e.g. its growth, distribution, components of change, and characteristics of individuals and families." Of particular interest within the context of the points I have tried to make in this essay are the discussions of migration patterns, urbanization and industrialization, and Canada in the context of world trends.

There are several collections that ought to be mentioned—most of them, alas! uneven in quality. They are "Canadian" to the extent that they deal with Canadian phenomena; they are "American" in terms of the models they use and the assumptions they make. Often, this serves to confuse more than it enlightens. Of the many that are now coming out, four representative books are listed as supplementary reading at the end of the summary bibliography.

Of a different order are *Canadian Society*, edited by R. Ossenberg, and *Social Space: Canadian Perspectives*, edited by D. I. Davies and K. Herman. The editors of these two volumes have, though in quite different ways, put together essays that constitute a coherent whole within an overarching framework that they hope is distinctively Canadian. Both frameworks point more to antagonisms, conflict and opposing interests than to consensus, harmony and equilibrium. Perhaps there is hope yet that we will be able to have a truly indigenous sociology that begins to ask the right questions about Canadian society.

SUMMARY BIBLIOGRAPHY
All are general.

Adams, Ian, William Cameron, Brian Hill and Peter Penz. *The Real Poverty Report*. Edmonton: Hurtig, 1971.

Cardinal, Harold. *The Unjust Society*. Edmonton: Hurtig, 1969.

Clark, S. D. *Church and Sect in Canada*. Toronto: University of Toronto Press, 1948.

———. *The Developing Canadian Community*. 2nd ed. Toronto: University of Toronto Press, 1968.

———. *Movements of Political Protest*. Toronto: University of Toronto Press, 1959.

———. *The Social Development of Canada*. Toronto: University of Toronto Press, 1942.

———. *The Suburban Society*. Toronto: University of Toronto Press, 1966.

Davies, D. I., and K. Herman, eds. *Social Space: Canadian Perspectives*. Toronto: New Press, 1971.

Elliott, Jean Leonard, ed. *Native Peoples*. Scarborough: Prentice-Hall, 1971.

Harp, John, and John R. Hofley, eds. *Poverty in Canada*. Scarborough: Prentice-Hall, 1971.

Hawthorn, H. B., ed. *A Survey of the Contemporary Indians of Canada*. 2 vols. Ottawa, 1966, 1967.

Hughes, Everett C. *French Canada in Transition*. Chicago: University of Chicago Press, 1943.

Innis, Harold A. *Essays in Canadian Economic History*. Toronto: University of Toronto Press, 1956.

———. *The Fur Trade in Canada*. Rev. ed. Toronto: University of Toronto Press, 1956.

———. *Problems of Staple Production in Canada*. Toronto: Ryerson, 1933.

Irving, John A. *The Social Credit Movement in Alberta*. Toronto: University of Toronto Press, 1959.

Kalbach, Warren E., and Wayne McVey. *The Demographic Bases of Canadian Society*. Toronto: McGraw-Hill, 1971.

Lieberson, Stanley. *Language and Ethnic Relations in Canada*. New York: John Wiley and Sons, 1970.

Lipset, Seymour Martin. *Agrarian Socialism*. Berkeley: University of California Press, 1950. Paper ed. New York: Doubleday, Anchor Books, 1968.

Lorimer, James, and Myfanwy Phillips. *Working People: Life in a Downtown City Neighbourhood*. Toronto: James Lewis & Samuel, 1971.

Lucas, Rex. *Minetown, Milltown, Railtown*. Toronto: University of Toronto Press, 1971.

Mackintosh, W. A., and W. L. G. Joerg. *Canadian Frontiers of Settlement*. 9 vols. Toronto: University of Toronto Press, 1934-40. Vol. 6, *The Settlement of the Peace River Country: A Study of a Pioneer Area*, by Carl Dawson and R. W. Murchie. Vol. 7, *Group Settlement: Ethnic Communities in Western Canada*, by Carl Dawson. Vol. 8, *Pioneering in the Prairie Provinces: The Social Side of the Settlement Process*, by Carl Dawson and Eva Younge.

Ossenberg, R., ed. *Canadian Society*. Toronto: Prentice-Hall, 1971.

Porter, John. *The Vertical Mosaic*. Toronto: University of Toronto Press, 1965.

Rioux, Marcel. *Quebec in Question*. Toronto: James Lewis & Samuel, 1971.

Rioux, Marcel, and Yves Martin, eds. *French-Canadian Society*. Toronto: McClelland and Stewart, 1964.

Robertson, Heather. *Reservations Are for Indians*. Toronto: James Lewis & Samuel, 1970.

Seeley, John R., et al. *Crestwood Heights*. Toronto: University of Toronto Press, 1956.

Waubageshig, ed. *The Only Good Indian*. Toronto: New Press, 1970.

Winks, Robin M. *The Blacks in Canada*. New Haven and Montreal: Yale University Press and McGill-Queen's University Press, 1971.

Supplementary Reading List

Blishen, B. E., et al., eds. *Canadian Society*. 3rd ed. Toronto: Macmillan, 1971.

Ishwaran, K., ed. *The Canadian Family*. Toronto: Holt Rinehart and Winston, 1971.

Mann, W. E., ed. *Canada: A Sociological Profile*. Toronto: Copp Clark, 1968.

———. ed. *Social and Cultural Change in Canada*. Toronto: Copp Clark, 1970. Vols. 1 and 2.

Women
Sandra Gwyn

Sandra Gwyn is a freelance writer and reviewer. She was a writer-editor for the federal Task Force on Government Information and the Secretary of State's Committee on Youth, and compiled a monograph, Women in the Arts in Canada, *for the Royal Commission on the Status of Women.*

There are plenty of women writers in Canada, but there is so little women's lit* that the only definitive account of how the vote was won (and, what is really more interesting, how the Imperial Privy Council's Judicial Committee was persuaded that "Persons" in the BNA Act meant women too) was written by a US scholar as her Columbia University PhD thesis. For lack of native-born de Beauvoirs or Greers, nearly everything that does exist—if this says a good deal about Canada it says more about Canadian women—is the work of civil servants. The hallmarks of their modestly impressive stack of reports, statistical analyses and pamphlets are solid research, cautious propagandizing—and a certain bloodlessness.

The place to begin, obviously, is the *Report* of the Royal Commission on the Status of Women in Canada. Unquestionably, this 499-page, information-crammed volume—the end product of four years' work, 468 briefs and $1.9 million—is a major achievement, the indispensable reference work in the field. It is also, unfortunately, dull and disjointed, put together without feeling or point of view. "A bleak and awkward document," Christina Newman has written, "so lacking in passion that it might be a report on freight rates, so devoid of personality that it might have been punched

---

*Defined, by the editors of *Read Canadian,* as nonfiction writing about Canadian women, in book form.

out by a computer."

The report's great strength—the reason that, for all its faults, it *is* indispensable—is the quality, even more, the sheer volume of its research. The total cumulative effect is to demonstrate, beyond argument, that women today as a class are having to cope with social change and upheaval as profound as our whole society endured during the Industrial Revolution. At the source, the evidence in the report suggests, is the squeeze that's developed between actual social and economic realities (between the cumulative impact of the pill, the decline of the extended family, the rural-urban shift, a labour force that's a third female, half a million mothers who work) and the traditional role and image women have always been assigned.

The trouble is, the reader almost has to figure this out for her(him)self. Bad organization and unnecessary repetition often blur the line of argument. And the commissioners, when they came to write about ideas and social forces, as opposed to presenting facts and figures, were frequently inclined to waffle.*

The best sections deal with those two areas where hard information was easiest to come by: women in the economy and women in the educational system. Together these account for well over half the text; they discuss everything from the way little girls are illustrated in grade-one readers to the numbers of women who are bank managers. Almost as effective is the short chapter on poverty. In fact, the single most important achievement of the report may well have been its unemotional depiction of the plight of women who are poor; the plight, in particular, of the sole-support mother.

But in 1536 numbered paragraphs, there are only three isolated references to the Women's Liberation Movement; there is virtually no discussion of female psychology; the chapter on women in politics and public life is painfully thin; and abortion and birth control are treated so circumspectly that they're listed

*For those who find the report heavy going, a forty-eight-page study guide, *What's In It?* has been prepared by the Canadian Association for Adult Education.

in the table of contents under "Responsible Parenthood." (To be fair, the actual recommendations in these areas, as throughout the report, are relatively tough.)

Another failing, in view of the report's importance as a document of national social policy, is that it treats Canadian women as if they were one homogeneous blob, taking virtually no account of regional characteristics, or what sociologists like to call "environmental factors." The persistent reader, though, can uncover at least some of the characteristics that set certain groups of Canadian women apart from others in studies the commission published separately.*

A useful introduction about the women of Quebec, for instance, can be found in Micheline D.-Johnson's essay, *History of the Status of Women in Quebec* and Francine Dépatie's analysis of the *Participation of Women in Politics in Quebec*. Neither delves very deeply into the Québécoise's psyche (by far the best exploration of this is Jean LeMoyne's essay, "Women and French Canadian Civilization" in *Convergences*) but together they provide a cogent account of the forces that have shaped her and the development of her political and legal consciousness. (Micheline Johnson is particularly good on the powerful role the single woman has played in Quebec society). *The Cultural Tradition of Canadian Women* by Margaret Wade Labarge, though skimpy in the Canadian context, is a lucid, literate historical summary of prevailing attitudes towards women from Aristotle to John Stuart Mill. Margaret MacLellan's *History of Women's Rights in Canada* is plodding and awkward but—in the absence of anything else in print—is a useful abbreviated guide to what act was passed when. And Sandra Gwyn's *Women in the Arts in Canada* is a comprehensive and quite detailed account of how and why Canadian women, now and in the past, have

---

*A dozen of these were published. Most, however, were fairly technical (i.e., *Patterns of Manpower Utilization in Canadian Department Stores; Taxation of the Incomes of Married Women*) and since the key findings were incorporated into the report, only those of general interest are mentioned here.

been more successful in the arts than any other competitive field.

Most other government publications about women concentrate on a single area: the whys and hows of their participation in the labour force. The two major studies—Sylvia Ostry's *The Female Worker in Canada*, and *Women Who Work*, a two-part survey by John Allingham and Byron Spencer—are based on 1961 census data; their principal findings centre around changing patterns of female employment that became evident in that survey, particularly the return of married women to the labour force. Two excellent examinations of how the nation's single largest employer of women behaves towards them are Stanislauw Judek's *Women in the Public Service* and Kathleen Archibald's *Sex and the Public Service*. The latter illustrates how, in federal circles, some people are more equal than others: in one experiment outlined, officials were asked to rate the paper qualifications of a number of candidates; given a male name, one candidate was rated first 86% of the time; with a female name, the same person ranked first only 58% of the time.

Seminal as they are, these four studies are of primary interest to the specialist. And since they also formed an important part of the research base for the royal commission report, most readers will probably find that excellent argument-settler, *Women in the Labour Force: Facts and Figures*, enough to be going on with. Published annually by the Women's Bureau of the Department of Labour, this handy paperback is brightly and concisely laid out; it contains easily comprehensible statistics and brief explanatory text on everything from the amount of time women lose on the job through illness (no more than men, as it turns out) to the percentage of female workers who belong to trade unions (around twenty per cent). The current edition includes, for the first time, comparative male-female wage rates for a wide range of occupations; these indicate that equal pay for equal work is still pretty much a platitude.

Two other useful Women's Bureau publications deal with the working mother. *Maternity-Leave Policies* is a comprehensive if rather dry summary of Canadian practices circa 1969; *Working Mothers and Their Child-Care Arrangements* is another factbook along the lines of *Women in the Labour Force*. For detailed information about such arrangements, the best source is *Day Care*, the report of a three-year survey carried out by the Canadian Council on Social Development. This includes a detailed analysis of a sample of 390 centres across the country; it outlines existing provincial day-care legislation, and provides an excellent summary review of existing Canadian and international studies of the effects of day care on children.

Apart from government or institutional products, books about the Canadian working woman amount to two how-to-cope manuals. Each is aimed at the mature woman thinking of going back to work, and each nicely complements the other. Sheila Kieran's *The Non-Deductible Woman* is full of reassuring advice on how to manage money, housekeeping and child care, and a husband's bruised ego. Sonja Sinclair's *I Presume You Can Type* concentrates on the job: she outlines a series of practical second careers and indicates where, across Canada, qualifying courses are available.

Another excellent how-to book is *Women and the Law* by Marvin A. Zuker and June Callwood. The opening chapter, "How To Get a Legal Abortion," is a useful abbreviated guide. Other sections thread through the complexities of divorce, provincial labour legislation and welfare regulations. This is a quick and easy handbook rather than a reference work, but the authors indicate in each case where to go for additional information. And for information about abortion in particular, that place is *Abortion in Canada*, by Eleanor Wright Pelrine. This book—the first offering in a promising New Press series called New Woman, edited by Adrienne Clarkson—contains comprehensive medical data, reviews Canadian law and discusses moral arguments pro and con. Also included are interviews with a number of doctors and reports of surveys the authors made of Canadian hospitals, and of women who have had personal experience with abortion.

Once one has been through the practical manuals, pickings become increasingly slim. On the Canadian woman in politics, the one book about the suffrage movement, Catherine Lyle Cleverdon's *The Woman Suffrage Movement in Canada*, is not only, as remarked earlier, the work of an American; it is also out of print. This account is a fairly typical example of the PhD thesis that becomes a book. It is earnestly factual and heavily footnoted, but a reader will learn next to nothing of the personalities of the women involved; still less of the ambience in which they lived. (Why, for instance, did nearly all the impetus for the movement come from Alberta?) Also out of print are two political biographies: Byrne Hope Sanders's official but none the less engaging *Emily Murphy*, the story of the Edmonton family-court judge who was probably our most interesting suffragette; and *Ask No Quarter*, Doris French and Margaret Stewart's lively, well-documented life of Agnes MacPhail, the Ontario farm girl who became our first woman MP. In fact, the only easily available work in the entire field is Judy LaMarsh's candid and idiosyncratic *Memoirs of a Bird in a Gilded Cage*. (And, a perceptive footnote, Adrienne Clarkson's review essay on Lamarsh, *The Female Style in Politics*, included in William Kilbourn's anthology, *A Guide to the Peaceable Kingdom*.)

In general biography, the work that stands out—good reading, say, for high-school students—is *The Clear Spirit*, edited by Mary Quayle Innis. This is a collection of short biographies of twenty outstanding Canadian women of the past; from the great Quebec mystic, Marie de l'Incarnation, to E. Cora Hind, the Winnipeg journalist who never failed to predict accurately the size of the wheat harvest. The contributions are a little uneven, but most authors managed to avoid sounding preachy. The best, perhaps, are Clara Thomas on the Strickland sisters (Susanna Moodie and Catharine Parr Traill), Doris French on Agnes MacPhail and Anne Montagnes on the outstanding Ottawa geologist, Dr. Alice Wilson.

For other glimpses of the Canadian woman, as she is and as she used to be, the reader has to rely, mostly, on scattered references in books whose central context is wider. Perhaps because they are more central to their culture the women of Quebec have been more imaginatively observed. In "Women and French Canadian Civilization" in his collection of essays, *Convergences,** Jean Le Moyne analyzes, profoundly and poetically, that powerful mythic figure, the fecund and at the same time virginal Quebec matriarch (". . . she stands on her linoleum, in calico, in front of a stove and a cooking pot, an infant on her left hip, a large spoon in her right hand. . . "). In her autobiography, *In an Iron Glove,* a kind of nonfiction equivalent of the novels of Marie-Claire Blais, Claire Martin writes with remorseless candour of her gothic Quebec girlhood. And Suzanne Paradis, in *Femme Fictive, Femme Réelle* (not available in translation), explores the consciousness of the Québécoise by analyzing female characters in novels by Quebec women writers.

English Canadian women usually turn up in accounts that are earnestly factual. The affluent pre-Friedan housewife of the fifties lingers in sections of that landmark sociological landscape, *Crestwood Heights;* the widow and divorcée of the late sixties reveals herself in interviews contained in *The One-Parent Family,* the report of a Council on Social Development survey. As for man-woman relationships, there are sharp insights into how men think of their wives in Adrienne Clarkson's collection of edited interviews, *True to You in My Fashion,* while Mary Van Stolk, in *Man and Woman* examines, in somewhat polemical fashion, the false premises on which these relationships can be based.

None of this, though, adds up to a solid body of work. There is a great deal more to be written, and felt, about Canadian women.

*An abbreviated version of this essay is included in *A Guide to the Peaceable Kingdom* under the title "The Strong Women of Quebec."

SUMMARY BIBLIOGRAPHY
General

Canada. Department of Labour, Women's Bureau. *Women in the Labour Force 1970: Facts and Figures.* Ottawa, 1971.

———. Royal Commission on the Status of Women in Canada. *Report.* Ottawa, 1970.

———. Royal Commission on the Status of Women in Canada. Studies.

   D.-Johnson, Micheline. *History of the Status of Women in the Province of Quebec* (1971).

   Gwyn, Sandra. *Women in the Arts in Canada* (1971).

   Labarge, Margaret Wade. *The Cultural Tradition of Canadian Women* (1971).

   MacLellan, Margaret E. *History of Women's Rights in Canada* (1971).

Canadian Association for Adult Education. *What's In It?* Ottawa: National Council of Women in co-operation with La Fédération des Femmes du Québec, 1970.

Clarkson, Adrienne. "The Female Style in Politics," in *A Guide to the Peaceable Kingdom,* ed. William Kilbourn. Toronto: Macmillan, 1970.

———. *True to You in My Fashion.* Toronto: New Press, 1971.

Cleverdon, Catherine Lyle. *The Woman Suffrage Movement in Canada.* Toronto: University of Toronto Press, 1950.

French, Doris, and Margaret Stewart. *Ask No Quarter.* Toronto: Longmans Green, 1959.

Innis, Mary Quayle, ed. *The Clear Spirit: Twenty Canadian Women and Their Times.* Toronto: University of Toronto Press, 1966.

Kieran, Sheila. *The Non-Deductible Woman: A Handbook for Working Wives and Mothers.* Toronto: Macmillan, 1970.

LaMarsh, Judy. *Memoirs of a Bird in a Gilded Cage.* Toronto: McClelland and Stewart, 1969.

LeMoyne, Jean. "Women and French Canadian Civilization," in *Convergences: Essays from Quebec.* Trans. Philip Stratford. Toronto: Ryerson, 1966.

Martin, Claire. *In an Iron Glove.* Trans. Philip Stratford. Toronto: Ryerson, 1968.

Pelrine, Eleanor Wright. *Abortion in Canada.* Toronto: New Press, 1971.

Sanders, Byrne Hope. *Emily Murphy.* Toronto: Macmillan, 1945.

Sinclair, Sonja. *I Presume You Can Type.* Toronto: CBC Publications, 1969.

Van Stolk, Mary. *Man and Woman.* Toronto: McClelland and Stewart, 1968.

Zuker, Marvin A., and June Callwood. *Canadian Women and the Law.* Toronto: Copp Clark, 1971.

Advanced

Canada. Department of Labour. *Maternity-Leave Policies, A Survey.* Ottawa, 1969.

———. Department of Labour. *Working Mothers and Their Child-Care Arrangements.* Ottawa, 1970.

———. Public Service Commission. *Sex and the Public Service,* by Kathleen Archibald. Ottawa, 1970.

Canadian Council on Social Development. *Day Care. Report of a National Study.* Ottawa, 1972.

———. *The One-Parent Family. Report of an Inquiry.* Ottawa, 1971.

Dépatie, Francine. *Participation of Women in Politics in Quebec.* In Studies of the Royal Commission on the Status of Women in Quebec. Ottawa, 1970.

Ostry, Sylvia. *The Female Worker in Canada.* Ottawa: DBS 1961 census monograph, 1968.

Paradis, Suzanne. *Femme Fictive, Femme Réelle.* Montreal: Editions Garneau, 1966.

Seeley, John R., R. Alexander Sim and Elizabeth W. Loosley. *Crestwood Heights.* Toronto: University of Toronto Press, Canadian University Paperbooks, 1963.

Professional

Canada. Department of Labour. *Women in the Public Service: Their Utilization and Employment,* by Stanislauw Judek. Ottawa, 1968.

———. DBS Special Labour Force Studies. *Women Who Work*, by John D. Allingham and Byron G. Spencer. Ottawa, 1967, 1968.

Urban Studies
Mike Goldrick

Mike Goldrick is an associate professor of political science at York University in Toronto. He is a former research director for the Bureau of Municipal Research and the co-editor, with L. D. Feldman, of Politics and Government of Urban Canada.

Literature on Canadian urban politics is sparse and relatively narrow. Far and away the largest volume of writing has been concerned with questions about legal powers and the structure and administration of urban government—in other words, with the formal machinery of government. The informal behavioural patterns that actually have more to do with urban politics—the process of determining who gets what, why and how—have been neglected.

The reason for this appears to have something to do with early traditions in the fields of political science and administration, fields from which urban politics has emerged. One tradition has been an implicit belief in and acceptance of the myths of liberal democracy, a position not restricted to municipal writers. Believing that self-interests operating in a free-market system produce the greatest good for the greatest number, students of urban politics have accepted the basic structures and processes of municipal government.

A second tradition has been linked to the first. Since the framework was sound, writers concerned themselves with studies about improving the administrative and fiscal efficiency of municipal systems. A plethora of prescriptive studies about the geographic size of municipalities, their tax bases, the division of responsibilities between them and the provinces, civil-service rules and so on tumbled forth—occasionally in books, but more often as government-sponsored studies.

Consequently, the literature over the years has been

innocent of works that confront vital problems of urban government and politics that press upon us today. Clearly, the contradictions of liberal democracy and their consequences in the cities of Canada must become the focus of contemporary research and writing. The literature will have to ask (even if it cannot yet answer) such questions as: Why are cities governed by and primarily for the benefit of large economic interests? Why are infant mortality rates in poor areas grossly in excess of those in wealthier areas? Why are welfare roles purged at the height of winter unemployment? Why are children labelled stupid if their school performance fails to conform to middle-class norms?

These questions have to do with the everyday life of urban residents and it is through the process of urban politics that they must be put. If this is to be done, the literature on urban politics must focus on at least four areas. The first has to do with identifying those who are involved in the exercise of power in urban governments. The second is concerned with how power is exercised; that is, with the recruitment of formal political leaders, with the process involved in policy making and the government machinery through which this is performed. The third involves the result of this process: how the product of public activity is distributed (that is, with the systems through which services are delivered to the public, and the impact they have on the people). Fourth and finally, future work must concentrate on examining new systems and processes of urban political activity—from the decentralization of conventional public action to extraparliamentary means of social change—in order to correct injustices in the existing order.

It is within this framework that available material will be surveyed. The short journey through it will emphasize the paucity of relevant literature and the considerable gaps that exist within it while at the same time introducing readers to what is available and what is useful.

The first area referred to above is concerned with the distribution of power in urban communities. But this concern cannot be abstracted from the broader one of how power and influence are distributed in the larger Canadian society. The classic work in this field is Porter's *Vertical Mosaic*. The book, a systematic analysis of institutionalized power, traces the origins and processes of socialization through which the élites of Canadian society pass. For a close observer of urban politics, the positions of influence described by Porter that are occupied by economic élites, the clergy, government officials and educational élites on a national level have their counterparts in the networks of influence that surround the governments of cities.

At a more specifically urban level, the question of who governs has been explored in a number of Canadian community-power studies. An early example of such work is the book *Crestwood Heights*, in which John R. Seeley et al. examine an upper-middle-class enclave in Toronto. Their analysis reveals much about the beliefs, values and behaviour of a group that in political terms exhibits manifest political efficacy. Shorter, article-length studies analyze many of the same matters. N. O. Matthew's study, "Small-Town Power and Politics," describes the network of influences in the educational system of an Edmonton suburb, while Guy Bourassa, in "The Political Elite of Montreal," reveals the transfer of power between élites in that city over the past 150 years. These studies are both concerned with the distribution of power between members of the middle class and appear in a collection of readings titled *Politics and Government of Urban Canada*.

Another series of works, most of them less "scholarly" in intent, are concerned with the working and nonworking poor of urban communities. These provide a partial explanation for élite dominance by implicitly referring to the so-called apathy of poverty, the condition that robs liberal democratic politics of its meaning for many working-class people and isolates them from urban politics. The recent book by Adams, Cameron, Hill and Penz, *The Real Poverty Report*, while not focusing directly upon political power, clearly shows the consequences of political exclusion.

Perhaps more poignantly, if not more explicitly,

Vallières's *White Niggers of America* and Butler's *Cabbagetown Diary* speak about the impact of oppression upon the ability of those cast outside the system to participate in its politics. *Working People*, an account of the lives of a group of working-class residents of Toronto, dramatizes strikingly in a chapter entitled "Political Life" the meaning of urban politics to one class of citizen. This is the politics not of expressways, skyscrapers and five-year capital budgets, but of across-the-counter harassment by minor officials, visitations by authoritarian agency workers and treatment by enforcers of middle-class laws.

The second area in which the literature of urban politics must focus is that which examines political leaders and the machinery and processes through which power is exercised. The Toronto Bureau of Municipal Research has published monographs dealing with political recruitment and the characteristics of elected representatives. *Parties to Change* is a series of studies dealing with the introduction of national and municipal parties into the 1969 Toronto civic elections. A second monograph, now several years old, analyzes the socioeconomic and attitudinal characteristics of aldermen from the boroughs and metropolitan government of Toronto. It is called *The Metro Politician.*

The one systematic treatment of urban policy making is presented in *Urban Political Systems* by Harold Kaplan. The book, touching on many areas of urban politics, contains an interesting analysis of the interplay between the bureaucracy, interest groups and elected representatives in the early days of metropolitan government in Toronto. A second book, a collection of articles originally published in the *Globe and Mail* by James Lorimer titled *The Real World of City Politics*, gets under the skin of policy making and reveals many of the "hidden agendas" that determine what municipal government will or will not do.

A study prepared for the secretary of state for Urban Affairs by Harvey Lithwick, titled *Urban Canada*, deals with a different dimension of policy making. Before offering the classic liberal solutions of more information and better technique, Lithwick describes the vacuum in urban policy making that is filled, at national, provincial and local levels of government, by the momentum of economic determinism.

The formal powers and structure of government, as previously noted, are the strong suit of the urban-politics literature. Starting way back with K. G. Crawford's contribution to the government of Canada series, *Canadian Municipal Government*, through D. C. Rowatt's *Your Local Government* to T. J. Plunkett's *Urban Canada and Its Government*, one can glean the nuts and bolts of municipal administration and organization. The most striking thing about this material is the implicit assumption that administrative arrangements apparently are benign and value' free. Yet one's intuition, verified by systematic studies relating these variables to differences in the type, level and quality of services produced by governments of varying arrangements, suggests that structure and organization in fact are highly influential in determining who does what for whom.

The third category of literature concerns the systems through which municipal services are delivered to recipients, services running through roads and schools to health and welfare services to rules governing land use, traffic regulation and early-closing by-laws. Mistakenly, many assume that "politics" ends when laws are duely passed. Yet the manner in which services are provided—or withheld—is highly political. Witness "Class Bias in Toronto Schools," appearing in the journal *This Magazine Is about Schools*; the brief to the Special Senate Committee on Poverty presented by the Social Planning and Research Council of Hamilton; the Bureau of Municipal Research monograph *Transportation: Who Plans; Who Pays;* or V. M. Anderson's "Infant Survival Differentials in the City of Toronto" in *Canadian Family Physician*. Each reveals clearly that middle-class politicians, elected by middle-class constituents and advised by professionally oriented bureaucrats, design delivery systems that maintain those unable to purchase independence and choice as dependent suppliants.

The final area concerns alternate processes and structures for governing urban areas. In one sense, the ground is thick with relevant works. For the past twenty years, there has been any number of government-sponsored reports aiming to reorganize particularly the metropolitan areas of Canada. A recent example, *Proposals for Urban Reorganization in the Greater Winnipeg Area*, is representative of this kind of study, which owes much to the "good-government" era of local government reform.

Less well known is the literature dealing with what is known variously as community organization or control, community development or, more broadly, participatory democracy. A recent collection of essays edited by Draper, entitled *Citizen Participation: Canada*, brings some of the available literature together. But much in the volume borders on the bland and conventionally acceptable. By contrast, *Participatory Democracy for Canada*, edited by Gerry Hunius, locates community control in a broadly based, ideological framework directed towards significant social change.

SUMMARY BIBLIOGRAPHY
All are general.

Adams, Ian, et al. *The Real Poverty Report*. Edmonton: Hurtig, 1971.

Anderson, V. M. "Infant Survival Differentials in the City of Toronto." *Canadian Family Physician* (September 1970).

Bureau of Municipal Research. *Transportation: Who Plans; Who Pays*. Toronto, 1970.

———. *Parties to Change*. Toronto, 1971.

———. *The Metro Politician*. Toronto, 1964.

Butler, J. *Cabbagetown Diary*. Toronto: Peter Martin Associates, 1970.

Canada. Special Senate Committee on Poverty. Submission of the Social Planning and Research Council of Hamilton. *Proceedings* 28 (March 1970).

Crawford, K. G. *Canadian Municipal Government*. Toronto: University of Toronto Press, 1954.

Draper, J. A., ed. *Citizen Participation: Canada*. Toronto: New Press, 1971.

Feldman, L. D., and M. D. Goldrick, eds. *Politics and Government of Urban Canada*. Toronto: Methuen, 1969.

Hunnius, G. *Participatory Democracy for Canada*. Montreal: Black Rose Books, 1971.

Kaplan, H. *Urban Political Systems*. New York: Columbia University Press, 1967.

Lorimer, James. *The Real World of City Politics*. Toronto: James Lewis & Samuel, 1970.

Lorimer, James, and Myfanwy Phillips. *Working People: Life in a Downtown City Neighbourhood*. Toronto: James Lewis & Samuel, 1971.

Manitoba. *Proposals for Urban Reorganization in the Greater Winnipeg Area*. Winnipeg, 1971.

Park School Council. "Class Bias in Toronto Schools." *This Magazine Is about Schools* 5, no. 4 (1971).

Porter, J. *The Vertical Mosaic*. Toronto: University of Toronto Press, 1965.

Plunkett, T. J. *Urban Canada and Its Government*. Toronto: Macmillan, 1968.

Rowatt, D. C. *Your Local Government*. Toronto: Macmillan, 1965.

Seeley, J. R. *Crestwood Heights*. Toronto: University of Toronto Press, 1956.

Vallières, Pierre. *White Niggers of America*. Toronto: McClelland and Stewart, 1971.

Poverty
James Lorimer

James Lorimer is one of the founding partners of James Lewis & Samuel. He is the author of The Real World of City Politics *and, with Myfanwy Phillips, of* Working People. *He teaches urban design in the School of Architecture at the University of Toronto.*

The subject of poverty in Canada is an American invention. Canadians became interested and concerned about poverty in this country in the early sixties because journalists, academics and policy makers in the US were in the throes of discovering there what they called the "poverty problem." It was a pure case of academic and media slopover from the US to Canada: Politicians, reading of the American "war on poverty," followed along with their pale imitation in 1965. Journalists read articles and books from the US on the subject and went off to do Canadianized versions. Students, noticing all the excitement in the media, started looking for poverty courses and academics rushed in to teach them.

It is important to understand the preconceptions about the way society works that are built into the concept of a "poverty problem." It is a help to remember that the problem was suddenly discovered and officially taken up in the US just at the time when low-income Americans, particularly blacks, were developing a much greater self-consciousness of themselves and of their economic and political oppression. Not only were they mainly working class, holding (or trying to find) blue-collar manual jobs; they were the least well-off members of the working class. By calling the problem one of poverty, US intellectuals went a long way to distracting attention from two important elements of this situation: first, the common racial background of many of the poorest Americans; and second, their common social class. By telling these people that they were, not blacks, not working-class Americans, but "poor," and by describing the situation in this way to each other, the pretence was maintained that the only difference between these people and other Americans was that they had lower incomes, less money. And the notion was being planted that everything would be all right again, fair and equal and so on, if the "poor" had somewhat more money so that they were no longer quite so low-income. Being pushed from view was the fact that they would of course still be working class, still be black or Chicano or Puerto Rican or native Indian, and still be faced with most of the same conditions of political and economic life that they experience now.

When Canadian academics, journalists and policy makers imported the idea of a "poverty problem" into Canada, they were importing this notion that we are all basically the same, and that the only important difference between us—and a difference that gives rise to all sorts of problems—is that some earn less money than others. The discussions of the poverty problem in Canada that have resulted, and the books that have been written, for the most part take this view.

The difficulty with it is that it is wrong. Its most serious flaw is that it allows us to ignore the realities of the structure of Canadian society—to ignore, for example, social classes, race and the status of Quebec as an internal colony of Canada.

What is generally described as the "poverty problem," the situation faced by people with low incomes and the accompanying difficulties, is a situation that is faced mainly by working-class people in urban Canada. Many of the characteristics that are described as part of the "poverty problem"—for instance, a cynicism about and detachment from political life—are in fact common to most working-class Canadians. Others—for instance, a very low level of health and dental care—are aspects of working-class life that are seriously exacerbated by low incomes. Not all working-class people are "poor"; in fact, incomes for the blue-collar worker range considerably and overlap with the incomes of middle-class families with white-collar jobs. But most people who are "poor" and who have the other characteristics that are supposed to go with low incomes to make up the "poverty problem" are working class.

That does not just mean that they have working-class backgrounds, and had blue-collar jobs when they were working and before they became "poor." One of the crucially important facts about low incomes in Canada is that about two of every three Canadians officially described as poor are employed. Only one in three rely mainly on government assistance of one kind or another for their incomes. The most common way to find yourself under the government's poverty line in Canada is to have a job, one that happens to pay relatively low wages.

Most of the books specifically written on the "poverty problem" in Canada ignore these facts about social classes. The most comprehensive of these poverty books is *The Real Poverty Report*, written by the four employees of Senator Croll's poverty committee who resigned with a flourish in the spring of 1971 and went on to write the poverty report they said the senator wouldn't allow them to produce for the government. Their book contains a good deal of smart semi-radical talk—about the "crummy apartments" people are forced to live in, the "unrelieved misery" of the poor, the need for a "social and political revolution" if poverty is to be ended—but underneath the polemic is an ordinary left-liberal analysis of the way the economic system produces low incomes for many people, and the way government programs of various kinds alleviate some of the worst conditions while perpetuating the system and harassing those who are being helped. Senator Croll's own report—*Poverty in Canada*—is now available, and it is instructive to compare the two books side by side. The major difference is that *The Real Poverty Report* does attempt an explanation of the existence of poverty, whereas Senator Croll does not look too closely at how his fellow senators, in their capacities as directors of the major Canadian and US corporations operating in Canada, are involved in an economic structure that inevitably yields low incomes, low wages and unemployment for many people. The Croll report is remarkable for its tear-jerking, exploitative and completely misleading set of half a dozen photographs.

There are other books that approach this subject from quite a different point of view. For one thing, instead of presenting statistical data and general analysis of economic and political conditions, they pin down the realities of life in Canada for people with relatively little money. For another, they provide information that helps to show what is inaccurate and misleading about the view that all Canadians are the same except that some of them earn less money than others.

One of these is *Working People*, a book Myfanwy Phillips and I did on an older, downtown neighbourhood of Toronto very much like the older working-class districts in every Canadian city. Most of the men living in the area have blue-collar jobs as truck drivers, warehousemen, electricians, packers and assembly-line workers; most are of Canadian or Anglo-Saxon background. Incomes in the area were about one-third less than average for the city as a whole; and many residents would fall below the official poverty line. The book describes the lives of people we became acquainted with, first in general terms and then through accounts of specific events like political meetings, evenings with friends and arguments between neighbours. Through this description it attempts to get at the basic characteristics of the life of working-class Canadians, to show what it means to be a member of that class and to show the implications of finding yourself with particularly low incomes.

Another book of this kind is *Reservations Are for Indians* by Heather Robertson, which describes in some detail life in four Indian communities in central and northern Canada. Indians and Métis are, without any doubt, the most oppressed and most victimized people of all in Canada, and there can be no doubt that this situation has been created by a combination of total government welfare bureaucracy and outside business, particularly the Hudson's Bay Company. The Robertson book describes this situation in precise and illuminating detail, and it is fascinating to read.

For more details on Indians and government policy, the best place to look is Harold Cardinal's *The Unjust Society*. Cardinal describes the attempts Indians are starting to make to organize themselves politically to change their situation. Similar things have, of course, been happening in towns and cities. Margaret Daly's *The Revolution Game* describes three such attempts, in Cape Breton, St. Jerome and Calgary, in a book that is devoted in part to exploring the attempt—and failure— of the Company of Young Canadians to provide working-class organizations with helpful organizing assistance.

Once launched into the literature on poverty, a reader with sufficient stamina could go on forever. There are several collections of articles by different authors on poverty, though generally these were created by publishers too lazy to find authors to write real books and are inferior in usefulness to the two poverty reports. Two bibliographies list in enormous detail the literature on the subject in Canada. To go further into the official poverty literature, one important book explains the distribution of income (though not wealth) in Canada, Jenny Podoluk's *Incomes of Canadians*. The Economic Council of Canada's *Fifth* and *Sixth Annual Reports* contain discussions of poverty.

The best thing that could happen to someone who was interested in reading about poverty in Canada would be that he discovered that he was really interested in a number of other subjects. For one, he would decide that he was really interested in working-class Canadians, and from *Working People* he would go on to films like Don Shebib's *Goin' Down the Road* and the NFB's *Pour la Suite du Monde*, to Claude Jutra's *Mon Oncle Antoine* and to novels like Hugh Garner's *Cabbagetown*, as well as Pierre Vallières's autobiography and political statement, *White Niggers of America*, while waiting for Canadian authors to add to the nonfiction literature on this subject. For another, he would decide that he had to learn more about the economic and political system that produces the conditions in which people on low incomes exist, and he would start with John Porter's *The Vertical Mosaic*, which sketches the structure of Canadian society and describes the élite that controls the country. He would probably also want to try to understand how Canada became the kind of society it is now, and for that purpose some history books would help. Stanley Ryerson's *Unequal Union* explores the vitally important nineteenth century; Marcel Rioux's *Quebec in Question* gives a brief history of Quebec that shows how the Quebec nation has always been colonized; Gustavus Myers's magnificently irreverent and revealing account in *A History of Canadian Wealth* of the connections between business and government shows how long is the story of domination of the political process by the economic élite; Kari Levitt's *Silent Surrender* defines the way in which Canada was taken over by the US.

That is the background that is necessary to understand why some Canadians have low incomes, and why the last decade of self-conscious soul-searching and discussion of the "poverty problem" has left many people somewhat better read but the situation itself unchanged.

SUMMARY BIBLIOGRAPHY
General

Adams, Ian, William Cameron, Brian Hill and Peter Penz. *The Real Poverty Report*. Edmonton: Hurtig, 1971.

Canada. Special Senate Committee on Poverty. *Poverty in Canada*. Ottawa, 1971.

Cardinal, Harold. *The Unjust Society*. Edmonton: Hurtig, 1969.

Daly, Margaret. *The Revolution Game*. Toronto: New Press, 1970.

Garner, Hugh. *Cabbagetown*. Toronto: Ryerson, 1950.

Levitt, Kari. *Silent Surrender*. Toronto: Macmillan, 1970.

Lorimer, James, and Myfanwy Phillips. *Working People: Life in a Downtown City Neighbourhood.* Toronto: James Lewis & Samuel, 1971.

Myers, Gustavus. *A History of Canadian Wealth.* Toronto: James Lewis & Samuel, 1972.

Porter, John. *The Vertical Mosaic.* Toronto: University of Toronto Press, 1965.

Rioux, Marcel. *Quebec in Question.* Toronto: James Lewis & Samuel, 1971.

Robertson, Heather. *Reservations Are for Indians.* Toronto: James Lewis & Samuel, 1970.

Ryerson, Stanley. *Unequal Union.* Toronto: Progress Books, 1968.

Vallières, Pierre. *White Niggers of America.* Toronto: McClelland and Stewart, 1971.

Advanced

Canada. Economic Council of Canada. *Fifth Annual Review.* Ottawa, 1968.

———. ECC. *Sixth Annual Review.* Ottawa, 1969.

Podoluk, Jenny. *Incomes of Canadians.* Ottawa: DBS, 1968.

Professional

Canadian Welfare Council. *Poverty: Annotated Bibliography and References.* Ottawa, 1966 and supplements.

Schlesinger, Benjamin. *Poverty in Canada and the United States. A Bibliography.* Toronto: University of Toronto Press, 1966.

Indians, Métis and Eskimos
Basil Johnston

Basil Johnston is a teacher in the Ethnology Department of the Royal Ontario Museum in Toronto.

For years the image of the Indian was either romanticized or vulgarized; his history was neglected and the merit of his ideas went unrecognized. As a result, books and accounts written about the natives were indifferent in tone and quality; most conveyed the notion that Indian life consisted of no more than teepees, canoes, wars and scalpings. At best the books engendered curiosity; at worst, prejudice.

In recent years the native peoples, like other minority groups, have begun to agitate for and demand justice. The tone and quality of books written and published has become correspondingly more responsible and, what is even more encouraging, an increasing number of native authors are making their contribution to Canadian literature. Hopefully, those who wish to know about the Indians will find more scope and depth in recent publications. The following books are recommended for all teachers at the public and secondary school levels as well as for general readers.

Forbidden Voice by Alma Green relates many aspects of Iroquois life, past and present: the important role of women in Iroquoian society; religious, social and political customs; the influence of Christianity and European civilization upon the Iroquois; the rejection of European culture and religion and the revival of native values and philosophy.

Particularly valuable are the author's accounts of the Iroquoian idea of the League of Peace. But because she does not amplify the Iroquois notion of the nature of man, the symbolism legends, dreams, visions and ceremonials as she describes them will not be adequately understood by white readers. As these occur in the realm of the imagination they will likely be dismissed as inconsequential. But they are replete with meaning and reflect the insight of the Iroquois peoples into the soul or spirit of both individuals and society, and their concern for the growth of personality and character.

If Alma Green refers to the Iroquoian disaffection and disappointment with Christianity and European culture, Peter Jones in his *History of the Ojibway Indians* is even more explicit in his disenchantment with certain aspects of Western civilization. At the same time, his role as missionary prevents him from criticizing the churches. The book reveals Peter Jones's dilemma and the problem of identity people face when they accept certain aspects of another culture but wish to retain their own.

Aside from his personal crisis of conscience, Peter Jones writes about that period extending from about the 1830s to the 1870s, an era of transition. During this time many Algonkian peoples were entering Canada from the United States, and many natives were transferring from one locality to another in Ontario. Reserves were founded: hunting declined in favour of agriculture; paganism was forsaken for Christianity; and education for industrial, vocational and agricultural purposes was encouraged. Indian life changed.

The account traces the material changes that occurred in the lives of the Ojibway and how they were influenced by European contact. Undergoing some form of adjustment or evolution were the role of women, patterns of training, family government, occupations, warfare, ideals, travel and dress; courtship and marriage; religious concepts and practices, feasts and burials, band government and council meetings; games and recreation. Unfortunately Peter Jones explains these matters from a Christian point of view, losing sight of the real and deep significance of Indian thought. Yet Reverend Jones recognized that not all European influences were good; he deplored alcohol and double moral standards, though his background withheld him from making critical comments about religion. Many current problems are illuminated by studying their origins and causes as described by Peter Jones. This book should be reprinted.

For all the fascination that they excite, the Inuit or the Eskimo are not well understood. It is because *People of the Deer* by Farley Mowat delivers new insights in pleasing and fluent prose that it is recommended. Mowat's account is not merely a description of a way of life of a portion of the Inuit; it is an explanation of the declining Inuit population, and an appeal for understanding and prudence in the kinds of assistance tendered to people in need.

The author argues persuasively that the fabric of a way of life is so fragile that any interference with but a part of it will bring about some form of disaster. The Eskimo's downfall was the fur trade. Seeking furs, the Inuit neglected his traditional skills, and when the fur trade diminished to the point where he had to return to his former way of life, he found that he was unable to live it with the same efficiency as before.

There was, of course, a related element that demonstrates how the impairment of a resource upon which people depend can lead to tragedy. The inland Eskimos depended upon the deer for sustenance and bodily heat. When the deer population diminished or was depleted, the Inuit faced hardship, and no medicine could stay the kind of starvation they endured.

Part Indian, yet not Indian; part white, yet not white; separated by law from the former and alienated by conduct from the latter; half and half, these are the Métis, the people in *Strange Empire* by Howard Kinzey.

Strange Empire is about a man, Louis Riel, and about a people, the Métis. Kinzey explores, but does not attempt to explain away, a basic ambiguity in the story of the man. On the one hand, Riel is seen as a victim of some mental disorder, a circumstance which seems not to have impaired his motives or the good he may have done. On the other, Riel becomes the victim of government procrastination and, in the end, of biased justice.

The book also analyzes from a sympathetic point of view the background of the Métis and the events that led to their uprising and eventual alienation. When

Canada acquired title to the West, the rights the Métis had in the land were ignored. They were dispossessed. As many were Catholic, the issues became religious; as the Canadian government vacillated, the issues became political; and as politicians became self-seeking or indifferent and the people neglected and uncertain, the issues became emotional. In Kinzey's presentation, the Métis experience thus becomes a study in the futility of integration and assimilation.

Studies of Indians should include the study of at least one outstanding man. *Tecumseth* by C. F. Klinck is recommended, because it best portrays the obstacles Indian leaders have always faced when they sought union of many tribes and because of Tecumseth's unique contribution to this nation.

Klinck's biography is an anthology of extracts from books, speeches, reports, letters, plays and poems, with questions for further study. These are fairly well balanced, combining opinion favourable and unfavourable to Tecumseth. Much of the book describes Tecumseth's endeavours to persuade the Indians to act in concert against the encroaching settlers; out of his arguments for resistance and union emerges the scope of Tecumseth's mind and vision, his capacity for grasping European law and for understanding the long-term consequences of disunity and conquest. That he failed does not detract from his stature as warrior and diplomat. What is less clear is his contribution to Canada as a nation. If it were not for Tecumseth's efforts this country or a large portion of Ontario might now be just another state of the United States.

The Unjust Society by Harold Cardinal articulates Indian and Métis attitudes and opinions as to the origin and nature of current difficulties encountered by the Indians. Cardinal suggests that certain of the causes are to be found in public indifference, bigotry and government betrayal and ignorance. He clearly understands that native resurgence and emergence will not be easy but he rejects the white man's politics and traditional manner of dealing with human problems and insists that solutions must come from the native peoples themselves. For their part, Mr. Cardinal suggests, white people and their government must do what they can to understand the native peoples, and then permit them the scope to resolve their destinies in their own way, at their own speed. The biggest single issue is trust. It must be re-established, and the onus for removing the pall of distrust that estranges Indians and the government falls upon the government. Treaties and rights must be restored. This plea, stated and reiterated several times, is directed to and intended for all Canadians of goodwill. This is required reading for an understanding of the native viewpoint.

In the collection of Indian speeches and writings compiled in *Touch the Earth* by T. C. McLuhan, there is a striking indication of the quality of Indian thought. These excerpts from the recorded speeches of Luther Standing Bear, Young Chief, Chief Weninock, Crowfoot, Okute and Big Thunder are characterized by perception of events and their consequences, by eloquence and logic of expression. From observation of the physical world and the interdependence of the various orders of existence, native thinkers posited the presence of a Master of Life; from the various and different modes and expressions of existence, the natives found harmony in the corporeal and incorporeal forms of being. The expression of attitudes suggests firm native concepts of ideals, rights and duties.

Black Hawk observed that if the natives had been forewarned of the disasters produced by the coming of the white man, they would not have believed. But Chief Joseph, Red Jacket, Tecumseth, Black Elk, Sitting Bull, Big Bear and many others clearly saw the consequences of contact: resistance by war, compromise by negotiation and trust in promises. They warned without avail, and no matter how logical, rational or moral their speeches, they were powerless.

The Canadian Indian by William Patterson is indispensable for anyone wishing to understand the native peoples. It is Indian centred and as such is a vast improvement on previous Indian history books.

Professor Patterson describes the experiences of

natives during colonial days, their reaction and attitudes towards the early settlers and their modes of resistance to European pressures and settlements. Many of the conflicts that occurred between native and European were, according to Patterson, cultural in nature. That the natives were unable to expel the invader or negotiate more equitable treaties was due to their division and want of physical power. The Indian eventually lost not only his lands but also his autonomy; in time, he lost his importance and his identity as well. Part of the struggle of the Indian is to recover his identity and to re-establish his importance and worth in a society far exceeding in size and population his own. The challenge lies in working out his destiny by adapting institutions and techniques from his own culture, and making a contribution to perhaps even influencing—white society through them. The protests of today and the rise of native organizations may be construed as forms of native resurgence and renaissance.

It should be understood that *Indians in Transition* by Gerald Walsh does not attempt to cover all aspects of difficulties the native peoples encounter in their relationships with other Canadians and in their experiences with the government. Nor does the author pretend to present the Indian viewpoint. But the book can be a very useful instrument for studying history backwards, by taking current issues such as prejudice, poverty, education and apathy and inquiring into their historical origins.

The origins of current problems are traced by Walsh from earliest contact between Indians and Europeans through promises, policies, practices, the fur trade and the changes brought by treaties, religion and technology. Indian people would include land acquisition as a long-standing source of tension. But the real merit and strength of the book rests in the section entitled "Solving the Problem." While three solutions are outlined, none is suggested as the most appropriate one for the natives. In fact, the selections intimate that none of the solutions generally recommended accomplish anything except create even more problems.

SUMMARY BIBLIOGRAPHY
All are general.

Cardinal, Harold. *The Unjust Society*. Edmonton: Hurtig, 1969.

Green, Alma. *Forbidden Voice*. Toronto: Hamlyn, 1972.

Jones, Peter. *The History of the Ojibway Indians*. London: Houlston and Wright, 1861.

Kinzey, Howard. *Strange Empire*. Toronto: Swan, 1966.

Klinck, Carl F. *Tecumseth*. Toronto: Prentice-Hall, 1961.

McLuhan, T. C. *Touch the Earth*. Toronto: New Press, 1971.

Mowat, Farley. *People of the Deer.* Toronto: McClelland and Stewart, 1952.

Patterson, William. *The Canadian Indian*. Toronto: Collier-Macmillan, 1971.

Walsh, Gerald. *Indians in Transition*. Toronto: McClelland and Stewart, 1971.

Drugs
Lynn McDonald

Lynn McDonald is a member of the Sociology Department of McMaster University in Hamilton. At the present time she is working, on a Canada Council grant, on research in the sociology of criminal law. In 1971 she worked as a research associate for the Commission of Inquiry into the Non-Medical Use of Drugs.

One of the best introductions to the subject of drugs can be found in Andrew Malcolm's *The Pursuit of Intoxication*. The title is something of a misnomer, for the book contains much material on drugs that do not intoxicate and discusses functions of drugs for other purposes: in religious ritual, for improved performance in sports and war, for brainwashing, murder and suicide, as well as for conventional medical purposes and recreation. The perspective is broad and the writing is good. The author (a medical doctor with the Addiction Research Foundation of Ontario) has written his book with a specific purpose. He objects to the use of drugs as a panacea for social ills and indeed ends the book with a plea for the development of constructive alternatives. This point is not intended to put the reader off; the overall tone of the book is informative rather than moralistic and the book is highly recommended.

The most recently published general book on drugs is Harold and Oriana Kalant's *Drugs, Society and Personal Choice*. It too provides a good introduction to drugs, both with respect to the nature of the drugs themselves and the decisions that have to be made regarding their control. The authors' purpose is to offer information so that citizens can make informed judgments regarding personal use and public policy. The authors are well-known researchers for the Addiction Research Foundation of Ontario.

Another well-written and relatively comprehensive

book is Reginald Whitaker's *Drugs and the Law*. The focus here is on illegal drugs rather than the whole lot, although illegal use is put into the perspective of medical drug use, and the nonmedical use of legal drugs like alcohol. There are chapters on the opiates, the marijuana scare and the hallucinogenic experience. Whitaker, however, also takes on the important moral and practical issues of attempting to control drug use by means of the criminal law. So he discusses the morality of putting young people in prison for using the drugs they prefer while their elders enjoy booze, tobacco and tranquillizers undisturbed. The author is not a "druggie" himself, but rather attempts to interpret the illegal drug scene to the middle-class, middle-aged world to which he belongs.

Another general introductory book is Sheila Gormely's *Drugs and the Canadian Scene*, a journalist's account of the illegal drug world. It is not of the same high calibre as the first three books discussed. The book is directed to parents and teachers, and especially non-users. It has chapters on dope dealing, Yorkville and some amusing comments on the drug commission, as well as the usual chapters on marijuana, speed, LSD and the other hallucinogenic drugs. The material covered consists largely of comments on the Toronto scene, briefs to the government commission and quotations from Toronto drug experts—all of which make the book seem already out of date. The tone is sympathetic in a way, but the drug world is taken very seriously and problems accorded an undue reverence.

Alcohol is still the most widely used drug in Canada, and the one causing the most problems by way of death, disease, violence and misery. It is curious, then, that there are so few books available on the subject; there are technical papers, government documents, pamphlets and periodicals, but few books. Furthermore, most of the nontechnical pamphlets and periodicals are not readily available to the general public, being directed to educational and treatment institutions.

One important book that is available is *Alcohol and Alcoholism*, a collection of articles published by the

Addiction Research Foundation of Ontario. The fifty papers in it were solicited from international experts for a conference in Chile. The book contains only a few articles by Canadians, and no material specifically pertinent to Canada, but the range of countries represented and the quality of the contributions is good. The papers report original research and some, especially the ones on biochemistry and psychopharmacology, would be difficult for the general reader. They give a review of the current state of knowledge in the field, however, and so would be very useful for people taking courses dealing with alcohol or working professionally with alcoholics. The topics include such matters as the role of alcohol in accidents and violence, the alcoholic employee, anti-alcoholism programs in schools, and the effect of nutritional deficiency on the appetite for alcohol (among rats).

Again, despite the important role tobacco plays in many diseases, there is very little published material on it in Canada. The Department of National Health and Welfare published *Smoking and Health* in 1964, a reference book for health-education purposes. It is well documented (largely relying on American and British studies) but very straight and boring in presentation. There is, more recently, a short report on cigarette smoking, produced by the Standing Committee on Health, Welfare and Social Affairs. It is again effectively a review of American and British studies, plus some very conservative recommendations for tobacco control in Canada. The committee was concerned, for example, about the losses advertisers would suffer if advertising were banned, yet neglected other obvious potential losses, such as those that morticians, coroners and cemetery workers would suffer if smoking were reduced.

There are several useful publications on heroin, although none of them are easily available to the public. One is a very good study of the results of treatment of heroin-dependent persons in a federal penitentiary built for those purposes. (Murphy, *A Quantitative Test of the Effectiveness of an Experimental Treatment Programme for Delinquent Opiate Addicts*.) The results show, among other things, that inmates subjected to more intensive treatment subsequently earned more money illegally and used heroin more often than those given less intensive treatment. Despite the enormously interesting findings, the report is a dry, technical document written for a specialist audience. It, like the next one to be noted, is discussed here primarily because it is a rare exception to the poor publication record of governments in the crime and corrections field.

The next study involves a comparison of certain inmates from the same institution with people who had not become heroin users, but who came from the same neighbourhoods in Vancouver. The comparison group was comprised of men who had been in the same class in school, in grade three, as the inmates. The excellent methodology of the study makes it a very important one in the field, and many of its findings are contrary to widely accepted theories on psychological causes of heroin use.

The drug commission's interim report is a very good source of information on the effects of the major drugs used nonmedically, including alcohol but not tobacco. It has one long chapter critically reviewing the research literature up to 1970. This is to be updated and expanded in the final report, notably with material collected by the commission itself. Otherwise, the interim report is a discussion of issues and recommendations. No original research is reported in it, but rather outlines of research in progress or being planned.

The drug commission is to publish a great deal of research findings, both in condensed form in its final report and in a series of research appendices. Assuming the research completed will be published, there will be much excellent material both for the public at large as well as specialists in the drug field. There are thorough and up-to-date accounts of the patterns of use (everyday life habits and the "social career" of use) for the major illegal drugs—cannabis, LSD, speed and heroin. There is a comprehensive analysis of sociological and psychological explanations as to why people use and become dependent on each of the major drugs. There are studies of hospital treatment for drug users, innovative services devised by young drug users themselves, drug education programs, marijuana use and driving and the psychological effects of marijuana—not to exhaust the list.

There is a whole series of commission studies covering all aspects of the administration of criminal justice in the drug field. It starts with a very sophisticated philosophical discussion of the use of the criminal law for the control of nonmedical drug use. There are then descriptive studies of each phase of the enforcement system, including statistical data and actual observational reports where possible. The police section, for example, includes material obtained by an observer going around with narcotics squads on duty. There is a thoroughly documented account of the international heroin market from beginning to end, necessarily from less direct sources. There is a study of the courts and sentencing practices, with data from interviews with the judges. There are studies of five correctional institutions dealing with drug offenders, including material collected by observers living in them and interviews with staff and inmates.

The fact of little publication on nonmedical drug use until the last few years is very much a function of government policy. The federal and provincial governments control access to major subjects of study, in the courts, hospitals and prisons. They also control access to statistical data on drug deaths, treatment of drug offenders, convictions and the like. In addition, the federal government has a virtual monopoly on experimental research for some drugs, through a strict research licensing procedure. (For example, it did not allow *any* experimental research to be done on cannabis use until 1970.) Further, local school boards control access to one of the major illegal drug-using groups, high-school students.

It has only been in recent years that any level of government has promoted research on nonmedical drug use (apart from alcohol), either by sponsoring it themselves or even allowing others to do it. Curiously, once governments did decide drug research was a good thing they financed it generously and without strings attached, which has not been the case in other countries, notably in the United States. This is probably the reason for the nonappearance, so far, of any anti-establishment, pro-drug literature in Canada. The attitude in Canada seems to be either to let researchers do their work in peace or not to let them do it at all.

Some kinds of research are thus still not permitted. The solicitor general's department still will not let researchers conduct studies in its prisons, or even release statistical data on offenders. The ban so far includes even the drug commission, established by the same government. Some provincial governments are still very restrictive in what access they will allow researchers to their institutions, and also refuse, in some cases, to release statistical material. Some school boards censor questions on drug use and some even insist on holding veto power over what results will be released.

SUMMARY BIBLIOGRAPHY
General

Canada. Commission of Inquiry into the Non-Medical Use of Drugs. *Interim Report*. Ottawa, 1970.
———. Department of Health and Welfare. *Smoking and Health*. Ottawa, 1964.
Gormely, Sheila. *Drugs and the Canadian Scene*. Toronto: Pagurian Press, 1970.
Kalant, Harold, and Oriana J. Kalant. *Drugs, Society and Personal Choice*. Toronto: General, 1971.
Malcolm, Andrew. *The Pursuit of Intoxication*. Toronto: Thorn Press, 1971.
Whitaker, Reginald. *Drugs and the Law*. Toronto: Methuen, 1969.

Advanced

Canada. Standing Committee on Health, Welfare and Social Affairs. *Report on Tobacco and Cigarette*

Smoking. Presented by M. Gaston Isabelle. Ottawa, 1969.

Popham, Robert E., ed. *Alcohol and Alcoholism.* Toronto: University of Toronto Press, 1970.

Professional

Canada. Department of the Solicitor General. *A Quantitative Test of the Effectiveness of an Experimental Treatment Programme for Delinquent Opiate Addicts,* by B. C. Murphy. Ottawa, 1970..

———. Department of the Solicitor General. *Rounders and Squares. Comparative Attitudes of Delinquent Addicts and Non-Delinquent Non-Addicts in Vancouver, BC.* Ottawa, 1968. .

Education
Douglas Myers

Douglas Myers is assistant professor in the Department of History and Philosophy at the Ontario Institute for Studies in Education. He is currently on full-time leave-of-absence from OISE to the Ontario Teachers Federation, working in the area of teacher education in the province.

It is doubtless not uncommon that, when asked to write about books in a particular field, most of the titles that come readily to mind are American or British in origin. Certainly this has been my experience in trying to compile a representative and contemporary list of Canadian books on education. Moreover, a few weeks' reflection on the problem has brought home to me, with wonderful clarity, some further characteristics peculiar, perhaps, to educational literature in this country.

To begin with the most obvious, there are ten distinct and independent educational jurisdictions in Canada. They have, of course, many things in common, but they also contain and reinforce some very important differences. A further complication is added by the federal presence, widely felt but constitutionally discreet. All this makes it difficult to write confidently or meaningfully about *Canadian* education. It also tends to encourage a lot of writing about provincial educational systems, which is likely to be of limited interest to readers in other regions of the country.

This may help explain why The Book—defined as a coherent, considered elaboration of one man's thoughts about some subject or other—seems such an unfamiliar concept to Canadian educational writers. Instead, the great bulk of information and opinion on education in Canada is contained in a vast and ever-increasing quantity of briefs, reports, studies and surveys. These are, to be sure, very useful, important and, sometimes, even interesting: the *Report* of the Royal Commission on the Status of Women in Canada and *It's Your Turn: The Committee on Youth Report*, to name only two examples, devote a good deal of attention to education. But in general, one does not exactly "read" such things; rather, one burrows into, rummages through or scrambles over them.

We do not, I think, lack potential authors but, for a variety of reasons, those whom one feels could write very lively and important books on Canadian education are not doing so. Many are too fully engaged in trying to reconstitute or reform the school system to take the time. Some no longer believe in the importance or effectiveness of books. Others, perhaps, are discouraged by the difficulties of publication and distribution. Those who are writing at all are either compiling or contributing to collections of articles, position papers or essays. Such collections often contain excellent snacks but they lack the satisfactions of a full-course meal.

Finally, there is the problem of how to deal with books that are primarily about something else, but have important educational implications—McLuhan's work, for example—or that devote some part of their attention to education—for instance, Harold Cardinal's biting chapter on "The Little Red Schoolhouse" in *The Unjust Society: The Tragedy of Canada's Indians*.

Taken together, these factors make it seem a bit difficult to rattle off a list of the top ten books in Canadian educational literature. The nature of the subject demands both a rather extensive listing of books and an active involvement for the interested reader who may have to hunt around before he finds precisely what he wants.

Let us begin then, with a general historical background. In *Canadian Education: A History*, edited by Wilson, Stamp and Audet, nine contributors provide twenty-one chapters covering the development of Canadian education from coast to coast and from the colonial period to the present. The book suffers, as such books do, from having to deal with so much material and is sometimes dull or superficial. But it attempts, with some success, to break out of the narrow institutional and inspirational tradition that has dominated educational history, and to place its subject in the wider context of Canadian social history. Most important for the general reader, it is crammed with references to other works and each chapter has a selected list of further readings. Another book of wide interest, because its theme is the complex and explosive controversies concerning French-speaking, English-speaking school rights in several provinces, is volume seven in the Canadian Historical Readings series, *Minorities, Schools and Politics,* which contains articles by Donald Creighton, W. L. Morton, Ramsay Cook and several other Canadian historians.

John Porter's *The Vertical Mosaic* was one of the most important Canadian books of the 1960s, and chapter six, "Social Class and Educational Opportunity," is essential reading for anyone interested in this crucial issue. Porter presents a forceful, well-documented critique of Canadian education which contends that the school system reinforces the position and power of the affluent section of the population and is inaccessible and unfair to lower-income groups. An illustration of how well the schools serve the needs of upper-middle-class communities in Canada is provided by the educational section of John Seeley's famous study in the 1950s, *Crestwood Heights,* which is included in *Canada: A Sociological Profile,* edited by W. E. Mann. At the end of a decade of unprecedented educational spending, however, both the *Report* of the Special Senate Committee on Poverty and, in somewhat more vigorous terms, *The Real Poverty Report* (written by four dissatisfied members of Senator Croll's staff), emphasize that the situation is depressingly unchanged. Lack of education and poverty are still closely linked; the improvements in public education of the 1950s and 1960s have failed to stop the transmission of poverty from generation to generation; and great regional disparity still exists.

Higher education, which, as the poverty reports point out, gets most of the federal money devoted to education but has the smallest proportion of lower-income students, has been the subject of a number of books of interest. Mainstream thought is well represented in *Changing Patterns of Higher Education in Canada*, a collection of four lectures dealing with the Atlantic provinces, Quebec, Ontario and the West, edited by R. S. Harris. A selection of the speeches and addresses from 1955 to 1967 of Claude Bissell, *The Strength of the University*, is an important record of a period during which retention of his post was a not inconsiderable achievement for a university president. *The University Game*, edited by Howard Adelman and Dennis Lee, is a collection in a very different vein, however, and reveals something of the soul searching, profound disillusionment and fundamental criticism that has affected such a significant section of the academic community. Julyan and Tim Reid, in *Student Power and the Canadian Campus*, have collected a wide variety of newspaper coverage and comment, speeches, manifestos and ultimatums that help record the protests and disturbances of the mid and late sixties. There it all is again—the Sir George computer, Stanley Gray and McGill, Dow Chemical on campus, Strax and Simon Fraser—and, though in a curious sense it seems a distant era, its influence was profound. The book that first focused attention on the problem of American influence on Canadian higher education, Robin Mathews's and James Steeles's *The Struggle for Canadian Universities*, conveys the emotional intensity of the controversy that has surrounded this important issue, and records some of the early battles on the subject.

After all the upheaval, however, the universities are still very much with us. To get a glimpse of what may be in store for them, and us, one should have a look at *Towards 2000: The Future of Post-Secondary Education in Ontario*. This paperback is the work of a special subcommittee of the Committee of Presidents of Universities of Ontario, and included John Porter, Bernard Blishen, John Evans and Pauline Jewett among its members. It was presented as a brief to the Commission on Post-Secondary Education in Ontario (the

Wright Commission), and its emphasis on making the university more accessible to all sections of the population, more responsive to community, provincial and national needs, and more diverse and flexible in its programs and organization seems to have made its influence felt, to judge by the draft report which that commission has just issued.

A notable exception to the non-book-producing tradition in Canadian education is provided by a group of authors who, over the past two decades, have put forward a consistent conservative critique of the public school system. Their aim has been to halt what they regard as the juggernaut of progressivist philosophy, which has dominated postwar Canadian education and which, according to them, is steadily undermining the time-honoured traditions of intellectual standards, achievement and discipline. Hilda Neatby's *So Little for the Mind: An Indictment of Canadian Education*, first published in 1953, is the most famous of these and its bold assertions and lively, erudite style made it one of, if not the best-selling books ever written in the field.* In 1960, Frank MacKinnon, from a similar point of view, launched a spirited assault upon the inviting target presented by the centralized and sprawling educational bureaucracy that controls and directs the schools. Though many contemporary critics of the education system would be unsympathetic to the political philosophy that motivates *The Politics of Education*, they share fully MacKinnon's distaste for educational bureaucrats and his concern for decentralizing the system and integrating schools more closely into local communities.

Nobody Can Teach Anyone Anything is the other side of the coin—a book based on the premise that the schools are dominated by conservative, knowledge-oriented élitists, and must be made *more* progressive. Its author, W. R. Wees, is an unrepentant publicist for this point of view and readers seem to find his writing either delightfully humane and compassionate or infuriatingly

---

*See also her collection of lectures on the subject, *A Temperate Dispute*.

romantic and hopelessly naïve. Official mainstream progressivist thought is perhaps best represented in *Living and Learning*, the Report of the Provincial Committee on Aims and Objectives of Education in the Schools of Ontario, otherwise known as the Hall-Dennis Report, published in 1968. This report, which attempted to look ahead and recommend some of the directions and forms public education should take, has been the subject of considerable controversy. In the conservative tradition, James Daly, a history professor at McMaster University, has issued a spirited tract under the title *Education or Molasses? A Critical Look at the Hall-Dennis Report*. Incidentally, Daly has set an example that others might well emulate in that he had this smart-looking and well-laid-out seventy-nine-page booklet produced by a small independent local printer. Perhaps the lost and noble art of pamphleteering can be revived. For a variety of other, more restrained reactions to Hall-Dennis, see also *Means and Ends in Education*, edited by Brian Crittenden, and a collection titled *Rethinking Education*.

Education in Quebec is a topic of great interest and importance, but unfortunately, for most of us it is very unfamiliar ground.* Louis-Philippe Audet and Armand Gauthier, in *Le système scolaire du Québec: Organisation et fonctionnement*, provide an excellent short survey of the 1960s that includes consideration of the two major government reports of the period, the Parent Report and the Rioux Report. Pierre Belanger and Guy Rocher's collection, *Ecole et société au Québec: éléments d'une sociologie de l'éducation*, contain both documentary materials and a wide selection of interpretative articles dealing with many aspects of Quebec education. *La grenouillère* by R. Haumont, a polemic directed against the Quebec ministry of education, was

*I am not, I hasten to add, an exception to this. I am therefore greatly indebted to André Le Blanc, secretary general of Vanier College in Montreal, for his suggestions. M. Le Blanc is at present preparing a retrospective review of education in Québec in the 1960s, with an annotated bibliography, for possible publication in the *McGill Journal of Education* in the fall of 1972.

the first substantial critical assessment, in book form, of the massive organizational and structural changes that had occurred in the early 1960s. The shift of concern and attention away from such matters towards questions of approach, content and quality is illustrated by C. H. Rondeau's *Pour une éducation de qualité au Québec*.

The number and range of publications in specialized areas of education—curriculum, administration, philosophy, psychology and so on—is far too enormous to be considered here. Mention must be made, however, of A. B. Hodgett's *What Culture? What Heritage?* which has had a very considerable influence in the area of Canadian studies at the public-school level. It is, in fact, a report of the most complete and thorough study ever undertaken of "civic education" (i.e., civics, social studies, history) in Canada, stamped with the highly individual imprint of its author and director, an experienced and talented teacher. The findings of this study, which were highly critical of the quality and nature of civic education in Canadian schools, received a remarkable response from teachers, academics and the public at large. A notable direct result has been the establishment of a unique, independent institution, the Canada Studies Foundation, which is supporting a number of interdisciplinary and interregional curriculum-development projects across the country.

A related phenomenon has been the increasing availability of published materials dealing with various aspects of Canadian life, aimed both at a school/college and a general readership. To mention only three examples: Clarke-Irwin has an Issues and Insights series; Maclean-Hunter is putting out a Canadian Issues series; and General Publishing will soon begin issuing its Canadian Critical Issues series.

Another rather specialized but important area that is currently attracting a great deal of attention is teacher education. Several provinces are reorganizing or attempting to redirect their teacher-education facilities and programs. In Ontario, following the recommendations of the 1966 Macleod report (*Report* of the

Ministers Committee on the Training of Elementary School Teachers), the thirteen teachers' colleges are in the process of being integrated or consolidated into university faculties of education. At UBC, the COFFE report (*Report* of the Commission on the Future of the Faculty of Education) is being implemented. The most lively and readable of the reports on the subject is the most recent, published in 1971 by the Committee on Teacher Education at the University of Prince Edward Island under the title *Teacher Education: Perseverance or Professionalism?* The most outstanding book in the field is John MacDonald's *The Discernible Teacher.* Set rather in the conservative tradition discussed above, though containing some radical proposals, this is an extremely thoughtful and well-argued treatment of the subject—the sort of book that forces the reader to focus and clarify his own views and theories.

As I said at the outset, most of those who could write extended radical critiques of our education system are far too busy to do so. Still, they have managed over the past few years to produce the most interesting and imaginative bits-and-pieces educational writing in Canada. Their main forum has been a journal called *This Magazine Is about Schools,* which has drawn together a variety of people involved in education, social work and community organizing—both inside and outside the established systems—whose common interest has been in changing, humanizing and liberating the schools. The tone of their work is highly personal, direct and subjective, indignant and irreverent, funny and sad. At its best their writing is inventive, stimulating and moving; at its worst, self-indulgent and naïve. Seldom is it dull. A selection of articles from the magazine has been edited by Satu Repo and published, ironically, by an American concern under the title, *This Book Is about Schools.* Particularly outstanding are the two superb articles by George Martell, the intriguing notions of Anthony Barton for altering the organization, curriculum and atmosphere of the schools, and excellent pieces by Satu Repo and Bob Davis. In the same category, though less passionate and spectacular, is another collection titled *Must Schools Fail?* scheduled for publication this year. Edited by Niall Byrne and Jack Quarter, this book contains a number of excellent articles on such subjects as educational alternatives, public and independent; the education of women; community control; the education of minority cultures; Americanization; moral education and a variety of other problems. The contributors include Ivan Illich, Krista Maeots, Loren Lind, John McMurtry and Robin Mathews and the collection will be of wide interest to a general readership.

As one who retains at least a residual faith in the power and importance of books, it seems to me appropriate to conclude with the fervent hope that the next few years will see the publication of more full-length books about education in Canada by some of the many people who are capable of first-rate writing on the subject—either the people who have already written something about it, like Martell, McMurtry, Barton, Lind, Repo and Davis, or the many others who have never quite got to the point of putting their ideas down on paper, but have something vital and important to say. Such a development would not only have a considerable impact on Canadian educational thought and practice, but would also make it possible for the next person who is asked to write a short guide to the most significant literature in Canadian education to dash it off in about half an hour with ease and confidence.

SUMMARY BIBLIOGRAPHY
General

Adams, Ian, et al. *The Real Poverty Report*. Edmonton: Hurtig, 1971.

Adelman, Howard, and Dennis Lee, eds. *The University Game*. Toronto: Anansi, 1968.

Audet, Louis-Philippe. *Elan de la reforme scolaire au Québec, 1939-1969*. Montreal: University of Montreal Press, 1969.

Audet, Louis-Philippe, and Armand Gauthier. *Le système scolaire du Québec: Organisation et fonctionnement.* Montreal: Librairie Beauchemin, 1969.

Belanger, Pierre, and Guy Rocher. *Ecole et société au Québec: éléments d'une sociologie de l'éducation.* Montreal: HMA, 1970.

Bissell, C. T. *The Strength of the University.* Toronto: University of Toronto Press, 1968.

Byrne, Niall, and Jack Quarter, eds. *Must Schools Fail?* Toronto: McClelland and Stewart, 1972.

Cardinal, Harold. *The Unjust Society: The Tragedy of Canada's Indians.* Edmonton: Hurtig, 1969.

Creighton, D. G., et al. *Minorities, Schools and Politics.* Toronto: University of Toronto Press, 1969.

Crittenden, Brian, ed. *Means and Ends in Education: Comments on Living and Learning.* Toronto: OISE, 1969.

Daly, James. *Education or Molasses? A Critical Look at the Hall-Dennis Report.* Ancaster, Ont.: Cromlech Press, 1969.

Eisenberg, J., and M. Levin, eds. Canadian Critical Issues Series. Toronto: General Publishing, 1972—.

Harris, R. S., ed. *Changing Patterns of Higher Education in Canada.* Toronto: University of Toronto Press, 1966.

Haumont, R. *La grenouillère.* Montreal: Editions du Jour, 1968.

Hewlitt, Alexander, and Stanley Pearl, eds. Canadian Issues Series. Toronto: Maclean-Hunter, 1970—.

Hodgetts, A. B. *What Culture? What Heritage? A Study of Civic Education in Canada.* Toronto: OISE, 1968.

MacDonald, John. *The Discernible Teacher.* Ottawa: Canadian Teachers Association, 1970.

MacKinnon, Frank. *The Politics of Education.* Toronto: University of Toronto Press, 1960.

Mann, W. E. *Canada: A Sociological Profile.* Toronto: Copp Clark, 1968.

Mathews, Robin, and James Steele. *The Struggle for Canadian Universities.* Toronto: New Press, 1969.

Neatby, Hilda. *So Little for the Mind: An Indictment of Canadian Education.* Toronto: Clarke, Irwin, 1953.

———. *A Temperate Dispute*. Toronto: Clarke, Irwin, 1954.

Ontario Institute for Studies in Education. Development Advisory Committee. *Re-Thinking Education: The Practical Implications of Living and Learning*. Toronto, 1969.

Porter, John. *The Vertical Mosaic*. Toronto: University of Toronto Press, 1965.

Porter, John, et al. *Towards 2000: The Future of Post-Secondary Education in Ontario*. Toronto: McClelland and Stewart, 1971.

Reid, Tim and Julyan, eds. *Student Power and the Canadian Campus*. Toronto: Peter Martin, 1969.

Repo, Satu, ed.*This Book Is about Schools*. Toronto: Random House, 1970.

Rondeau, C. H. *Pour une éducation de qualité au Québec*. Montreal: Presses Libre, 1971.

Saywell, J. T., ed. Issues and Insights Series. Toronto: Clarke, Irwin, 1971—.

Wees, W. R. *Nobody Can Teach Anyone Anything*. Toronto: Doubleday, 1971.

Wilson, J. D., R. M. Stamp and L.-P. Audet, eds. *Canadian Education: A History*. Toronto: Prentice-Hall, 1970.

Government and Committee Reports

Canada. Royal Commission on the Status of Women in Canada. *Report*. Ottawa, 1970.

———. Secretary of State. *It's Your Turn: The Committee on Youth Report*. Ottawa, 1970.

———. Special Senate Committee on Poverty. *Poverty in Canada*. Ottawa, 1971.

The COFFE Report: The Report of the Commission on the Future of the Faculty of Education, University of British Columbia. Vancouver: University of British Columbia Press, 1969.

Ontario. Provincial Committee on Aims and Objectives of Education in the Schools of Ontario. *Living and Learning*. Toronto: 1968.

———. Department of Education. *Report of the Minis-ters Committee on the Training of Elementary*

School Teachers, 1966. Toronto, 1966.

Quebec. Commission d'enquête sur l'enseignement des arts. *Rapport.* 4 vols. Quebec, 1967. (The Rioux Commission)

———. Royal Commission of Inquiry on Education. *Rapport.* 5 vols. Quebec, 1963-1966. (The Parent Commission)

University of Prince Edward Island. Committee on Teacher Education. *Teacher Education: Perseverance or Professionalism?* Charlottetown: University of PEI, 1971.

Crime and the Criminal Justice System
Lynn McDonald

Lynn McDonald is a member of the Sociology Department of McMaster University in Hamilton. At the present time she is working, on a Canada Council grant, on research in the sociology of criminal law. In 1971 she worked as a research associate for the Commission of Inquiry into the Non-Medical Use of Drugs.

Publications on crime and the criminal justice system in Canada are very limited in terms of coverage of the field and very mixed in quality. There is some good material, even some that is original and controversial. But most of the material reflects an uncritical, law-and-order orientation, and most of this material is mediocre in quality or bad. The general reading public could well be unaware of the existence of the whole field, for little is done to make such material known. Some of the material is difficult to obtain, being published in academic journals, government documents and research monographs from relatively obscure centres of criminology.

There is one general textbook on the subject, *Crime and Its Treatment in Canada*, a book of readings published in 1965. It is geared largely to people in correctional work. The various components of the correctional process are systematically covered: police, courts, probation, training schools, prisons and parole. Only four of the seventeen articles reflect an academic purpose, those on the nature of crime and the criminal law, causes of crime and crime rates.

The articles vary considerably in purpose, comprehensiveness and quality. The article on crime gives a reasonable introduction to some of the basic issues of interest to academic criminologists. The article on causes of crime covers a number of the major traditional theories, but seems dated even in 1972 since it fails to mention the more recent and now fashionable ones. The

article on criminal law by Ryan is fairly comprehensive
and ends with a modest critique of the flaws of the
legislation, although judging it largely meritorious. The
companion criminal-law article, by McLeod, then
commissioner of penitentiaries, is entirely uncritical of
Canadian legislation; indeed, the possibility of doubt
does not appear to have been entertained. The article on
prisons includes a strong attack on the whole system,
the only article to be so forthright in criticism. The
articles on probation, parole and training schools are
largely uncritical descriptions of those practices as they
were in the early 1960s, practices that have since
changed substantially. There are recommendations for
improvements which only amount to more of the traditional correctional approach: more staff, more staff
training and better facilities. It is assumed that money
can buy rehabilitation. No evidence is offered to justify
these recommendations, or to show that correctional
methods produce successful results at all.

An uncritical acceptance of correctional philosophy
appears in the academic articles in this book as well as in
those on the correctional system. This is really not
surprising when one realizes that most of the articles of
both types were written by members of the correctional
establishment. The book was edited by the head of the
Canadian Correctional Association, who was also a
member of the federal government's Canadian Committee on Corrections, and the book was introduced by
the head of that committee. Almost all of the articles
were written by persons who were employed by government correctional services at some level. The exceptions
also happen to be the contributors who were the most
critical of the system.

There is another book of readings on crime and corrections in Canada in preparation at the time of writing
of this review, *Deviance and Societal Reaction in
Canada*, by Craig Boydell and others. It is a longer book,
with many more, usually shorter articles, largely reprints
of papers from academic journals. The orientation is still
law and order for the most part, although the style is
more sophisticated. There is some criticism of the

existing system, probably more than in *Crime and Its Treatment in Canada*. But the reader will still not find fundamental criticism of the criminal justice system, or find fundamentally different approaches to the subject, which are now appearing in Canada as well as elsewhere.

The best book on criminal justice in Canada, in terms of the quality of the work done, is a book on sentencing, John Hogarth's *Sentencing as a Human Process*. It is expensive ($15) and long (432 pages) but technical material is confined to appendices, which are sold separately. Very complex material is explained in straightforward unmathematical language, which should be understandable to people without any special knowledge of the field. (Indeed, social scientists will have to buy the appendices to get what they will want out of the book.)

The book is an attempt to explain how judges decide what sentences they will give in criminal cases. The author began by attempting to understand how judges define their own tasks, what they are trying to accomplish in sentencing, how they look at offenders, what information they consider important and what they do with conflicting information and objectives. A large number of questions were derived to capture these various components and these were ultimately narrowed down to a number of scales. The scales were used in the next stage of the research to predict (with remarkable accuracy) what sentences the judges would give under various circumstances.

The book is written in a tone that is sympathetic but not naïve; judges are human beings trying to do a difficult job conscientiously. So, while the judges were not consistent with each other in actual sentences (a familiar finding), they were found to be highly consistent with respect to their own objectives (which was not known before). Many sobering results appear nevertheless. For example: only thirty per cent of the judges claimed to have read even as much as one social-science book on crime and delinquency, and the judges that stated the greatest concern for rehabilitation were also the judges who gave the longest sentences.

A short but good account of the criminal justice system from the perspective of its subjects is given in a publication of the Canadian Civil Liberties Education Trust, *Due-Process Safeguards and Canadian Criminal Justice*. The book reports a study of people who appeared in provincial courts in five major cities (Vancouver, Winnipeg, Toronto, Montreal and Halifax) in a one-month period. The findings show that due-process guarantees were often violated, in letter and in spirit. There were claims of accused being denied permission to telephone, delays in being able to request bail, excessive use of arrest and jail over summonses and claims of pressure in the taking of police statements. Of the people arrested, a quarter claimed to have been injured by the police, usually with no witnesses but other police being present.

Justice was found to be speedy. More than half the accused who pleaded guilty had their cases disposed of in less than ten minutes and most of those who were sentenced to penitentiaries were processed in less than twenty minutes. This, the report points out, cannot be justified on grounds of a heavy workload, for the courts sat on average only two hours and twenty minutes per day.

The book is largely a report of findings without any attempt to explain *why* such unsavoury practices as were allegedly uncovered occurred. The existing system is described and judged in the light of certain stated objectives, the constitutional guarantees of due process. This makes it a much more valuable source of information than the more detailed government reports, to be reviewed later, which also fail to explain *why* anything happens, yet do not even let us know *what* is going on.

Other Canadian books on aspects of the criminal justice system are *The Prosecutor*, by Brian Grosman, and *Detention before Trial*, by Martin Friedland. Both are written by lawyers but both are suitable books for general readers. The book on prosecutors reports information collected on prosecutors in Ontario and gives a reasonably comprehensive description of the background and views of prosecutors. The book on the bail system is a thoroughly detailed indictment of the bail system in Canada as it was in the 1960s, a system that has only very recently been changed.

The only other book to be considered here is *Society behind Bars* by W. E. Mann, a study of an Ontario prison for men, the Guelph reformatory. The standard basic features of institutional life are described: inmate subculture, the process of "institutionalization," inmate leadership and staff-inmate relationships. There is not much new in the book for the person who has read American and British prison studies, which is not necessarily a criticism since prisons are very much the same everywhere. People who believe Canadian prisons to be places for soft living will find much to the contrary in this book.

Government departments are not a source of worthwhile information on crime so far as their regular publications are concerned, but committees and commissions established for special tasks have been. Government departments at both the federal and provincial levels publish a lot of material on crime and corrections, but mostly annual reports heavy on statistical tables and light on interpretation. The departments, in fact, have little of interest to publish since they conduct little research. Further, of the research they do sponsor, less still is released to the public in any form. Information is almost never made easily available by, for instance, publishing it in a book and selling it. Commissions, on the other hand, can be relied upon at least for a report with some substance to it, and some appendices if we are lucky.

The Department of Justice Committee on Juvenile Delinquency published a report in 1965 that gives reasonable descriptive material on delinquency and how authorities deal with it. The tone of *Juvenile Delinquency in Canada* is more cautious and apologetic than is usual even in government publications. Almost everything mentioned in an unfavourable light is qualified; for example, the probation officers are overworked and the juvenile-court judges have other responsibilities. There were no social scientists on the committee, and no social-science research was commissioned for it, which probably explains why the nonlegal aspects were covered in such a simplistic way.

The Canadian Committee on Corrections, reporting in 1970, came up with a much more ambitious report, *Towards Unity: Criminal Justice and Corrections*, but rather similar otherwise in style and orientation. It also employed no social scientists and commissioned no original research. It did, however, study trends in crime rates and showed that the crime rate in Canada was not increasing, a fact that appears to have been ignored in the report itself, and by justice ministers, solicitors general and the like since. The report contains sections of all the standard correctional divisions: police, courts, institutions, probation and parole. Nowhere is there any fundamental criticism of the existing system, although numerous relatively minor faults are pointed out. Indeed, there is no assessment of the existing system with respect to any criteria.

The report begins with the committee's philosophical approach, which is apparently conceived of as a radically humanitarian one. It states that the first consideration in determining criminal-justice objectives should be minimal interference with human liberty. In subsequent sections of the report, however, this principle seems to lose priority. For example, the committee recommends a type of preventive detention, that is, imprisonment of people for crimes they *might* commit. Yet at the same time it is admitted that there is no known way of treating potential criminals, so preventive detention cannot even be defended on grounds of rehabilitation.

A Quebec government commission on the administration of justice is a better source of information than either of these federal committees. Its final report appears in three volumes (fundamental principles, legal security and crime), the third of which is published in three parts (crime trends, peaks of criminality and organized crime). The commission had research conducted for it, although hastily and with relatively superficial analysis as a result. These research appendices (there are eight) are unfortunately available only in French. Five are reports of public-opinion surveys (on attitudes to the police, corrections and the criminal justice system); one is on the views of the police themselves (with regard to work satisfaction) and one is on the views of prosecutors and defence lawyers. There is one appendix reporting on an investigation of prison escapes and one on the role of teaching and research in the administration of criminal justice.

The problem in the field of crime and criminal justice is not so much that good material is not published as that good research is not done that could be published. Publishers who spent money commissioning books would help considerably, but there would still be a substantial gap. For that, the government is the culprit. Private money cannot buy access to correctional institutions, court records or Statistics Canada. So research requiring access to those places, which amounts to a substantial proportion of the crime and criminal justice field, still cannot be done.

Governments in Canada hamper research more diligently than do governments anywhere else in the Western world. Rarely are people allowed into institutions for data-gathering purposes, which is also the case in many countries. But in Canada, government departments refuse access even to statistical records, which does not happen to that extent elsewhere. Further, the statistical material published in Canada is of very little use to researchers, which is certainly not the case in many countries, notably the United Kingdom. Ironically, the federal government and many of the provinces spend a great deal of money on crime and corrections research. Most of the departments concerned now have research sections within them, but the function of such sections is not readily apparent and the number of publications issuing from them is negligible.

SUMMARY BIBLIOGRAPHY
General

Canadian Civil Liberties Education Trust. *Due-Process Safeguards and Canadian Criminal Justice—A one-month inquiry.* Toronto, 1971.

Friedland, Martin L. *Detention before Trial.* Toronto: University of Toronto Press, 1965.

Grosman, Brian A. *The Prosecutor.* Toronto: University of Toronto Press, 1970.

Mann, W. E. *Society behind Bars.* Toronto: Social Science Publishers, 1967.

McGrath, W. T., ed. *Crime and Its Treatment in Canada.* Toronto: Macmillan, 1965.

Advanced

Boydell, Craig L., Carl F. Grindstaff and Paul Whitehead. *Deviance and Societal Reaction in Canada.* Toronto: Holt Rinehart and Winston, 1972.

Canada. Department of Justice Committee on Juvenile Delinquency. *Juvenile Delinquency in Canada.* Ottawa, 1965.

Canadian Committee on Corrections. *Towards Unity: Criminal Justice and Corrections.* Ottawa, 1969.

Hogarth, John. *Sentencing as a Human Process.* Toronto: University of Toronto Press, 1971.

Professional

Quebec. Commission of Inquiry into the Administration of Justice on Criminal and Penal Matters in Quebec. *Crime, Justice and Society.* 3 vols. Quebec, 1968-69; Annexes 1-8, University of Montreal.

The Media
Donald Gordon

Donald Gordon has been a research consultant for the Senate Committee on Mass Media in Canada, the Task Force on Government Information, the Royal Commission on Bilingualism and Biculturalism and the Brookings Institute in Washington. The author of two books, he is at present an associate professor with the interfaculty program board at the University of Waterloo.

Canada is almost uniquely a nation forged by its media. Its original economics, politics and boundaries were very largely determined by the interplay of existing and proposed communications systems—often in defiance of both people and nature. Its subsequent patterns of development have been equally heavily media-flavoured, both defensively in terms of the artificial fostering of Kulture, and offensively in their waves of whipped-up nationalism, sectarian malice and, ironically, susceptibility to cut-rate Americanization.

Such broad themes are extensively and well documented in published Canadian material. With the exception of film, any mildly interested browser can put together a reading program for himself (or others) on Canadian mass media that is informative, infuriating and illuminating. There won't, alas, be quite the bawdiness or brashness available in vintage American and British memorabilia, and some careful ferreting and between-the-lines reading may be required to reveal all the facets of greed and nastiness, but the canvas still is detailed and reasonably incisive.

What follows, then, is one media-worn veteran's version of a reading program. It is subject to some value judgments (mostly unintentional), some omissions (all unintentional) and, in all probability, some errors. But, by the grace of what recommended writers do have to say and the variety of bibliographies they provide, such flaws can be corrected by readers to their own taste.

The fact that a good five-foot shelf of Canadian media books can be put together is the result of people and politics. The understandable narcissism of media practitioners has been combined with a mixture of heroic and hilarious probing by governments to produce historical, descriptive, theoretical and anecdotal publications in abundance.

General background and some snapshots of the development of Canadian media are to be found in several basic books. W. H. Kesterton's *A History of Journalism in Canada* provides a comprehensive overview of the development of print journalism. It can be enriched and supplemented with more specialized offerings, such as *Brown of the Globe* by J. M. S. Careless, *News and the Southams* by Charles Bruce, *Dafoe of the Free Press* by Murray Donnelly and the *Report* of the Special Senate Committee on Mass Media, volume one.

A browse through libraries and second-hand book shops should also serve to turn up at least four other useful books: M. E. Nichols's *(CP) The Story of the Canadian Press,* Carlton McNaught's *Canada Gets the News,* J. H. Cranston's *Ink on My Fingers* and the brief but important volume by George V. Ferguson and F. H. Underhill, *Press and Party in Canada: Issues of Freedom.*

Lighter touches hinting at some of the real flavour of newspapering can be turned up in Roy Greenaway's *The News Game,* Gordon Sinclair's *Will the Real Gordon Sinclair Please Stand Up,* and (if you can find it) Arthur Ford's *As the World Wags On.*

Other aspects of print are not yet served very well in Canada. A volume of background papers on book publishing is being issued in conjunction with the Ontario royal commission study of the field in 1972—and this will mark the first survey collection to appear in print in more than a decade. Weekly newspapers and magazines are best dealt with through direct references, since the handful of memoirs and musings that have been published are out of print and largely out of date. Advertising, as a facet of print, is best approached via an apologia—*The Economic Implications of Advertising* by O. J. Firestone—and by leafing through any of the copies you can find of the *Annual of Advertising and Editorial Art* put together by the Art Directors Club of Toronto.

In addition, volume three of the *Report* of the Special Senate Committee on Mass Media has some succinct sections on magazines, student papers and the "underground" papers in Canada. (Tucked away in the libraries at the University of Western Ontario and Carleton University, however, there is even more useful material in the form of the actual briefs submitted to the senators.)

Electronic media are well covered. Frank W. Peers's *The Politics of Canadian Broadcasting, 1920-1951* is one of the most comprehensive summations in print and is well worth its sometimes heavy prose.

The *Report* of the Committee on Broadcasting, the *Report* of the Task Force on Government Information and (if you can ever pry a copy loose from a cautious bureaucrat) the three-volume *Report* of the Consultative Committee on Program Policy (1967-68) combine to provide interesting history and glimpses of the views of government and its advisors in Canada. These, at least, will provide a representative sampling of urgent and sometimes inventive recommendations brought forward which, in turn, can be compared with actual progress achieved.

Then, when you have dried your eyes, you can turn to more theoretical publications as a way of preparing for eventual (and inescapable) confrontation with McLuhanland. John A. Irving has edited an overview, *Mass Media in Canada,* which remains timely despite its age—it was originally published in 1962. Two other books, *Language, Logic and the Mass Media* and *The New Literacy,* have been put together by D. R. Gordon for readers able to cope with woolier prose.

All these suffer, to some extent, from considering the media apart from influences around them. It's probably easier to consider print or TV as ends in themselves, for instance, but the gains in simplicity, focus and perhaps even clarity are diluted by qualities of unreality.

So, at about this point, some attention to the setting in which Canadian media operate is really necessary. One set of sources might include volume one of the historic Rowell-Sirois Report (available in a reprint); John Porter's *The Vertical Mosaic*, another landmark effort; Mildred A. Schwartz's *Public Opinion and Canadian Identity*, a much-neglected study of great worth; and the readings edited by Richard Laskin, *Social Problems: A Canadian Profile*. Taken in their entirety, such books provide enough of history, sociology, economics and politics to indicate the harsh realities within which Canadian media exist. Used selectively, they can provide shorter dabblings sufficient for at least a workable sense of the lay of the land.

Now for McLuhanland. Right away, somewhat belated acknowledgment of the contributions of the late Harold A. Innis is essential. Dr. Innis wrote in a style almost as compact as that of his star pupil and one somewhat more comprehensible. At least one of *The Bias of Communication* or *Changing Concepts of Time* is required reading for anyone determined to go on to contemporary McLuhan.

And then it would be wise to consult some translators. Among the many who have sprung up to explain, laud, castigate and confuse us about Marshall McLuhan, two Canadian writers seem to have done reasonably well. A slim volume entitled *Marshall McLuhan* by Dennis Duffy is a well-written and sensibly impartial explanation of main themes. *The Medium Is the Rear-View Mirror* by Donald F. Theall is much more extensive and thorough and probably one of the most intellectually sophisticated of current offerings.

Dr. McLuhan himself is best grappled with through perusal of *The Gutenberg Galaxy, Understanding Media, The Mechanical Bride* and, just for the fun of it, *Counterblast*.

At about that point, you might consider getting back down to earth. Juxtaposition of any of the McLuhan soarings with, for instance, the *Report* of the Royal

Commission on Taxation, might suggest that all media theorizing is a little mad.

Finally, it is also worth keeping Canadian periodicals in mind to supplement and update published books. The field of film, for instance, is really best considered via periodical sources—at least until some rather more enterprising books come on the scene. In particular, *Take One, Broadcaster, Content, National Film Board Newsletter, Last Post, Canadian Dimension,* the *Mysterious East, Saturday Night* and *RPM* are useful as reasonably consistent chroniclers of the Canadian media scene. They are all prone to biases of various kinds, but they at least help you to keep up with current uproars.

SUMMARY BIBLIOGRAPHY
All are general.

Bruce, Charles. *News and the Southams.* Toronto: Macmillan, 1968.

Canada. *Report of the Committee on Broadcasting.* Ottawa, 1965.

———. *Report of the Task Force on Government Information.* 2 vols. Ottawa, 1969.

———. Royal Commission on Taxation. *Report.* Ottawa, 1966.

———. Special Senate Committee on the Mass Media. *Report.* 3 vols. Ottawa, 1970.

Careless, J. M. S. *Brown of the Globe.* 2 vols. Toronto: Macmillan, 1959.

Cranston, J. H. *Ink on My Fingers.* Toronto: Ryerson, 1953.

Donnelly, Murray. *Dafoe of the Free Press.* Toronto: Macmillan, 1968.

Duffy, Dennis. *Marshall McLuhan.* Toronto: McClelland and Stewart, 1969.

Ferguson, G. F., and Frank H. Underhill. *Press and Party in Canada.* Toronto: Ryerson, 1955.

Firestone, O. J. *The Economic Implications of Advertising.* Toronto: Methuen, 1967.

Ford, Arthur. *As the World Wags On.* Toronto: Ryerson, 1950.

Gordon, Donald R. *Language, Logic and the Mass Media.* Toronto: Holt Rinehart and Winston, 1966.

———. *The New Literacy.* Toronto: University of Toronto Press, 1971.

Greenaway, Roy. *The News Game.* Toronto: Clarke, Irwin, 1966.

Innis, Harold A. *The Bias of Communication.* Toronto: University of Toronto Press, 1968.

———. *Changing Concepts of Time.* Toronto: University of Toronto Press, 1952.

Irving, John A. *Mass Media in Canada.* Toronto: Ryerson, 1962.

Kesterton, W. H. *A History of Journalism in Canada.* Toronto: McClelland and Stewart, 1967.

Laskin, Richard. *Social Problems: A Canadian Profile.* Toronto: McGraw-Hill, l964.

McLuhan, Marshall. *Counterblast.* Toronto: McClelland and Stewart, 1969.

———. *The Gutenberg Galaxy.* Toronto: University of Toronto Press, 1962.

———. *The Mechanical Bride.* Toronto: Saunders, 1968.

———. *Understanding Media.* Toronto: McGraw-Hill, 1964.

McNaught, Carlton. *Canada Gets the News.* Toronto: Ryerson, 1940.

Nichols, M. E. *(CP) The Story of the Canadian Press.* Toronto: Ryerson, 1948.

Peers, Frank W. *The Politics of Canadian Broadcasting, 1920-1951.* Toronto: University of Toronto Press, 1969.

Porter, John. *The Vertical Mosaic.* Toronto: University of Toronto Press, 1965.

Schwartz, Mildred A. *Public Opinion and Canadian Identity.* Scarborough: Fitzhenry and Whiteside, 1967.

Sinclair, Gordon. *Will the Real Gordon Sinclair Please Stand Up?* Toronto: McClelland and Stewart, 1966.

Smiley, D. V., ed. *The Rowell-Sirois Report, Book One.* Toronto: McClelland and Stewart, 1963.

Theall, Donald F. *The Medium is the Rear-View Mirror.* Montreal: McGill-Queen's University Press, 1971.

4 Literature and the Arts

Nineteenth Century Literature
Gordon Roper

*Professor Gordon Roper gave graduate courses in
Canadian fiction at the University of Toronto before
moving to Trent University in 1969. He has contributed
three chapters to the* Literary History of Canada,
*established the Massey College Collection of Canadian
fiction, and now directs the Shell Fund for acquiring
Canadian literature at Trent.*

Poetry in nineteenth century Canada was more widely
regarded as a public art than it is today. Most poems
were written to affect the reader, not for self-
expression. Poems were composed for many reasons: to
celebrate communal events such as weddings, births,
feast days or Great Cheeses; to console suffering or the
loss of loved ones; to praise God, the Queen, Nature or
young women; to teach temperance or to jollify; to ease
the tedium and strain of work; to inspire reflection or
contemplation; to commemorate people, places and
events; to share the writer's sense of the new life in the
new land, his hope for a great future or his homesick-
ness for the old land he had left. Poems were like axes
against the wilderness; they preserved and reinforced the
human bonds with the people and ways left behind, and
they bound together new neighbours.

Poems were written by all classes of people: by
emigrant ploughboys, mechanics, newspaper printers,
undertakers, clergymen and their wives, by politicians
and governors general. They were written by blue-
stockings and local bards and sweet singers and, increasingly in the closing decades of the century, by classically
trained university graduates. Poems were written in all
forms: ballads, hymns, rhyming couplets, even Spen-
serian stanzas; there were lyrics, satires, long narrative
poems, epics and verse dramas. They were written in
many moods: in the tender and sentimental, the

tough-minded and savage, the patriotic, the devotional, the erotic, comic, Gothic and the lugubrious.

Poetry was more commonly available then than now. Expensive or cheap editions could be had in the bookstores or by mail of all the favourite poets in English—Goldsmith and other later eighteenth century poets, Scott, Byron, Moore, Tupper, Mrs. Hemans, Longfellow, Lowell, Holmes, Bryant, Whittier, Tennyson. And even while local publishing conditions inhibited the production of books of verse by Canadian poets, more than five hundred writers did publish more than eight hundred volumes of verse—almost all at their own expense, and self-distributed. But most readers read the local poets in their newspapers, for newspapers then carried a poetry column on their front page. Or they read them in the literary journals that were born and died, such as Mr. and Mrs. Moodie's *Victoria Magazine* (1847-1848), or the more successful *Literary Garland* of Montreal.

These volumes of nineteenth century poetry are all out of print now, although a few copies may linger like late April snow on the literature shelves of older public libraries and a few universities. But generous samplings of the work of these poets are to be found in three large collections made in the nineteenth century, while selections from the major poets of the time are reprinted in several modern anthologies.

The largest sampling of poems written in Canada before Confederation is in *Selections from Canadian Poets* by Edward Hartley Dewart (1864). Dewart's long introduction is an important document on mid-nineteenth century views on poetry in Canada, and it is a classical argument for the need of a national literature to help build a sense of national identity. It is out of print now, but will be reprinted shortly. *Songs of the Great Dominion,* edited by William Douw Lighthall (1889), printed about two hundred poems, many of them written after Dewart's collection. Lighthall's book was published in London and was intended as a poetic showcase of the new land for readers in Great Britain. It has been reprinted in facsimile in Cole's Canadiana collection. *A Treasury of Canadian Verse,* edited by Theodore Rand (1900) is less nationalistic and more aesthetic in its principle of selection. It contains poems by the more sophisticated literary men of the 1880s and 1890s. It is out of print now but copies are to be found on some library shelves.

The most comprehensive modern anthologies containing selections of major nineteenth century Canadian poets are Carl Klinck and R. E. Watters's *Canadian Anthology* and A. J. M. Smith's *The Book of Canadian Poetry.* The Klinck and Watters volume allots 175 pages to both prose and poetry before 1900; it has the most comprehensive bibliography on the period and on individual writers as an aid to further study. The Smith anthology devotes about two hundred pages to pre-1900 poetry, and has an excellent long introduction on Canadian poetry. Its bibliography is extensive but less useful than the Klinck and Watters bibliography.

A. J. M. Smith also edited *The Oxford Book of Canadian Verse in English and French,* which superseded the much less critically responsible volume of the same name edited by W. W. Campbell in 1913. Smith joined F. R. Scott in editing *The Blasted Pine: An Anthology of Satire, Invective, and Disrespectful Verse,* which contains a scattering of anti-establishment nineteenth century poems. Ralph Gustafson gave about one hundred pages to pre-nineteenth century poetry in his excellent paperback anthology, *The Penguin Book of Canadian Verse.*

Reprints of individual volumes of nineteenth century poems are few as yet. William Henry Drummond's *Habitant Poems* has appeared in the New Canadian Library, and they will print a volume of Charles Sangster's poems in 1972. Individual volumes of the work of Isabella Valancy Crawford, Charles Mair, Archibald Lampman, Charles G. D. Roberts, Bliss Carman and Duncan Campbell Scott will be published in the near future by another press. A generous selection of the poems of Roberts, Carman, Lampman and Scott is available in the New Canadian Library *Poets of Confederation,* edited by Malcolm Ross.

For nineteenth century folk and work songs, see Edith Fowke and Alan Mills's *Canada's Story in Song*.

The most seminal study of nineteenth century Canadian poetry probably has been E. K. Brown's *On Canadian Poetry*. The most comprehensive historical and critical study is to be found in the *Literary History of Canada*, edited by Carl Klinck and others, parts two and three, and in the conclusion by Northrop Frye. About half of the essays in A. J. M. Smith's anthology of critical articles, *Masks of Poetry*, are on nineteenth century Canadian poetry. See also R. E. Rashley's *Poetry in Canada: The First Three Steps*, and Desmond Pacey's *Ten Canadian Poets*.

Even more than poetry, fiction in nineteenth century Canada was a popular art. Most fiction writers wrote to make money, and so wrote to move their readers by a mingling of sentimental and sensational appeals. They emulated the kinds of fiction fashionable in the English-speaking world in Great Britain and the United States. They found it difficult to compete with British and American writers, for Canada was flooded with cheap editions and story weeklies from the United States. A few Canadians—May Agnes Fleming, the Sadliers (mother and daughter) and James De Mille—succeeded in supplying New York publishers with a stream of fashionable sentimental and sensational serials; most Canadian writers could only place fiction with the domestic newspapers and literary magazines that accepted, at little or no pay, sketches or short stories. A few hundred volumes of fiction by Canadians were published in Canada before the closing decades of the century, most of them at the author's own risk. In the 1880s and 1890s, however, the demand for fiction in North America soared. International copyright agreements were achieved; a Canadian publishing industry grew, and Canadians found a more open market in American magazines. Almost all of this fiction published in the last century is long out of print, but a dozen landmarks of various kinds have been reprinted in the New Canadian Library; others will be reprinted in the near future.

The first fiction to use the North American scene was Frances Brooke's *The History of Emily Montague* (1769), a lively, sophisticated novel of sensibility in letter form. Mrs. Brooke was a temporary resident of Quebec while her husband was garrisoned there; her other novels are about English life.

The next landmark is an example of a more violent kind of fashionable fiction. Major John Richardson's *Wacousta: or, the Prophecy* (1832) is a three-decker variety show of sensation and sensibility, essentially Gothic in nature, modelled partly on Scott's historical romances and more on Cooper's Indian romances. It exploits the Pontiac conspiracy at Detroit.

A very different mode of fiction was developed by Thomas Chandler Haliburton in his Clockmaker series (1836, 1838, 1840) and in later books, especially in *The Old Judge* (1849). Haliburton wrote the first of the Clockmaker newspaper letters primarily to wake his fellow Nova Scotians up politically and economically. He combined with unique skill the Irvingesque sketch (in his English squire character) and varieties of popular, oral American humour (in his Sam Slick character). He opened a rich vein of humorous satirical writing in which later men like Mark Twain and Stephen Leacock worked. Mrs. Susanna Moodie's *Roughing It in the Bush* (1852), usually read as a series of autobiographical sketches, probably owes much of its freshness to her skillful heightening of personal experience by fictional devices and affective prose. Mrs. Moodie was a practiced fiction writer, for she published more than fifteen novels of domestic sentiment and children's stories, none of which have anything to do with the Canadian scene.

Very few Canadian writers wrote in the spirit called for by Dewart in the introduction to his *Selections from Canadian Poets*. William Kirby was one who did consciously try to create a splendid myth about the past of his new country, in *The Golden Dog (Le Chien D'or)* (1877). Kirby drew less on the Gothic patterns of historical romance and more on those of Dumas and Scott. But his inspiration flagged and Gothic sensation takes over in the latter part of this work. The New Canadian Library edition reprints an abbreviated version. Other myths of Canada were created more successfully by the English writers Ballantyne, Marryat, Kingston and Henty, who established visions of the Canadian North and Northwest that became endemic in fiction at the turn of the century. Gilbert Parker exploited this myth of the Northwest, mixed with the sentiment of Bret Harte, the exotic of Kipling and his rhetorical flair, in his popular Pierre tales in the 1890s. Parker also exploited the keen interest in North America for local-colour tales fed by the publishing of many stories about French Canadian life in American magazines. Of these, his *When Valmond Came to Pontiac* (1895) is the most charming; it may be reprinted shortly. Parker's historical romance, *The Seats of the Mighty* (1896) has been reprinted in the New Canadian Library. It owes little to Kirby's attempt to create national myths, and much more to the current vogue for high historical romance.

Another fashionable form of fiction at the end of the century was the fable of muscular Christianity in the open air. Ralph Connor (the Reverend Charles Gordon) met with instant success with his *Black Rock* (1898) and *The Sky Pilot* (1899), both set in the foothills of the Rockies. All of Connor's fiction is now out of print except *The Man from Glengarry* (1901), reprinted in the New Canadian Library.

The last quarter of the century also saw the rising fashion of science fiction, best exemplified in the work of Jules Verne. The versatile James De Mille, who had become one of the most successful of *Harper's* stable of writers in New York, scored with his last book, *A Strange Manuscript Found in a Copper Cylinder* (1888), reprinted in the New Canadian Library.

The most significant literary development in the last quarter of the century was the drive for a fiction that would tell the truth about human experience, unsensationally and unsentimentally. Henry James, William Dean Howells and George Eliot led the way. Two Canadians distinguished themselves in this new realism.

Francis William Grey's *The Curé of St. Philippe* (1899) is an honest and perceptive picture of life in a French Canadian village, and makes one regret that Grey wrote little other fiction. Sara Jeannette Duncan combined affection and hard-headedness, in a way that is unique among nineteenth century Canadian writers, to portray the social, religious and political life of an Ontario town like Brantford in *The Imperialist* (1904). Unfortunately for Canadian readers, Miss Duncan married an Englishman in India, and most of her twenty fictions are concerned with Anglo-Indian life or with the international scene in England. Only *The Imperialist* is set in Canada; it has been reprinted in the New Canadian Library.

Historical and critical writing about nineteenth century Canadian fiction is not extensive. The fullest account is in parts two and three of the *Literary History of Canada*, edited by Carl Klinck and others. Articles appear occasionally in the issues of the scholarly quarterlies *Canadian Literature* and the new *Journal of Canadian Fiction*, both of which compile annual bibliographies of historical or critical writing on this field.

SUMMARY BIBLIOGRAPHY
Books containing nineteenth century Canadian poetry

Dewart, Edward Hartley, ed. *Selections from Canadian Poets, with occasional critical & biographical notes.* Montreal: Lovell, 1864.

Drummond, William Henry. *Habitant Poems.* Toronto: McClelland and Stewart, New Canadian Library, 1959.

Fowke, Edith, and Alan Mills. *Canada's Story in Song.* Toronto: Gage, 1960.

Gustafson, Ralph, ed. *The Penguin Book of Canadian Verse.* Harmondsworth: Penguin, 1958.

Klinck, Carl F., and R. E. Watters, eds. *Canadian Anthology.* Toronto: W. J. Gage, 1955. Rev. and enlarged ed. 1966.

Lighthall, William Douw, ed. *Songs of the Great Dominion: Voices from the Forests and Waters, the Settlements and Cities of Canada.* London: Walter Scott, 1889. Reprinted in Coles Canadiana Collection, 1971. Also reprinted by Scott in 1892 as *Canadian Poems and Songs,* and in a shorter form as *Canadian Poems and Lays.*

Rand, Theodore H., ed. *A Treasury of Canadian Verse.* Toronto: Briggs, 1900.

Ross, Malcolm, ed. *Poets of the Confederation.* Toronto: McClelland and Stewart, New Canadian Library, 1960.

Sinclair, David, ed. *Nineteenth-Century Narrative Poems.* Toronto: McClelland and Stewart, New Canadian Library, 1972.

Smith, A. J. M., ed. *The Book of Canadian Poetry.* Chicago: University of Chicago Press, 1943. Rev. and enlarged ed. 1948. 3rd ed. Toronto: Gage, 1957.

———, ed. *The Oxford Book of Canadian Verse in English and French.* Toronto: Oxford University Press, 1960.

Smith, A. J. M., and F. R. Scott, eds. *The Blasted Pine: An Anthology of Satire, Invective, and Disrespectful Verse Chiefly by Canadian Writers.* Toronto: Macmillan, 1957.

Books about Canadian poetry

Brown, E. K. *On Canadian Poetry.* Toronto: Ryerson, 1943. Rev. ed. 1944.

Klinck, Carl F., et al. *Literary History of Canada: Canadian Literature in English.* Toronto: University of Toronto Press, 1965. See parts 1 and 2, and the conclusion.

Pacey, Desmond. *Ten Canadian Poets.* Toronto: Ryerson, 1958.

Rashley, R. E. *Poetry in Canada: The First Three Steps.* Toronto: Ryerson, 1958.

Smith, A. J. M., ed. *Masks of Poetry.* Toronto: McClelland and Stewart, 1962.

Nineteenth century
Canadian fiction in print

Haliburton, Thomas Chandler. *The Old Judge; or, Life in a Colony* (1849). Toronto: Clarke, Irwin, 1968.

Ross, Malcolm, ed. New Canadian Library. Toronto: McClelland and Stewart.

    Brooke, Frances. *The History of Emily Montague* (1769). 1961.

    Connor, Ralph (pseud. of Charles Gordon). *The Man from Glengarry* (1901). 1960.

    De Mille, James. *A Strange Manuscript Found in a Copper Cylinder* (1888). 1969.

    Duncan, Sara Jeannette. *The Imperialist* (1904). 1961.

    Grey, Francis William. *The Curé of St. Philippe* (1899). 1970.

    Haliburton, Thomas Chandler. *The Clockmaker: or, The Sayings and Doings of Samuel Slick, of Slicksville* (1836). 1958.

    Kirby, William. *The Golden Dog (Le Chien D'Or)* (1877). 1969.

    Moodie, Susanna. *Roughing It in the Bush* (1852). 1962.

    Parker, Sir Gilbert. *The Seats of the Mighty* (1896). 1971.

    Richardson, Major John. *Wacousta; or, the Prophecy* (1832). 1967.

Books about nineteenth century
Canadian fiction

Klinck, Carl, et al., eds. *Literary History of Canada.* Toronto: University of Toronto Press, 1965.

See also the scholarly quarterlies, *Canadian Literature* (Vancouver: University of British Columbia Press, 1959—), and *Journal of Canadian Fiction* (Fredericton: University of New Brunswick, 1972—).

Bibliographies

Watters, Reginald Eyre. *A Check List of Canadian Literature and Background Materials, 1628-1950.* Toronto: University of Toronto Press, 1959. Rev. and enlarged ed. 1972.

Watters, Reginald Eyre, and Inglis Bell. *On Canadian Literature. A Check List of Articles, Books and Theses on English Canadian Literature, Its Authors, and Language.* Toronto: University of Toronto Press, 1966.

See also the checklist of new editions, reprints and critical and scholarly work on Canadian literature compiled annually in *Canadian Literature*, beginning with no. 3 (1960).

Modern Fiction
W. H. New

W. H. New teaches English at the University of British Columbia. Associate editor of the critical quarterly Canadian Literature, *he has contributed essays to several journals, edited* Four Hemispheres *(an anthology of Commonwealth short stories), and written a monograph entitled* Malcolm Lowry.

A history of modern English-language Canadian fiction traces a journey into "realism" and out of it again. Whereas earlier nonfiction had been descriptively realistic, nineteenth century fiction largely relied on the stock figures and the elevated style of romantic adventures. Twentieth century writers, for about five decades, tried to make their landscapes more specific, to lock them, for example, in southern Saskatchewan, Halifax, Montreal or Manitoba. They tried also to ensure that their characters were fully motivated and behaved credibly in such locales. The commitment to psychological motivation, however, led a number of writers by the 1960s to explore the nature of the mind itself, to examine such abstractions as vision, knowledge, perception, imagination and power. Often a highly stylized fiction resulted. Symbolic and mythic landscapes overlapped regional geographies. The heart of such work was no less real than that which "realism" sought to represent, and certainly it exerted no less powerful a hold upon its readers. But it more openly admitted the artifice of its technique and as one of its aims held language itself up to contemplation.

A concern for linguistic pattern characterizes in another way much humorous writing. Incongruities controlled within a writer's style can at once render the foibles of life and parody the flaws of overused literary forms. Of the many Canadian writers who have employed the techniques of wit—Sara Jeannette Duncan,

Robertson Davies, Paul Hiebert, Robert Kroetsch, to name a few—none has appealed more widely than Stephen Leacock. In his most coherent and sustained work, a book of eleven episodes entitled *Sunshine Sketches of a Little Town* (1912), the sense of the absurd is compounded by a genuine sympathy for imperfect mankind. Leacock consciously insists that man's ironic dimensions lead at once to laughter and to tears, and the tonal ambivalence that he managed to master conveys Canadian prose into the twentieth century. The pressures of the time seemed contradictory. "Progress" proved unsettling, yet to pretend that change had not taken place was absurd. Between the two attitudes lay a belief in, and a search for a simpler life, a lost innocence that might, for the duration of a work of literature, be retrieved.

The lurking danger in that approach is sentimentality, but Leacock's writings never wholly escaped the empirical world. His invented town of Mariposa is rooted in the real one of Orillia, Ontario. Readers are made conscious not only of the "sunshine" of his sketches but also of the frame of shadow around them. And even though his characters are largely flat caricatures—trying to commit suicide on bromo-seltzer or resigning their position because they don't know the meaning of "mugwump"—their idiosyncrasies merely exaggerate the experience of everyday life. Together their elaborate entanglements and mundane solutions portray the fabric of a genuine small town—not by the absurdity, but because they probe genuine aspirations and limitations and evoke genuine emotional response. One function of the humour is to make the limitations acceptable, to accustom people to the fact that they do live in an imperfect world. Life then seems a human comedy—no less serious for that, but, for all its distress, not without happiness either.

A more militantly earnest response to relative values and modified ideals permeates Frederick Philip Grove's *A Search for America* (1927). A fictional autobiography of Phil Branden, a Scandinavian immigrant from a decayed gentle family (educated, literate, yet limited by his cultural standards), *A Search for America* traces the partial change in character that results when the America Branden had dreamed of collides with the America he experienced. Longer and less deliberately entertaining than Leacock's book—Branden is by turns spirited, forthright, egotistical and priggish—*A Search for America* none the less engages the attention. Like so many Canadian books (other writers who explore the theme include Laura Salverson, Frederick Niven, Henry Kreisel and Will Bird), it reveals the monetary expectation and disillusion of many immigrants. What concerns Grove more is the nature of North America itself. His character must face the petty graft of a waiter's life in a second-rate Toronto restaurant, the more elaborate corruption of a New York encyclopedia sales racket, illness, poverty, middle-class prejudices against strangers and hoboes and, above all, the acquisitive naïveté of the North American people. Ready to adapt to anything, they adapt to corruption easiest of all. Yet beneath the surface of the acquisitive society lay the individualistic and egalitarian ideals—ideals which Grove ultimately felt were more likely to be realized in Canada than in the United States. If systems impeded the realization of such a dream, they did not prove its impracticality. When Branden resolves to speak socialism to the bosses and intone conservative virtues to the men, and to take on a teaching job in Manitoba and tell the true story of immigrants, the autobiographical element of the book surfaces. The solution smacks of expedient compromise, but even more it insists on the unity of the moral quest and the search for knowledge. As a kind of forerunner of the transcontinental youth migrations of the 1960s and 1970s, the book serves also as a goad to remind society of the nature of morality and the reality of imaginative dreams and ideals.

Like Grove's work, Morley Callaghan's probes moral behaviour, affirms conservative values, but unremittingly berates the institutions that have become arbiters of behaviour in modern society. The church, municipal government, prisons, business enterprises—all come under fire. What matters is the individual, but as *Such Is*

My Beloved (1933) makes clear, the very individuality of any attempt to adhere to a genuine morality will doom it; the combined power of institutions—at least for the moment—will inevitably win. Thus when the central character of that novel, a young Roman Catholic priest named Father Dowling, goes out into his parish and in apparent Christian charity befriends two prostitutes, he is pilloried by his superiors and by the community at large. To have left the situation at that, however, would have been grossly simplistic. Callaghan compounds the problem by leaving Father Dowling's basic motives largely in doubt: is he saintly, or guilty of enormous pride? The resulting dubiety, as much as the urban setting and deprived characters, communicates the reality of the life Callaghan wanted to convey.

To throw an emphasis on the facts of that life, and to avoid the romanticizing processes of traditional Canadian narrative, Callaghan devised a deliberately flat style, which he learned largely in the international literary community of Paris in the 1920s. (His contemporary there, John Glassco, has written in *Memoirs of Montparnasse* [1970] one of the finest and most ingenuous portraits of that time, displaying also one of the most exemplary styles in modern Canadian prose.) Callaghan's own style has been the subject of critical controversy, but the conscious craftsmanship he sought marked the more general movement of Canadian writers in the 1940s towards convincing explorations of point of view and human subjectivity.

The illusion of reality was the issue. English-language writers learned in part from their French-speaking counterparts, such as Ringuet, Roger Lemelin and Gabrielle Roy. They learned also from their direct experience of the depression and, on the prairies, the drought and crop failure that accompanied it. The natural barrenness of Saskatchewan in the 1930s became for Sinclair Ross a symbol of sterile human relations. In his major novel, *As for Me and My House* (1941), an unbelieving churchman and his wife, Philip and Mrs. Bentley, find themselves endlessly ministering to towns they detest and for their pains discover that they are no longer capable of reaching each other. Masks have become their way of life. As all the characters project their masks on to others, creating in their own image, the world becomes difficult to interpret; its "truths" are ambivalent. Ross communicates such a view by involving readers in Mrs. Bentley's perspective—the book takes the form of her diary—only to undercut their sympathy by reminding them that she creates in her image too. Absolute judgments are impossible in such a world, and values—accordingly, perhaps—become increasingly important as their common acceptance disappears.

The numerous books about growing to maturity (by W. O. Mitchell, Ernest Buckler, Martha Ostenso, Adele Wiseman, Mordecai Richler, Hugh MacLennan and others) pursue that search for values in a disordered world. Richler's *The Apprenticeship of Duddy Kravitz* (1959), with irreverent but lively iconoclasm, traces the rise of a Montreal ghetto boy to financial success and shows how he must sacrifice friends, ideals and traditions in his pragmatic struggle to survive. The comedy of the author's method and the pessimism of his vision painfully interact. Duddy's choices are not between virtue and vice, but only "among enemies"; a kind of success is therefore also a kind of failure, and the tensions of life go unresolved.

For MacLennan, who of all Canadian writers has been the most directly concerned with (and committed to) the developing maturity of the nation itself, the internal tensions between English and French cultures seem equally life-denying. *Return of the Sphinx* (1967) indicates by its title an acceptance of the enigma. A semi-allegorical novel of the conflict between fathers and sons, it pits a federalist cabinet minister against his separatist child, explores the genuinely held philosophies of both, and ends in violence. All that remains is the land, still withstanding its occupants, enduring; but endurance alone in the face of such chaos seems a bleak prospect, with only a slim hold on a stable future.

The land acquires a distinct, personal character in Ethel Wilson's fiction also, but her characters are ultimately more capable of living in harmony with it. In *Swamp Angel* (1954), Maggie Vardoe abandons her shallow husband, becomes Maggie Lloyd again, heads for the interior of British Columbia to find an identity of her own in a fishing camp, and gains "a special value in a landscape with trees." One of the most masterfully subtle Canadian stylists, Ethel Wilson concentrates on character rather than on event, and quietly, gently, insists on the power of commitment itself, the enduring human capacity for choice even in apparently constricting social environments and in the face of ineluctable time. The novel thus probes the limits of freedom. In so doing it examines the options that women have in modern Canadian society. Male writers like Sinclair Ross and Brian Moore have attempted to consider that question; more recently Audrey Thomas, Mavis Gallant, Alice Munro, Margaret Atwood, Marian Engel and Margaret Laurence have passionately and with searing wit written from the intensity of female experience. Laurence's *The Stone Angel* (1964), about the dying days of Hagar Shipley (told from her admirably raging point of view), communicates all the frustration, all the emotional energy and physical weakness of the aged, while celebrating the tenderness of human sympathies and the worth of life itself. Hagar misjudges people around her, is used by others, yearns for understanding and seeks outside herself the identity she already possesses; she emerges as a fallible human being, in other words, whose passion is engrossing.

The concern for exploring the nature of identity has led a number of other writers into quite different fictional techniques; the result has been the panoramic questing cultural histories of Abraham Klein and Rudy Wiebe, the mythic landscapes of Sheila Watson and Gwendolyn MacEwen, the metaphysical and political mindscapes of Malcolm Lowry and Dave Godfrey, and various recent works about the nature and function of art. Taking as its centre the nature of man's search for his soul rather than the behaviour of a man searching, Lowry's brilliant *Hear Us O Lord from Heaven Thy Dwelling-Place* (1961) demands an appreciation of its deliberately allusive, complex, repetitive, rhythmic technique; its meaning lies in its method. Action is less important to it than idea, character less important than the processes of thought or the processes of characterization. In creating a novelist *persona* named Sigbjørn Wilderness (who in turn creates a novelist-character Martin Trumbaugh), Lowry is exploring the fragmentation of identity, the fact that the mind knows itself in various ways. Such knowledge inevitably leads to chaos before the individual finds his way back to Edenic peace, a cyclical journey that is represented by voyages from British Columbia and the Isle of Man to Panama and volcanic Italy and back again. Hence immigration forms, canals, book-jacket biographies, and even the seven stories of the book, all lock single identities away; the progress of the novel—for the stories blend into that—demonstrates the cumulative unity of the fragments, the *necessary* tension between chaos and paradise if man is to find mortal harmony. He must accept the "Wilderness" in himself; then the tension acquires some meaning, and laughter becomes not an escape from discord but a joyous ability to transcend it.

The multiple perspectives of Godfrey's *The New Ancestors* (1970), set in immediately pre-revolutionary Lost Coast, West Africa, display an equally complex technical blend of empirical, external, political truths with visionary, internal, metaphysical ones. Centring on a political murder, the destruction of one "cell" by another, it postulates that such an "Africa" is within everyone, that the ordered but unpredictable process of cell division (biological as well as political) describes the development both of individual identity and of national culture. The metaphor also insists on the contemporaneity of the past *in* the present, and the cast of minor characters reveals different aspects of the quest for present meaning. Their language strives to evoke religious experience as well as empirical fact; their need for tradition and their ability to face the future coalesce; their talent for re-creating the truth of dream and fable utters their capacity to remain independent. The search for "ancestors" thus acquires distinct

national importance. To celebrate the cultural dream of
his own society becomes Godfrey's goal; to accept the
unpredictability of the future concurrently with an
active engagement in the present becomes his central
character's willing role; in the interpenetration of
science and art (but the distinction between truth and
utility) lies his method. If it utters a new form of
realism in Canadian literature, it also indicates one
possible direction for the continued development of the
novelist's craft.

Standard primary and secondary bibliographies of
Canadian fiction are by R. E. Watters and by Inglis Bell
and Susan Port; supplementary serial bibliographies are
published annually in the critical journals *Canadian
Literature* and *Journal of Commonwealth Literature;* an
annual review of Canadian fiction appears in the
*University of Toronto Quarterly.The Oxford Com-
panion to Canadian History and Literature,* edited by
Norah Story, provides useful biographical and historical
data, and the *Literary History of Canada,* edited by C.
F. Klinck, provides a more comprehensive general
survey.

SUMMARY BIBLIOGRAPHY
General

Callaghan, Morley. *Such Is My Beloved* (1934). Toronto: McClelland and Stewart, 1957.

Grove, Frederick Philip. *A Search for America* (1927).
Toronto: McClelland and Stewart, 1971.

Laurence, Margaret. *The Stone Angel* (1964). Toronto:
McClelland and Stewart, 1968.

Leacock, Stephen. *Sunshine Sketches of a Little Town*
(1912). Toronto: McClelland and Stewart, 1965.

MacLennan, Hugh. *Return of the Sphinx* (1967).
Toronto: Macmillan, 1970.

Richler, Mordecai. *The Apprenticeship of Duddy
Kravitz* (1959). Toronto: McClelland and Stewart,
1969.

Ross, Sinclair. *As for Me and My House* (1941).
Toronto: McClelland and Stewart, 1957.

Wilson, Ethel. *Swamp Angel* (1954). Toronto: McClelland and Stewart, 1962.

Advanced

Glassco, John. *Memoirs of Montparnasse.* Toronto and New York: Oxford, 1970.

Godfrey, David. *The New Ancestors.* Toronto: New Press, 1970.

Lowry, Malcolm. *Hear Us O Lord from Heaven Thy Dwelling-Place.* Harmondsworth: Penguin, n.s., 1961.

Professional

Bell, Inglis F., and Susan Port, eds. *Canadian Literature/ Littérature Canadienne 1959-1963.* Vancouver: University of British Columbia Press, 1966.

Klinck, Carl F., ed. *Literary History of Canada.* Toronto: University of Toronto Press, 1965.

Story, Norah, ed. *The Oxford Companion to Canadian History and Literature.* Toronto: Oxford, 1967.

Watters, R. E., ed. *A Check List of Canadian Literature and Background Materials 1628-1950.* Toronto: University of Toronto Press, 1959.

Watters, R. E., and Inglis F. Bell, eds. *On Canadian Literature 1806-1960.* Toronto: University of Toronto Press, 1966.

Modern Poetry
Dennis Lee

*Dennis Lee has taught at Victoria College, the University
of Toronto, and at Rochdale College, and is now chief
editor at the House of Anansi Press. He has published
four books of poetry:* Kingdom of Absence, Civil
Elegies *(1968),* Wiggle to the Laundromat *and* Civil
Elegies and Other Poems *(1972).*

Whenever a friend asks me how to Come to Grips with
Canadian Poetry, I tell him to forget about Canadian
Poetry and go read some Canadian poets. That way he
will almost certainly enjoy himself. He will also, if he
persists, end up better attuned than many specialists.

If he is a particular kind of friend I lend him Michael
Ondaatje's *Collected Works of Billy the Kid* or Margaret
Atwood's *Power Politics.* To other friends I might give
George Johnston's *The Cruising Auk,* Alden Nowlan's
Playing the Jesus Game or a book by Al Purdy. My
point is not that these are the best poets in Canada
(though each is pretty good). All I have in mind is that
they are poets who write for real; that they're accessible
to people with a wide range of consciousness; and that
most of these books are unified—reading them in one
sitting is a self-contained pleasure.

There's a deeper reason for starting in without a master
plan, though, and it grows out of the particular nature
of our poetry. Since Confederation, poetry has been our
liveliest art. Canadians have written and read poetry
without grants or exhortations, instinctively, to bring
their lives to some kind of focus and to enjoy themselves. Hence there has always been a sense of ongoing
vitality to it: new poets appear uninvited year after year;
magazines start up and fold; poetry presses launch themselves into messianic existence. The first fact about
Canadian poetry is that it is a living process; its most

exciting feature is its messy, sprawling, gloriously various self-renewals. If you miss the chance to take part in that process, you miss one of the few civilized pleasures in the country.

How good is it? So far as I can tell, Canada has produced more good poetry than any other nation with a comparable history and population. And if you read for a while, you will find several poets you consider excellent by the same standards you'd apply anywhere in the world. At the same time, I do not see that we have yet thrown up that handful of poets around whose work a people's deepest realities can take shape and become articulate. While our best poets have travelled superlatively well, there have been very few arrivals.

These two facts about our poetry dictate the best way to read it: forget about Great Monuments, and dive into the ongoing process for yourself. Borrow something a friend has enjoyed, and make up your own mind. Leaf through books and little magazines at a store or library, and take home something that looks intriguing. Follow up stray remarks or magazine articles, and don't be too impressed by anybody's reputation—there is a lot of well-meaning hype. If you need scholarly reassurance, reflect that Canlit is a very recent "discipline"; all the reigning experts got that way by passionate random reading. There are areas of our literature where a Great-Books approach may be relevant, but poetry is just not one of them. Use whatever haphazard method comes to hand.

There is a time for a systematic approach, of course—after you have scouted the territory for yourself. So assume that my friend has been out foraging in bookstores, libraries and friends' shelves for a year or so. He has found half a dozen poets he likes, one or two who speak to him very deeply, and a good many who put him to sleep. Some magazines he trusts; others he now ignores. He is becoming aware that the west coast has its own style—in the poetry scene as much as in poetry. He is getting some sense of the continuity in Montreal and the Maritimes, the discontinuities in Toronto. He is even

beginning to separate the excitement of the writing/
reading process from its more solid achievements. Where
does he go next, to see what he's missed?

The obvious place to begin is with the anthologies.
But the same basic caution applies: while there are a
number of beautifully edited collections, they are (for
me at least) sabotaged by accepting the monuments-of-
Canadian-poetry approach. Each poet is interred, in
chronological order and at whatever length the editor
considers appropriate, in a kind of premature pantheon.
I keep finding that poets whose work gives me an
adrenalin rush as it comes into print have the opposite
effect in our anthologies. If you make your starting
point here you may never go any further, and you will
certainly not discover our poetry as a living process.

At the moment there are two basic collections. The
more important is A. J. M. Smith's *Modern Canadian
Verse*. Bilingual, it starts with E. J. Pratt and Paul Morin
and ends up with the young poets of the mid-sixties. It
launders out a lot of the wildness in recent poetry—what
a succession of minor Christian humanists we turn out
to be!—but it is still a fine collection. For the poetry of
the last two decades, the best starting point is Gary
Geddes and Phyllis Bruce's *15 Modern Canadian Poets;*
it runs from Earle Birney to Victor Coleman. (I have not
yet seen Eli Mandel's *Poets of Contemporary Canada*,
which covers some of the same territory.)

A second approach through anthologies is to get four
McClelland & Stewart collections which span the last
one hundred years; since fewer poets are included, each
is more fully represented. The four are *Poets of the
Confederation, Poets between the Wars, Poetry of Mid-
Century* and *Poets of Contemporary Canada.*

A third approach is to look at the collections of new
poets that have been pouring out in the last five years,
in an attempt to keep readers in touch with the
avalanche of new writers. The best known is Al Purdy's
Storm Warning; the one I've enjoyed most is Ann Wall's
Mindscapes, which breaks the usual format by presenting only four, relatively mainstream new poets. John
Colombo's *New Direction in Canadian Poetry* is an

elegant, lightweight introduction to concrete poetry.

Even though Canadian anthologies seem to lose most of the unpredictable, adventurous quality of our poetry at large, they do provide good leads to individual writers you may not know. But look elsewhere too—every reader has his own list of poets whom these modern anthologies have served badly. The first five on my list would be Milton Acorn, David Helwig, George Johnston, George Jonas and Dennis Lee. And if you find a collection that hasn't left out all of Al Purdy's best poems, please write . . . Eventually you'll become the editor of your own imaginary anthology. That is not pretentious; it is the only sensible response to the wildly various pleasures of our poetry.

But my friend is becoming a pest. He has read on his own, devoured every anthology on the market, and keeps asking for more leads. I have tried to fob him off with literary criticism; he has now subscribed to *Canadian Literature* (plus half a dozen poetry magazines). He has read the *Literary History of Canada* from cover to cover (though I find he remembers nothing of the articles on modern poetry), and Northrop Frye's *The Bush Garden* and Doug Jones's *Butterfly on Rock* and Dudek and Gnarowski's *Making of Modern Poetry in Canada* and Eli Mandel's *Contexts of Canadian Criticism*. He bought a slew of critical paperbacks— reader's guides to single authors, collections of articles— but gave most of them away for recycling, claiming that eighty per cent were a waste of time.

I didn't argue, though I hope he finds the other twenty per cent. Instead I agreed, reluctantly, to draw up a short-list of ten modern poets he mustn't overlook—a list compiled, with great self-effacement, from my sense of who the most informed readers consider to be our major poets. But I warned him that if he showed it to anyone who hadn't already got the knack of exploring on his own, I would give him a complete set of *Canadian Poetry Magazine*. The list was still not a substitute for reading on his own; it was a final check that he hadn't missed anyone obvious.

E. J. PRATT. Poets of my generation spent much of their early careers quarrelling silently with the landmark known as E. J. Pratt. My conclusion today is fairly banal: Pratt wrote what he wrote, and a reader either enjoys blank-verse narratives or he doesn't. Approached as the Great Canadian Poet, Pratt is hard to swallow. Approached in any saner way he makes awfully good reading.

EARLE BIRNEY. After publishing his intelligent, humane poetry for three decades, Birney has done everything from verse drama to concrete. The readiest sampler is his *Poems of Earle Birney.*

IRVING LAYTON. Layton defies all his editors, particularly himself. There are such stretches of clumping bathos between his moments of magnificence that reading him entire is utter torment. Yet nobody has figured out how to get his best poems tied down in one place satisfactorily. The current attempt is a super-fat, super-expensive *Collected Poems.* Since his best work is just splendid, you probably can't avoid wading through the whole book to find it.

AL PURDY. For my money, this is the best poet we have produced. A bad Purdy poem is in a class by itself, but a good Purdy poem is irreplaceable: bawdy, bittersweet, alive in the time we inhabit. His selected poems is in preparation; I would not be without it for anything.

MARGARET AVISON. Avison's austere, sure-footed craft is very deeply meditated; she is to be sipped, not taken in gulps. She writes of what used to be called the spiritual life, with the understatement that comes from direct experience. I re-read *The Dumbfounding* each year, and find that two or three more poems open up each time—you might look first at "The Swimmer's Moment," "Meeting Together of Poles and Latitudes," and "A Story."

RAYMOND SOUSTER. Pick up any volume by Souster— he publishes almost a book a year, latterly with Oberon Press. If his quiet, decent perceptions of urban life and passing time chime with your own sense of things—as they do for many readers—you can read your way

through his books with unchanging pleasure. If they don't, you won't find anything different in his other books. There is no single-volume digest of Souster, though *The Colour of the Times* attempted to be that.
MILTON ACORN. Although it's a description that would startle anyone who has met him, Acorn is the invisible man of Canadian poetry; everyone likes his work, but nobody remembers to anthologize him, governor-generalize him, or even to praise him adequately. Look at *I've Tasted My Blood:* his early work is social realism of a fine, nitty-gritty kind, but in his best poems his brawling vigour reaches towards the sublime.
ALDEN NOWLAN. Playing the Jesus Game is one of the most satisfying selected poems in Canadian literature—it's hard to find though, as it was published by a small press in New York State. Nowlan's poems are more muscular and ambitious than Souster's, but if you like one poet you'll probably enjoy the other.
LEONARD COHEN. Cohen's *Selected Poems* is one of the basic documents of sensibility from the last fifteen years. For me, the parallels with Bliss Carman grow stronger every year—which restrains my enthusiasm. But his lyricism remains the purest we've ever had. His three albums arc very uneven, but his best songs—like "Suzanne" and "Bird on a Wire"—are going to be permanent.
MARGARET ATWOOD. By the time she was thirty Atwood had published five remarkable books of poetry—cool, devastating, at times almost unforgivably knowledgeable. She is probably the most widely read poet in Canada at present, certainly among younger readers. Her books are *The Circle Game, The Animals in that Country, The Journals of Susanna Moodie, Procedures for Underground* and *Power Politics.* The third and the fifth are perhaps the most striking points of entry, but if you like one you'll end up with all five.

My friend has come back at me one more time— somewhat shamefaced, I'm glad to say. He began by asking whether I had been completely candid with him;

he has had three good years reading Canadian poetry, but something is apparently missing. Somehow it hasn't jelled yet. Am I sure I'm not holding somebody back on him? . . . if I stopped reacting diplomatically, and spoke as a partisan, as a publisher and—most of all—as a poet?

Now this was perceptive of him, you say. But I have been in that situation before. I didn't fool around. Sternly I asked him what he was hiding behind his back, in the brown manila filing folder. He cracked, and in the moments that ensued I gathered that not only did he have another manuscript at home twice as good as the one he had just handed me, though not quite complete but in a couple of weeks; he was also thinking of setting up a small publishing venture because all the most exciting poets were young and still unrecognized and not in the anthologies and there was a conspiracy among the established writers to keep them down and Canadian poetry had barely *begun.*

I could see his point. I gave him a manuscript of my own, which I happened to have behind my back at the time, and we settled down to read each other's work.

His wasn't bad. Mine was great. And the process is still going on. Between us, like the generations of our predecessors, I swear we will get Canadian poetry on the right track at last.

SUMMARY BIBLIOGRAPHY
Points of Entry

Atwood, Margaret. *Power Politics.* Toronto: Anansi, 1971.

Johnston, George. *The Cruising Auk.* Toronto: Oxford, 1959.

Nowlan, Alden. *Playing the Jesus Game.* Trumansburg, N.Y.: NEW/BOOKS, 1970.

Ondaatje, Michael. *The Collected Works of Billy the Kid.* Toronto: Anansi, 1970.

Purdy, Al. *Selected Poems.* Toronto: McClelland & Stewart, 1972.

Anthologies

Colombo, John. *New Direction in Canadian Poetry*. Toronto: Holt Rinehart and Winston, 1971.

Geddes, Gary, and Phyllis Bruce, eds. *15 Modern Canadian Poets*. Toronto: Oxford, 1970.

Mandel, Eli, ed. *Poets of Contemporary Canada*. Toronto: McClelland & Stewart, 1972.

Purdy, Al, ed. *Storm Warning*. Toronto: McClelland & Stewart, 1971.

Ross, Malcolm. *Poets of the Confederation*. Toronto: McClelland & Stewart, 1960.

Smith, A. J. M., ed. *Modern Canadian Verse*. Toronto: Oxford, 1967. (Not to be confused with the *Oxford Book of Canadian Verse*.)

Wall, Ann, ed. *Mindscapes*. Toronto: Anansi, 1971.

Wilson, Milton, ed. *Poets between the Wars*. Toronto: McClelland & Stewart, 1967.

———, ed. *Poetry of Mid-Century*. Toronto: McClelland & Stewart, 1964.

Criticism

Canadian Literature. Ed. George Woodcock. Vancouver: University of British Columbia Press, 1959–. Quarterly.

Dudek, Louis, and Michael Gnarowski, eds. *The Making of Modern Poetry in Canada*. Toronto: Ryerson, 1967.

Frye, Northrop. *The Bush Garden*. Toronto: Anansi, 1971.

Jones, Douglas. *Butterfly on Rock*. Toronto: University of Toronto Press, 1970.

Klinck, Carl, et al., eds. *Literary History of Canada*. Toronto: University of Toronto Press, 1965.

Mandel, Eli, ed. *Contexts of Canadian Criticism*. Toronto: University of Toronto Press, 1971.

Major Poets

Acorn, Milton. *I've Tasted My Blood*. Toronto: Ryerson, 1969.

Atwood, Margaret. *The Animals in that Country.*
Toronto: Oxford, 1968.
———. *The Circle Game.* Toronto: Anansi, 1967.
———. *The Journals of Susanna Moodie.* Toronto:
Oxford, 1970.
———. *Power Politics.* Toronto: Anansi, 1971.
———. *Procedures for Underground.* Toronto: Oxford,
1970.
Avison, Margaret. *The Dumbfounding.* New York:
Norton, 1966.
Birney, Earle. *The Poems of Earle Birney.* Toronto:
McClelland and Stewart, 1968.
Cohen, Leonard. *Selected Poems.* Toronto: McClelland
& Stewart, 1968.
Layton, Irving. *Collected Poems.* Toronto: McClelland
& Stewart, 1971.
Nowlan, Alden. *Playing the Jesus Game.* Trumansburg,
N.Y.: NEW/BOOKS, 1970.
Pratt, E. J. *Collected Poems.* Ed. Northrop Frye.
Toronto: Macmillan, 1958.
———. *Selected Poems.* Ed. Peter Buitenhuis. Toronto:
Macmillan, 1968.
Purdy, Al. *Selected Poems.* Toronto: McClelland &
Stewart, 1972.
Souster, Al. *The Colour of the Times.* Toronto:
Ryerson, 1967.

The Literature of Quebec in Translation
Ronald Sutherland

Ronald Sutherland teaches comparative Canadian literature at l'Université de Sherbrooke. He is a musician and translator as well as the author of five books, among them Second Image: Comparative Studies in Quebec/Canadian Literature, *and* Lark des Neiges, *a novel.*

The art of translation is very much like marriage—it works best when there is a high degree of compatibility, understanding and shared interests. And like marriage, despite many pitfalls and imperfections, translation is something we will probably have to live with for a long time to come.

When the French poet Charles Baudelaire first discovered the works of Edgar Allan Poe, as he later explained, he saw "with terror and rapture not only subjects I had dreamt about, but phrases which I had thought and Poe had written twenty years before." Now *that* is compatibility! And perhaps it explains why Baudelaire's translations of Poe are often more effective than the originals. But, unfortunately, not all translations are as good as Baudelaire's. Some translators, naturally, are more competent or more compatible in particular instances than others, and some writers are harder to translate than others. Whatever the case, however, translation is a cultural bridge, a passageway through the language barrier, a chance to increase one's understanding of how other people think and feel. And for Canadians, of course, it is a question of understanding how large numbers of other Canadians think and feel.

English-speaking Canadians interested in Canadian books written in French are lucky. A lot luckier than their French-speaking counterparts. Only five modern Canadian novels in English have so far been translated into French (three of them Hugh MacLennan's), whereas some forty Quebec novels are available in English translation. And what is more important, these novels provide a good picture of the evolution of Quebec literature, its variety, its changing attitudes and its current trends.

French Canadians were once a largely rural, largely homogeneous community, and until quite recently the leaders of this community—clergymen, historians, teachers and politicians—were determined that it should stay that way. They were afraid of the urbanization and industrialization that had taken place in Europe and the United States. They felt that these movements would cause the old rural, Christian values of obedience, hard work, resignation to the miseries of life and supreme duty to prepare oneself for heaven, 'to be replaced by materialism and godlessness.

Many Quebec authors have celebrated the old rural values, but probably the most successful was a French immigrant, Louis Hémon, who came to Quebec precisely because he was fed up with the decadence of the sophisticated societies of Europe. Hémon went to the uninviting region of Lac Saint-Jean in northern Quebec, worked on the land and eventually wrote his classic novel *Maria Chapdelaine*. A measure of its impact is the fact that not long after the novel became known, two separate English translations were published, both appearing in 1921.

Maria Chapdelaine is a near-perfect illustration of the old rural values of Quebec. Maria's father, Samuel, is almost masochistic in his wish always to start again once he has completed the back-breaking work of making a farm from the wilderness. Despite her secret wish to live an easier life in a settled community, the mother is dutifully obedient to her husband's pioneer passion. The conviction that they are performing God's will sustains the Chapdelaines through all crises. Even when the mother dies before her time, wasted from a hard life and the production of children with the regularity of the farm animals, Samuel and Maria experience no great sorrow. They are secure in the "certainty" that their loved one has been called to paradise according to the divine plan. When later Maria has a choice between marrying a neighbour and repeating the pattern of her mother's life, or marrying another young man who will take her to prosperity in the United States, she picks the former.

The Chapdelaines believe that it is their duty to preserve the Quebec life they know. As Hémon put it, "Nothing changes and nothing will change." The future of Quebec, according to this attitude, was assured by what was called "the revenge of the cradle." French Canadians would simply multiply until they numerically overwhelmed other Canadians. And if all Quebeckers had followed in the footsteps of the Chapdelaines, it might have happened.

The novel that perhaps best illustrates why it didn't happen is Ringuet's *Thirty Acres*. Dealing with a period a few years later than that of *Maria Chapdelaine*, this book depicts how the old system began to break up. It is the story of three generations of the Moisan family. The first two subscribe entirely to the values of the Chapdelaines, and the book is rich in detail of the Quebecker's former attitudes to life, the land and the divine plan. It is when Ringuet deals with the third generation, however, that a new dimension emerges. We see the daughters and sons abandoning the established traditions, becoming interested in new techniques, leaving for the city, emigrating to the United States, embracing change with the same determination that their ancestors showed in resisting it. *Thirty Acres*, then, illustrates the transition between the old order and the modern period. Urbanization and industrialization were happening after all. And the hope of the revenge of the cradle, despite the dictates of the church, was fading as fast as couples could find out about birth control. The introduction of the pill, of course, administered the *coup de grâce*.

Gabrielle Roy's *The Tin Flute* dramatizes the transition period as it took place in the city, telling of the Lacasse family's struggles in the slums of Montreal. The mother, Rosanna, is still trying to live according to the old values, and she suffers crushing hardship with too many children, an unemployed husband and no way to provide the basic necessities. Her oldest daughter, Florentine, is a perfect contrast to Maria Chapdelaine. Being in the city, she can see that there are easier ways of life than that of her mother, and she decides to use every means at her disposal to improve her lot. *The Tin Flute* shows the impracticality of the old values under urban conditions, and it also shows them being replaced by blatant, often ruthless materialism. Florentine has no hesitation in luring Jean Lévesque, a capable and ambitious young man with a future, into making love to her. But she doesn't fit into Jean's idea of his future. Jean thus becomes the forerunner of the tough, heartless hero of so many modern novels, to whom success means more than anything else in life.

There are a number of other novels of Quebec's transition period, wherein values are being reassessed and individuals are trying to cope with a rapidly changing society. One can mention Gabrielle Roy's *The Cashier*, a psychological study of the life of an insignificant, sick little man trapped by his circumstances. André Langevin's *Dust over the City,* set in the mining town of Thetford Mines, tells the story of a young doctor and his unfaithful wife against the background of a group of people trying to adapt to the choking grip of big industry. Roger Lemelin's *The Town Below* and *The Plouffe Family* are entertaining and more general novels of life in Quebec City. The church and priests, to be sure, have always been prominent in Quebec life and literature. Complex problems created by evolving attitudes towards the church and within the church are explored by Lemelin in his *In Quest of Splendour,* by Gérard Bessette in *Not for Every Eye* and by Gilles Marcotte in *The Burden of God,* the last two heavier reading than the first.

In recent years, since about 1960, the Quebec novel has been generally moving in two directions. Some young novelists have been looking back, re-evaluating the past in general or childhood in particular, and frequently interpreting what they see in dark tones and by the use of black humour and the grotesque. Marie-Claire

Blais, who began her writing career as a teenager, is perhaps the best known of these novelists. Her translated works include *Mad Shadows, The Day Is Dark, Tête-Blanche* and *A Season in the Life of Emmanuel*. Much less limited and more entertaining than Blais is Réjean Ducharme, whose novel *The Swallower Swallowed* has been highly acclaimed in the French-speaking world, almost winning, in fact, the famed Prix Goncourt. The novel tells the story of a sensitive, intelligent, unloved child of an unsuccessful marriage, who builds an elaborate shell around herself to compensate for the normal emotional growth she cannot have. Bérenice is an intricate, bizarre and engaging characterization on the part of Ducharme, whose imaginative powers seem almost limitless. There is an extraordinary intensity about the whole novel, which perhaps explains why it won the Governor General's Award for poetry!

Along with Blais and Ducharme, Roch Carrier must also be mentioned. His *La Guerre, yes sir* is certainly one of the funniest books to grace Quebec literature in recent years. The plot is simple, a group of English Canadian soldiers escorting the body of a dead comrade back to his home village in Quebec. But Carrier has a diabolical sense of humour and a penetrating vision of what he calls the Middle Ages of the province. He dissects the values of the old order and places them under a darkly coloured glass, and he comes up with scenes—children playing hockey with a severed human hand, for instance—that cannot fail to engage the reader's attention. Each in his own way, then—Blais, Ducharme and Carrier—have provided arresting insights into Quebec society and the human condition.

The second general trend among contemporary novelists has to do with Quebec separatism. Claude Jasmin's *Ethel and the Terrorist* is a short, dramatic study of the thoughts and actions of a young man who has committed a terrorist act and is escaping to New York with his Jewish girlfriend. Jacques Godbout's *Knife on the Table* is painted on a much broader canvas and has more symbolic significance. The hero represents the young people of Quebec, plagued by indirection and the need for a viable *raison-d'être*. His beautiful blonde girlfriend, Patricia, is symbolic of the allure and comfort of the affluent North American society.

A third novel concerning separatism, however, is undoubtedly more revealing than the other two, if at the same time more demanding in terms of the reader's attention. Hubert Aquin supposedly began to write *Prochain Épisode* (The Next Step) when he was in prison. His hero is a modern Hamlet, a would-be terrorist who is grounded by the incapacity to take definitive action when the situation requires. Actually, the novel is a spy story that takes place largely in Switzerland, but by skillfully interweaving the thoughts of the hero into the action line, Aquin produces an eloquent expression of the frustrations and anxieties that have long haunted French-speaking Canadians.

Of particular interest is the striking contrast between *Prochain Épisode* and the first novel mentioned here, *Maria Chapdelaine*. Whereas the Chapdelaines live by "certainty," Aquin's hero is certain of nothing, including himself. And whereas the prime motivation of the Chapdelaines is preservation of the past unchanged, *Prochain Épisode* proclaims that Quebec has no history, that the past is covered in shame and that only a positive revolutionary act will generate essential self-respect and self-confidence. Quebec has come a long way in fifty years, and novels from *Maria Chapdelaine* to *Prochain Épisode* have faithfully reflected the growing pains. In these books, I will go so far as to say, one can find the true picture of what has happened.

Poets, of course, have also expressed these growing pains, from the tormented, Jansenistic introspection of Saint-Denys-Garneau to the post-October-crisis proclamation of Paul Chamberland that "Love shall overcome." For those who do not know French, perhaps the most effective approach to Quebec poetry is through John Glassco's recent *Poetry of French Canada in Translation* and Fred Cogswell's *One Hundred Poems of Modern Quebec*. The various numbers of Sherbrook University's parallel-text journal *Ellipse* provide a valuable supplement, as does John Glassco's translation of the *Journal of Saint-Denys-Garneau.*

For the literature of Quebec in translation there is no complete bibliography as such. My critical volume *Second Image: Comparative Studies in Quebec/Canadian Literature* does contain a complete list of novels in translation up to 1970, as well as a detailed "Note on Translation and Comparative Studies in Canada." In an article in *Meta* called "French-Canadian Literature in Translation," the critic Philip Stratford, himself the translator of works by Claire Martin and Jean Le Moyne, published all the information he could gather about stories, poetry, drama, autobiography and belles-lettres, in addition to novels in English translation, up to 1968. The translation of Quebec literature, however, like Quebec literary production itself, continues to gain momentum, and the interested reader wishing to keep up to date must simply watch for announcements of new translations as they become available.

SUMMARY BIBLIOGRAPHY
All are general.

Aquin, Hubert. *Prochain Episode.* Trans. Penny Williams. Toronto: McClelland & Stewart, 1967.

Bessette, Gérard. *Not for Every Eye.* Trans. Glen Shortliffe. Toronto: Macmillan, 1962.

Blais, Marie-Claire. *The Day Is Dark.* Trans. Derek Coltman. New York: Farrar Straus & Giroux, 1967.

———. *Mad Shadows.* Trans. Merloyd Lawrence. Toronto: McClelland & Stewart, 1960.

———. *A Season in the Life of Emmanuel.* Trans. Derek Coltman. New York: Farrar Straus & Giroux, 1966.

———. *Tête-Blanche.* Trans. Charles Fullman. Toronto: McClelland & Stewart, 1961.

Carrier, Roch. *La Guerre, yes sir.* Trans. Sheila Fischman. Toronto: House of Anansi, 1970.

Cogswell, Fred, ed. *One Hundred Poems of Modern Quebec.* Fredericton: Fiddlehead, 1970.

Ducharme, Réjean. *The Swallower Swallowed.* Trans. Barbara Bray. London: Hamish Hamilton, 1968.

Ellipse. Eds. D. G. Jones, Joseph Bonenfant, Sheila Fischman, Georges-V. Fournier, Monique Grandmangin. Sherbrooke: Faculté des Arts, 1969—.

> Number 1—trans. of Gaston Miron, Paul-Marie Lapointe, Fernand Ouellette, Gérald Godin, Paul Chamberland.
>
> Number 2—trans. of Roland Giguère.
>
> Number 3—trans. of Michèle Lalonde.
>
> Number 4—trans. of Roch Carrier (stories).
>
> Number 5—trans. of Gaston Miron.
>
> Number 6—trans. of various poems and comments on October Crisis.
>
> Number 7—trans. of Jacques Brault.

Godbout, Jacques. *Knife on the Table*. Trans. Penny Williams. Toronto: McClelland & Stewart, 1967.

Glassco, John, trans. *The Journal of Saint-Denys-Garneau*. Toronto: McClelland & Stewart, 1962.

———, ed. *Poetry of French Canada in Translation*. Toronto: Oxford, 1970.

Hémon, Louis. *Maria Chapdelaine*. Trans. W. H. Blake. Toronto: Macmillan, 1921.

Jasmin, Claude. *Ethel and the Terrorist*. Trans. David Walker. Montreal: Harvest House, 1965.

Langevin, André. *Dust over the City*. Trans. John Latrebe and Robert Gottlieb. Toronto: McClelland & Stewart, 1955.

Lemelin, Roger. *The Plouffe Family*. Trans. Mary Finch. Toronto: McClelland & Stewart, 1950.

———. *In Quest of Splendour*. Trans. Harry Lorne Binsse. Toronto: McClelland & Stewart, 1955.

———. *The Town Below*. Trans. Samuel Putnam. Toronto: McClelland & Stewart, New Canadian Library, 1961.

Marcotte, Gilles. *The Burden of God*. Trans. Elizabeth Abbott. Toronto: Copp Clark, 1964.

Ringuet (pseud. of Philippe Panneton). *Thirty Acres*. Trans. Felix and Dorothea Walter. Toronto: McClelland & Stewart, New Canadian Library, 1960.

Roy, Gabrielle. *The Cashier*. Trans. Harry Lorne Binsse. Toronto: McClelland & Stewart, New Canadian Library, 1955.

———. *The Tin Flute*. Trans. Hannah Josephson. Toronto: McClelland & Stewart, New Canadian Library, 1958.

Stratford, Philip. "French-Canadian Literature in Translation." *Meta* 13, no. 4 (December 1968).

Sutherland, Ronald. *Second Image: Comparative Studies in Quebec/Canadian Literature*. Toronto: New Press, 1971.

Drama
Jack Gray

Jack Gray is a playwright. He is also secretary general of the Canadian Theatre Centre, chairman of the Writers Council of ACTRA, and on the executive of ACTRA and of the Playwrights Guild. He is currently writing "a lot of plays," a history of Hart House Theatre, and is editor of the University of Toronto Press Canadian Play Series.

Strictly speaking, the drama is made to be seen and not read. Many dramas that do read well, play badly, and there are most effective stage works that are impossible on the printed page. In addition to this, much of the best modern drama appears on radio, film and television—media that have not yet really been accepted as "literature"—and have not, therefore (in Canada at any rate), been immortalized in print.

When we do come to stage works, we find that only a small number of the estimated three to four hundred new plays that have been produced in Canada since 1945 have been published. While several of the best plays are available, these cannot really be said to be representative of the vitality and experiment that is going on.

Four writers dominate the printed play market at the moment: Robertson Davies, Gratien Gélinas, James Reaney and George Ryga. Other plays by John Coulter, John Herbert, John Thomas McDonough, Len Peterson and Lister Sinclair are also available.

Fortunately, this situation seems to be changing. Brian Parker is editing a New Drama series for New Press, the first volume of which, *The Ecstasy of Rita Joe and Other Plays* by George Ryga, is published. The next New Drama volume will be a collection of James Reaney's plays, and further collections of Quebec and Ontario plays are planned. At least two larger anthologies of Canadian plays are being prepared. And this year the University of Toronto Press begins publishing its Canadian Play Series, which is designed to make available, quickly and economically, published texts of recently produced Canadian plays. The first item in this will be David Freeman's *Creeps*. One of the most active publishers of new plays in the past few years has been Talonbooks, in Vancouver, whose Talonplay series is edited by Peter Hay, and which has Reaney's *Colours in the Dark*, and Ryga's *Ecstasy of Rita Joe* and *Captives of the Faceless Drummer* in print.

A common fault of those who comment on the Canadian play is excessive praise on the one hand (most often from the playwrights), and excessive criticism on the other (most often from the critics). Only a few of the new plays produced in Canada in the last twenty-five years have been genuinely popular, and these not necessarily the "best." Significantly, solid dramatic work, like that we get from Gélinas (who has written sparingly, and mainly for himself as an actor) has proved enduring.

Ageless and venerable, John Coulter has made Riel (who was the hero of the Canadian hippies—when there were hippies) his own. His earlier play on the subject, *Riel*, published in 1962 by the Ryerson Press that was, is a rambling work that has proved itself both on television and the stage, and as a mine for Mavor Moore when preparing the libretto of the opera *Louis Riel*, composed by Harry Somers. Coulter's later *The Trial of Louis Riel* is based on the records of Riel's trial, held in Regina in 1885, at which the Métis leader was condemned to death. First staged in Regina in the summer of 1967, it has continued to be a sell-out summer attraction in that city ever since.

Robertson Davies (who is also a novelist, a diarist, an essayist, a humourist *and* the Master of Massey College) has written many plays. One of these, *Overlaid*, is among the most successful one-act plays yet written by a Canadian. Three other of Davies's one-act plays, *Eros at Breakfast, The Voice of the People* and *At the Gates of the Righteous*, are gathered together with his best-known full-length play *Fortune My Foe*, in *Four Favourite Plays*. *At the Gates of the Righteous* is a neglected but delightful and irreverent romp, and makes us wish that Davies had at least once tackled a hard-edged satire on a matter of substance. *Fortune My Foe* is now somewhat out of date—it deals with a Canadian professor struggling with himself not to go and work the goldfields in the United States—but it remains a lively and attractive work.

While Gratien Gélinas seems somewhat old-fashioned in terms of today's Quebec, he has written three of the most commercially successful plays ever written by a Canadian. They have all been translated into English, and they are all in print. (We do not have English versions of Marcel Dubé, or Michel Tremblay, or most of the other important French Canadian dramatists, which is our great loss.) Gélinas writes mainly for himself, and his plays, with their basically sentimental heroes, reflect the particular requirements this outstanding actor-writer sets himself. The title role in *Tit-Coq*, the Bousille of *Bousille and the Just*, and Pierre Gravel, the tortured lawyer and aspiring federalist politician in *Yesterday the Children Were Dancing* whose son is the leader of a terrorist plot, each gave Gélinas a chance to reinforce his place in the Canadian theatre.

John Herbert's *Fortune and Men's Eyes* is the most successful play yet from a Canadian writer, and an international hit. Herbert himself has now left Canada to live in England. *Fortune and Men's Eyes* takes a hard, highly theatrical look at a loss of innocence, at the brutal degradation of a young man sentenced to a reformatory.

John Thomas McDonough took one of the best potential subjects in recent Canadian history, the conflict between Maurice Duplessis and Bishop Joseph Charbonneau, as the text for his play *Charbonneau & le Chef*. The play as written in English poses many stage problems, but its power is great. A French translation-adaptation staged at Quebec City's Trident Theatre in 1971 did one hundred and three per cent business.

Len Peterson is one of Canada's most accomplished

dramatists, but his only published play is *The Great Hunger*, which uses the structures of classical tragedy to portray a theme from traditional Eskimo lore, a son's revenge for the murder of his father.

James Reaney has published five plays, four that are collected in *The Killdeer and Other Plays*, and more recently, his highly successful *Colours in the Dark*, first done at Stratford in 1967. Reaney is not writing plays in any of the traditional senses in which that word is used. These works are really dramatic poetic games, and the stage is merely a convenient place to present them. Reaney is a better poet than dramatist. In fact, his poetry is so attractive that it usually doesn't matter too much about his play, as such. The success of works like *Colours in the Dark* suggests that Reaney knows quite a lot about his Canadian audiences. "Surely one of the things theatre could be about is the relaxed awareness that comes when you simply play," he suggests in his note to the original production. That is one of the approaches he has taken in his work for the theatre, but there are others, and all repay study.

George Ryga has been fortunate in his mentors and interpreters. His best play, *The Ecstasy of Rita Joe*, has been enthusiastically received all over the country, and even transformed into a ballet version. Ryga is another poet who seems to be using the theatre (and television) partly because it is one of the more popular or prestigious forms in our period. His use of it remains uneasy, however, and his command of the medium, while continually experimental and devoted to his committed concerns, is unsure. Ryga may be taken as representative, however, of a group of younger playwrights, very few of whom have been published (Herschel Hardin is one such, John Palmer another), who have real talent, deep social commitment and a furious desire to write stageworthy plays. The works of these writers are worth hunting down. You will find one by Hardin—*Esher Mike and His Wife, Agiluk*—in the fall 1969 issue of *Drama Review*.

Lister Sinclair has not written for the stage for some years, but two of his earlier works, *Socrates* and *The*

Blood Is Strong, are of interest. *Socrates* was written during the notorious McCarthy years, when Senator Joseph McCarthy was conducting his political witch hunts in the United States, and the play reflects this. *The Blood Is Strong* is a drama set in Nova Scotia in the early nineteenth century; it tackles the ageless and universal problem of the generations, and how they differ.

One problem that must be faced regarding the drama in English Canada is that it is, in the main, trivial; and when not trivial, too often below that level of technical accomplishment that allows it to find a significant audience. Canadians need not feel any special pain because of this, for our dramatists share this problem with most of their contemporaries writing in the European languages—if that is any consolation.

In examining the extant printed texts of our English plays we find, first, that little has been reprinted at all. This reflects the general lack of either public or intellectual interest in our drama to this time. Second, we find that among those plays that are (temporarily) preserved, there are no masterpieces. These remarks are not intended to slight our dramatists, for they have worked in such an atmosphere of hostile indifference in Canada that it is remarkable there are any Canadian dramatists at all. Their basic achievement has been to survive.

During the last twenty-five years most of our theatrical effort has gone into the equipment, including buildings, and the training of a corps of actors, directors, designers and technicians. This necessary first stage of achievement now makes it possible for Canadians in most major centres to enjoy some, usually highly accomplished, professional theatre. But the establishment of this base, with its attendant colonial bias in its repertoire, its narrowly based audience, and its limited ability to accommodate the growing number of young people anxious to be part of the Canadian theatre, has already begun to spark the growth of a series of alternate theatres of varying accomplishment, vitality and commitment.

Strangely, it is this alternate theatre that has plunged most enthusiastically into new plays by Canadians, with some theatres devoting their whole effort to such work. Only now is such work beginning to be published. Those interested in the new drama should keep their eye on this theatre, and its writers, from whom we can hope to hear much more.

SUMMARY BIBLIOGRAPHY
All are general.

Coulter, John. *Riel*. Toronto: Ryerson, 1962.

———. *The Trial of Louis Riel*. Ottawa: Oberon, 1968.

Davies, Robertson. *Four Favourite Plays*. Toronto: Clarke, Irwin, 1968. Contains *Eros at Breakfast, The Voice of the People, At the Gates of the Righteous* and *Fortune My Foe*.

Gélinas, Gratien. *Bousille and the Just*. Toronto: Clarke, Irwin, 1966.

———. *Tit-coq*. Toronto: Clarke, Irwin, 1966.

———. *Yesterday the Children Were Dancing*. Toronto: Clarke, Irwin, 1967.

Herbert, John. *Fortune and Men's Eyes*. New York: Grove Press, 1967.

McDonough, John Thomas. *Charbonneau & le Chef*. Toronto: McClelland and Stewart, 1968.

Peterson, Leonard. *The Great Hunger*. Agincourt, Ont.: Book Society, 1967.

Reaney, James. *Colours in the Dark*. Vancouver and Toronto: Talonplays with Macmillan, 1969.

———. *The Killdeer and Other Plays*. Toronto: Macmillan, 1962. Contains *The Killdeer, The Sun and the Moon, One-Man Masque, Night-Blooming Cereus*.

Ryga, George. *Captives of the Faceless Drummer*. Vancouver: Talonbooks, 1971.

———. *The Ecstasy of Rita Joe and Other Plays*. Edited and with an Introduction by Brian Parker. Toronto: New Press, 1971. Contains *The Ecstasy of Rita Joe, Indian, Grass and Wild Strawberries*.

Sinclair, Lister. *The Blood Is Strong.* Agincourt, Ont.: Book Society, 1956.

———. *Socrates.* Agincourt, Ont.: Book Society, 1957.

Art and Architecture
Barry Lord

Barry Lord is co-ordinator of education services at the National Gallery of Canada in Ottawa. Formerly critic for the Toronto Daily Star *and one-time editor of* artscanada *magazine, he continues to write criticism for various publications. His catalogue for the exhibition* Painting in Canada, *which he organized for theCanadian pavilion at Expo 67, has been distributed as a book by Information Canada.*

The demand for good books on Canadian art and architecture continues far greater than the supply. Art books generally are expensive to produce, so the effects of cultural imperialism on the book trade are particularly oppressive here. British- and American-owned publishers can't see a great market outside Canada for books on Canadian art, and can't justify the expense of a book with a great many colour plates for their Canadian buyers alone. The same economics inhibits the few Canadian publishers, with their slimmer and shakier capital base, even more.

The solution is evidently something like a "people's publishing house," or as close to it as we can get so deep inside the US empire. Indeed, most of our publications on art—especially when we include exhibition catalogues and magazines—are either heavily subsidized or actually originate from government institutions like the National Gallery. A more genuine popular basis for Canadian art books may have to await the successful conclusion of a struggle for Canadian independence.

Meanwhile, it remains appalling that, as of this writing, there is still no cheap, available paperback history of Canadian art suitable for the beginning student. University and college department chairmen cite the lack of such a book as justification for their failure to offer students adequate courses in our own art history.

Since so many of the teachers in their departments are American or British, with neither knowledge nor concern about Canadian art, the rationale is more than a little suspect. Yet clearly Ryerson's 1967 paperback reprint of William Colgate's *Canadian Art; Its Origin and Development* won't do. It's unchanged from the original 1943 edition, and of course doesn't reflect subsequent scholarship even on the limited 1820-1940 period it does discuss.

Russell Harper's hardback *Painting in Canada: A History*, subsidized as a Centennial project, is usually considered too expensive to require of undergraduates or community-college students, but it is the standard authority on painting. A reliable compilation of facts linked together in readable manner, it seldom sparkles with incisive analysis but at least manages to cover the ground comprehensively. From the seventeenth century down to 1945, it is the indispensable sourcebook with which to begin; for the past quarter-century, unfortunately, it is not nearly as good.

The equivalent to Harper for architecture, based on an earlier book but published in this revised and enlarged version in the same year as Harper's text, is Alan Gowans's *Building Canada; An Architectural History of Canadian Life.* More systematic than Harper in grouping his material according to period and style, Gowans sensibly placed his emphasis on what matters most in Canadian architecture, the domestic and "vernacular" tradition. In this it's a perfect complement to Ritchie's *Canada Builds*, where you can find out how these churches and homes were constructed. Ritchie's book provides rich photographic and descriptive details of the material and technical basis of the styles that Gowans describes. Gowans's own text is cogent enough, although it's all at the front of the book, so that the serious student must continually interrupt his reading to consult the plates and their informative captions at the back.

In the decorative arts there are several books that at least partially avoid such faults of design. Jean Palardy's

The Early Furniture of French Canada, translated by Eric McLean, is a handsome and generously proportioned volume with a discursive text at the outset, but also descriptions of each type of furniture—armoires, buffets, commodes—before each cluster of photographs. Like Harper and Gowans, Palardy manages to function as both standard authority and introductory guide to his subject. Scott Symons's *Heritage: A Romantic Look at Early Canadian Furniture*, with its brilliant photographs by John de Visser, ought to have been as definitive for the furniture of the rest of the country, but it's ruined by Symons's raving prose that insists on personifying each corner cupboard and cabinet in gushing allegories of sensuality and quasi-religious fervour. ("Furniture is faith!")

Of all the books available on the smaller useful objects, the one I like best is Donald Webster's *Early Canadian Pottery*. While authors on these applied arts often try to write volumes that will satisfy at the same time both general readers and specialist collectors, Webster has the advantage of writing four years after Elizabeth Collard's exhaustive scholarly study, *Nineteenth Century Pottery and Porcelain in Canada*, which includes an analysis of the economics of the trade and extends its scope to ceramics imported by Canadian dealers. As a result, Webster is content to produce a warm little book that begins by explaining how earthenware is made, and then proceeds to survey the history of pottery fired in Canada. The style is not distinguished, but the good illustrations and excellent colour plates make this book well worth having.

Gerald Stevens's *Early Canadian Glass* is my favourite of books on that topic, particularly because it includes an intriguing chapter on the archaeology of early glass-factory sites. Stevens is an "amateur" in the best sense of the term, and rather than classifying each specimen, he brings his subject to life by relating his own discovery of it. Unfortunately there's nothing comparable from a Canadian publisher on Canadian silver, and nothing at all in book form on Canadian textiles.

F. St. George Spendlove's *The Face of Early Canada*

is out of print, but it's still the best guide to the early etchings, engravings and lithographs recording Canadian scenery and events. Subtitled *Pictures of Canada which Have Helped To Make History*, it includes a brief but accurate account of the evolution of print-making techniques from woodcut to rotogravure, and an inclusive survey of the artists and the "views" they drew and published, mostly before the camera could do the job.

For the succeeding period, when photographers set out to document the land and its people for the first time, Ralph Greenhill's *Early Photography in Canada* is the standard text. It includes a representative survey of the early pictures, and is a readable revelation of the days when "Notman and Sons" flourished in every city in Canada, and was even known as a leading photographic firm internationally.

If you're tired of surveys and want to proceed to books on more specific topics, Peter Mellen's *The Group of Seven* is undoubtedly the finest single volume on painting that I can recommend to you. It's well written and imaginatively conceived—rare for a book on Canadian painting—with a thoroughly researched and stimulating text aptly related to ample illustrations. Mellen discusses all aspects of the fabled Seven, dismisses the legends deftly, presents the historical evidence and interprets their style with a sensitive, knowledgeable eye. I happen to think he is wrong when he depreciates their relative originality, but there is no question that Mellen's is a thoroughly enjoyable and important book.

Of all the books by and about the Group painters and their precursor, Tom Thomson, A. Y. Jackson's *A Painter's Country* should be required reading, if only because the odyssey it describes has become almost as much a part of the legend as Thomson's canoe or Harris's icebergs. It is Jackson's autobiographical account of his life-long encounter with Canada, one of those books that stubbornly claims a place in our awareness of what it is to be Canadian.

Most of the books published on Thomson and the Group are biographies larded with uncritical appreciations of the painting. *Lawren Harris,* like the artist and his work, is a patrician exception. Edited by his widow, Bess Harris, and R. G. P. Colgrove, with an irrelevant introduction by Northrop Frye, the text includes rather too much of Harris's transcendental philosophizing. But the pictures and their reproduction are superb; the boxed volume is a beautiful example of the book-maker's art, and stands as a credit to publishing in Canada.

Good books on individual artists earlier than the Group are harder to find. Russell Harper has recently given us *Paul Kane's Frontier*, a suitably lavish publication that includes many fine colour plates, a biography of the artist by Harper and a complete reprint of Kane's own journal, *Wanderings of an Artist among the Indians of North America*. Harper's *catalogue raisonné* of Kane's paintings in this book, incredibly enough, is the only such complete listing for any Canadian artist that is now in print.

Of a much less colourful subject, *Robert Harris, 1849-1919,* Moncrieff Williamson has written what he calls "an unconventional biography." It's not so un-conventional; Williamson has carefully selected and assembled the artist's correspondence to reconstruct his Victorian life, from his origins in Charlottetown through his training in Europe to his successful career in Toronto and Montreal. It's too bad there aren't enough illustra-tions in this otherwise most attractive volume.

The outstanding study of the architecture of a parti-cular place is Eric Arthur's *Toronto: No Mean City.* Arthur relates his subject not just to architectural history, but to the whole complex process of Toronto growing up. His prose is vigorous, his pictures well selected and especially full of fascinating information for anyone who knows the city as it is today. We need ten or more books like it, one for every major city in Canada.

If you want to read specifically about contemporary Canadian art, you'll have to turn to the art magazines and to exhibition catalogues, not books. There is no adequate history available in English of the past thirty years of Canadian painting, and monographs on major figures simply don't exist. The only contemporary survey is British and can't be trusted completely as to facts, interpretation or the colour of its plates. In such conditions the appearance of a lush publication devoted to *Harold Town Drawings* is almost criminal; Town's celebrity may justify the attention, but his drawings don't.

Carol Moore Ede's *Canadian Architecture, 1960-70* is a great disappointment. It offers no insight or analysis, crowding its pages with too many photographs of "outstanding examples" of current building. The cult of the architect and the building as his artefact is sustained, rather than any serious examination of the social problems of architecture and their possible solutions today.

The only book on contemporary Canadian art that I must recommend is about neither painting nor sculpture nor architecture. It's the National Film Board's *Canada: A Year of the Land*, with a slight text by Bruce Hutchison but magnificent pictures by our many excellent photographers of landscape. Designed by Allan Fleming, this magnificent boxed volume quickly sold out when it first appeared from the Queen's Printer in Centennial year; it's available now in a reprint from Copp Clark. The selection of pictures, their disposition on the page, their sequence, colour, size; all is judiciously managed so that the designer discreetly gets out of the way, and allows you to see not only the photographs, but the country they record. Keep this book for evenings when you have a sense of Canada, when your eyes crave sensibility and reward, and when you care about art only because it leads you to life.

SUMMARY BIBLIOGRAPHY
All are general.

Arthur, Eric. *Toronto: No Mean City*. Toronto: University of Toronto Press, 1964.

Colgate, William G. *Canadian Art; Its Origin and Development*. Toronto: Ryerson, 1967.

Collard, Elizabeth. *Nineteenth Century Pottery and Porcelain in Canada*. Montreal: McGill University Press, 1967.

Ede, Carol Moore. *Canadian Architecture, 1960-70*. Toronto: Burns and MacEachern, 1971.

Fulford, Robert, ed. *Harold Town Drawings*. Toronto: McClelland and Stewart, 1969.

Gowans, Alan. *Building Canada; An Architectural History of Canadian Life*. Toronto: Oxford, 1966.

Greenhill, Ralph. *Early Photography in Canada*. Toronto: Oxford, 1965.

Harper, J. Russell. *Painting in Canada: A History*. Toronto: University of Toronto Press, 1966.

———. *Paul Kane's Frontier*. Toronto: University of Toronto Press, 1971.

Harris, Bess, and R. G. P. Colgrove, eds. *Lawren Harris*. Introduction by Northrop Frye. Toronto: Macmillan, 1969.

Jackson, A. Y. *A Painter's Country*. Toronto: Clarke, Irwin, 1967.

Mellen, Peter. *The Group of Seven*. Toronto: McClelland and Stewart, 1970.

National Film Board. *Canada: A Year of the Land*. Text by Bruce Hutchison. Toronto: Copp Clark, 1969.

Palardy, Jean. *The Early Furniture of French Canada*. Trans. Eric McLean. Toronto: Macmillan, 1963.

Ritchie, T. *Canada Builds*. Toronto: University of Toronto Press, 1967.

Spendlove, F. St. George. *The Face of Early Canada*. Toronto: Ryerson, 1958.

Stevens, Gerald. *Early Canadian Glass*. Toronto: Ryerson, 1961.

Symons, Scott, and John de Visser. *Heritage: A Romantic Look at Early Canadian Furniture*. Toronto: McClelland and Stewart, 1971.

Webster, Donald. *Early Canadian Pottery*. Toronto: McClelland and Stewart, 1971.

Williamson, Moncrieff. *Robert Harris, 1849-1919: An Unconventional Biography*. Toronto: McClelland and Stewart, 1970.

For reference

Harper, J. Russell. *Early Painters and Engravers in Canada*. Toronto: University of Toronto Press, 1970.

Reid, Dennis. *A Bibliography of the Group of Seven.* Ottawa: National Gallery of Canada, 1971.

In addition, the catalogue to the exhibition *Three Hundred Years of Canadian Art* (Ottawa: National Gallery of Canada, 1967), and the catalogues of the permanent collections of the National Gallery of Canada (Ottawa, 1960, out of print) and the Art Gallery of Ontario (Toronto: McGraw-Hill, 1970) are useful references.

5 Books and Publishers

The Ten Best Canadian Books

The jury was composed of the editors and the contributors to *Read Canadian*. Canadian books were defined as books by Canadian authors published originally in English only. The argument about "best" still rages among the jurors and will continue, we hope, everywhere Canadian books are read.

The books appear alphabetically by author. They are all in print and, except where otherwise noted, are available in paperback editions. If any of these books are not easily available from your local bookstore, they may be ordered through the Readers' Club of Canada (17 Inkerman St., Toronto 5) at the prices indicated, postpaid.

Morley Callaghan. **Morley Callaghan's Stories** (1959). $1.25 paper.

Donald Creighton. **The Empire of the St. Lawrence** (1956). First published in 1937 as *The Commercial Empire of the St. Lawrence, 1760-1850.* $8.95 cloth; $5.50 paper.

Northrop Frye. **Anatomy of Criticism: Four Essays** (1957). $3.25 paper.

George P. Grant. **Lament for a Nation: The Defeat of Canadian Nationalism** (1965). $4.50 cloth; $1.50 paper.

Harold Adams Innis. **The Fur Trade in Canada: An Introduction to Canadian Economic History** (1930). $12.50 cloth; $2.75 paper.

Margaret Laurence. **The Stone Angel** (1964). $7.50 cloth; $2.50 paper.

Stephen Leacock. **Sunshine Sketches of a Little Town** (1912). $7.50 cloth; $1.50 paper.

Marshall McLuhan. **The Gutenberg Galaxy: The Making of Typographical Man** (1962). $10.00 cloth; $2.25 paper.

E. J. Pratt. **Collected Poems** (second edition, 1958). $9.95 cloth; no paperback available.

Mordecai Richler. **St. Urbain's Horseman: A Novel** (1971). $7.95 cloth; no paperback available.

Publishing in Canada
David Godfrey and James Lorimer

David Godfrey, who received the 1970 Governor General's Award for his novel The New Ancestors, *is the co-founder of three independent Canadian publishing houses. He teaches English at the University of Toronto.*

James Lorimer is one of the founding partners of James Lewis & Samuel and the author of two books, The Real World of City Politics *and, with Myfanwy Phillips,* Working People. *He teaches urban design in the School of Architecture at the University of Toronto.*

If, having come to the end of this book, you find yourself with an embarrassingly long list of essential Canadian books you never knew existed, determined to get through them all in the next couple of weeks and quite pleasantly bewildered about where to begin in the midst of such unexpected abundance; then you are reacting the way most readers will, even people who have long taken an interest in Canadian literature. Of course there are areas where little has been written in Canada, or where only peripheral work has been done while central issues and subjects have been ignored. Nevertheless, we have a respectable and wide-ranging national literature: that much is proved by this book.

Although many people will be pleasantly surprised to find that it is possible to fill a book this size with articles about Canadian books—and it was only limitations of size and time that prevented the editors from exploring many more subjects in this edition—others will be offended at the idea of saying, even softly: Read Canadian. They will rush to the conclusion that this is "narrow nationalism," urging that Canada be cut off from the great international free flow of ideas.

Of course no one is saying that people should stop reading American books or British books, or Dutch or

Swedish or Belgian books for that matter. What we both would say, however, is that Canadians should learn about themselves and their own country, and that they have an obligation to do that before they become better informed than most Americans about the US, or more English than the English. Only in a country as colonialized and as deprived of its own sense of itself as this one would such a position be regarded as anything other than obvious.

It is perfectly clear that, for Canada, internationalism has in practice meant submerging our own reality, first in favour of British culture and more recently, American. Nowhere is this more clear than in the field of books. Writing and publishing is at the heart of every country's cultural and intellectual life, and book publishing is a key activity whose importance to national life is far greater than the small contribution it makes as an industry to a country's gross national product. Yet the best estimates available suggest that no more than five per cent of the books bought every year in Canada are books written by Canadians and published by Canadian-owned firms. The book-publishing industry is at present dominated by foreign branch plants, some of them British but most of them American. Publishing is not quite in the same category as the oil industry, the auto industry or the computer industry, which are almost totally American owned. But it has come perilously close.

The price we are forced to pay for this situation is clearly illustrated by a very simple set of figures. In other industrialized nations, book publishing as an industry accounts for .21-.24% of annual gross national product. In Canada, book publishing accounts for only .06% of GNP. These may seem to be tiny fractions, but when a GNP of $100 billion is being forecast for Canada in 1972, this means that the national book-publishing industry—including the output of those foreign subsidiaries operating in the country—is producing something like $60 million worth of books instead of $210 million. Think of the tremendous difference it would make to people who read, write and publish books in

Canada if there were $150 million more books being produced every year in this country. The present gross underdevelopment of our branch-plant-dominated publishing industry connects directly to the gross under-development of our national cultural life at every level, from books on gardening and travel to poetry and philosophy.

Many people understand very clearly how important it is to Canada that its book publishers be owned and controlled by Canadians. That was the reason for the storm of protest that arose in late 1970 over the sale of Ryerson Press by the United Church of Canada to McGraw-Hill. Ryerson had been for 141 years a Canadian-owned publishing firm, producing a wide range of titles from cookbooks to school textbooks to fiction. Its sale to American interests, together with the fact that this left Canada with nothing more than the remnants of a Canadian-owned publishing industry, at last focused attention on the importance of book pub-lishing and on the central matter of ownership.

The same concern is understood and expressed in Quebec, where the threat is more from expanding French publishers than from US firms. This lay behind the public controversy in early 1972 over the takeover by a large and powerful French firm, Hachette, of Quebec-owned publishers and distribution houses.

One positive result of the controversy surrounding the Ryerson sale was that it brought together some of the remaining Canadian-owned English-language pub-lishers, who began for the first time to talk to each other and to understand their common problems and interests, faced by the immediate threat of a total US takeover of the industry. In a matter of months these Canadian-owned publishers formed a new trade associa-tion, the Independent Publishers' Association, which agitated for government measures to halt the US take-over and to make available the capital that these firms needed in order to continue to operate and to expand their activities.

Almost all the Canadian-owned book-publishing firms in the country affiliated themselves with this new group.

It embraced both the small, relatively new young houses like Peter Martin Associates, Hurtig Publishers, Tundra Books and the House of Anansi, and the few remaining large, Canadian-owned firms like Clarke, Irwin and the University of Toronto Press. Only McClelland and Stewart stood aloof, apparently considering itself big and important enough not to need the strength of a trade association for protection.

At first these Canadian-owned publishers focused their attention on the need for immediate government measures to protect them from being driven into bankruptcy, not because of losses but because of the desperate shortage of capital to finance the industry or from being forced to sell out to a willing US buyer. More recently, however, the focus of their attention has centred on the question of ownership, and on the need for complete Canadian ownership and control of the country's book-publishing industry.

Why is this question of ownership so important? There are, after all, people who argue that it doesn't matter who owns a publishing firm. What counts, they say, is whether a firm is publishing books by Canadian writers, in Canada, printed by Canadian printers on Canadian paper. The federal Department of Industry, Trade and Commerce, which concerns itself with the book-publishing industry, puts it in the wood-products division, along with the pulp and paper industry. The only concern of the department's officials seems to be that books be printed on Canadian paper, and they show not the slightest concern about whether the publisher is the House of Anansi or the Columbia Broadcasting System, through its publishing subsidiary, Holt Rinehart and Winston.

People are right to feel—as they demonstrated that they did feel in the Ryerson-sale controversy—that the question of ownership is crucial. The main impact of foreign ownership on a Canadian subsidiary seems to be that all the Canadian employees become fixated, nervously guessing at what it is that head office would like to see them doing, and then nervously trying to do it. Their main reference point becomes the big-time US head-office people. What they have to do is find ways of producing and selling books to Canadians that will please and gratify their US employers.

Occasionally, of course, the control that goes with ownership is not so gently exercised. It may—and in some cases does—mean that the local subsidiary's manager has to ask his Chicago head office for specific permission to go ahead with each one of the Canadian books he produces. Or a branch-plant manager is liable to find—as one man did recently—that he can be fired on twenty-four hours' notice by a board of directors of the parent company sitting in London.

The style of the branch plants operating in Canada reflects foreign vested interests. Decisions about what books to commission and publish in Canada are made after very careful consideration of how these will influence the branch plant's much more profitable sales of books imported from the parent company abroad. When, for example, a branch-plant manager is producing educational books for university students, he is very likely to look for Canadian books to publish that will support and extend the market for the American texts he is already selling, rather than for Canadian books that will replace US works. That is exactly the logic of the books of "Canadian readings" that have been flooding the university markets in recent years. Most of these are from branch plants like Methuen, Copp Clark, Holt Rinehart and McGraw-Hill. From the point of view of a branch-plant manager, the delightful thing about a book of Canadian readings on, let us say, Canadian economic policy is that it must be used in conjunction with basic texts on economic policy, and invariably the branch plant has exactly such a text to sell from its US parent.

Book publishing of this kind invariably exploits the efforts of Canadian writers and scholars in order to produce profits for the branch plants, both from the sales of these books themselves and from the sales of imported books that continue unimpeded. The exploitation is even more blatant in the field of literature. Thus, for instance, Holt Rinehart and Winston is planning a book titled *The Evolution of Canadian Literature*, covering the period from 1945-1970. In the anthology are to be pieces of work by Canadian writers who were first published and made their reputations, not with Holt Rinehart, but with other firms, most of them small and Canadian owned. Holt Rinehart, in fact, did not publish originally the work of even one of the writers who will be included in this anthology. But it is quick to leap into the field as soon as it sees money to be made, and it can do so much more easily than any small Canadian-owned house because of the way in which the branch plants have succeeded in recent years in monopolizing the field of educational publishing for schools and universities.

Foreign-owned publishers are, it is quite true, producing books written by Canadians. As a result of the recent public controversy about the industry, they will be producing more of them in an attempt to establish their credentials as "good" corporate citizens. But the very Canadian books they produce are often books that in fact further our dependence on foreign materials, that strengthen the impression that all important thought and all great creative work is done somewhere else, usually in the US, sometimes in Britain, but certainly not right here at home in Canada.

Canadian-owned publishers are also producing more books, but these are usually of a quite different kind, particularly in nonfiction fields. One of the revealing indications of this is the fact that a very high proportion of the books mentioned in this book have been brought out by Canadian-owned firms. The proportion is many times greater than would be expected, simply on the basis of the number of titles in print from Canadian-owned companies compared to the number from foreign-owned publishers. That is as good an indication as any of the crucial importance of who owns our publishing companies.

This issue of ownership is bound to be at the centre of future public discussion of the book-publishing industry. At its first general meeting, the IPA agreed that no further sales of Canadian-owned firms to foreign owners should be permitted. In a brief to the Ontario

Royal Commission on Book Publishing in June 1971, the Canadian-owned firm of James Lewis & Samuel called for complete repatriation of the industry, and for one hundred per cent Canadian ownership of all book-publishing firms operating in the country. By early 1972, the government-action committee of the IPA was recommending to the organization that it demand from government a firm commitment to one hundred per cent Canadian ownership of the industry by 1977.

Needless to say, the branch plants are feeling the pressure and are doing their best to belittle the relevance of this issue of ownership. The branch plants have their trade organization, ironically called the Canadian Book Publishers' Council, which is of course much better funded than the IPA. The CBPC numbers some of the larger and longer-established Canadian-owned book publishers amongst its members, but they are in a minority. The branch plants' dominance is well-illustrated by the 1972 slate of CBPC officers. There is not a representative of Canadian-owned firms among them; the organization is being run by the local managers of Prentice-Hall, McGraw-Hill and Holt Rinehart and Winston. A search to find a token Canadian willing to serve in this group was unsuccessful.

As things have been changing inside the book-publishing industry, conditions have also been changing outside. We are all aware of the growing interest of Canadians in their country, and accompanying this has been a growing interest in Canadian books of all kinds. Good work is being done in a wide range of fields; new writers are appearing all the time; and publishers—almost without exception the Canadian-owned houses, particularly the small and relatively new ones—are bringing out more and more books and managing not to lose money in the process.

Nevertheless, the presence of foreign books and foreign publishers is obvious, and is being strongly felt. When you walk into a good bookstore, there is still shelf upon shelf stacked with books classified by subject on sociology, travel, science fiction, art. The bulk of them are not masterpieces, not great literary works—they are ordinary books, by ordinary American and (to a much lesser extent) British writers. Canadian books have by no means pushed these foreign books off the shelves; in fact, they are usually segregated off into a separate little compartment that the bookstore inevitably labels "Canadiana." In Britain, you don't find special little book departments labelled "Britannia." In Sweden, no set of shelves labelled "Swedenia." We have a long way to go yet.

Some progress has, however, already been made in the battle to save the Canadian publishing industry from total American takeover and to create conditions in which Canadian-owned firms can rapidly expand their publishing. In the late 1960s many Canadian firms were, like Ryerson, facing serious difficulties brought on by a severe shortage of working capital, capital to finance ongoing operations and expansion. It was not that Canadian-owned firms were losing money, though some were; it was rather that their profits were not as high as those earned by other industries, and that as a consequence they didn't attract financial support from the usual sources of capital for business operations in the country.

The chartered banks were unwilling to lend money to Canadian-owned firms. But they were quick to provide McGraw-Hill with a loan to finance the purchase of Ryerson.

It took the Ryerson sale to get provincial and federal governments to believe that the problem was serious. Since November 1970, Ottawa has announced several times that it is just about to announce measures to assist the book-publishing industry. It has actually done nothing. The Manitoba government offered long-term capital to publishers willing to move to Manitoba, and one textbook firm took up the offer.

The most important constructive step came from Ontario. Faced with tremendous public criticism because of its refusal to halt the Ryerson sale, the Roberts government took the traditional step of setting up a royal commission. The commissioners, instead of burying the problem they were charged to investigate, got their operation going, produced three interim reports in only a few months, and got Ontario to lend one million dollars, interest free, to McClelland and Stewart when Jack McClelland threatened to sell, and refused to rule out the possibility of a US purchaser.

Then the royal commission got the Ontario government to set up a program to guarantee long-term capital loans to other Canadian-owned firms. The fruits of this measure will be seen by Canadian readers before the end of 1972, and it will enable Ontario-based firms to produce a much wider range of new, interesting and useful Canadian books.

People who like to read Canadian books have a clear vested interest in the internal affairs of the publishing industry. So do teachers, university lecturers, librarians, aspiring writers, printers, designers and a whole host of other people. We all have a stake in seeing the branch plants and foreign subsidiaries replaced by independent Canadian-owned publishers. We need government measures that change the rules of the game, and we need more books and more book publishers.

There are many different ways for people to help create a more vigorous and lively Canadian-owned book-publishing industry. Here is a short check list of things you can do.

- Next time you're in your public library, look at the shelves of new acquisitions and complain if you don't see all the important new books from Canadian-owned houses.
- Look at the books your kids are bringing home from school, and complain to your school trustees if they are American in origin.
- If you're a student, refuse to buy books published by branch plants even if they're required reading. Rely on library copies or xeroxes instead.
- Ask your local librarian to check the library to see if every book mentioned in *Read Canadian* is there, and suggest that the missing ones be purchased and put on the shelves.
- Join the only all-Canadian book club, the Readers'

Club of Canada (17 Inkerman Street, Toronto 5), and, if you feel so inclined, cancel your membership in the Book-of-the-Month club.

- Put yourself on the mailing lists of Canadian-owned publishers whose books interest you, so you're sure to find out about their new titles.
- Write letters of complaint to the editor of your daily newspaper if the paper doesn't carry regular reviews of important new Canadian books.
- If you're a student and someone suggests that you buy and read a US text, check to see if there aren't Canadian books on the same subject and, if there are, unilaterally substitute the Canadian for the American.
- If you're at a Canadian university, give an inscribed presentation copy of *Read Canadian* to every one of your US professors.
- If you're a writer, always discuss your manuscripts and projects with Canadian-owned firms first and avoid the branch plants.
- If you're a Canada Council administrator, don't give publication grants to publishers that aren't one hundred per cent Canadian owned.
- If you're a cabinet minister, persuade the cabinet to enact legislation immediately requiring that all book publishers operating in Canada be one hundred per cent Canadian owned by 1977.

Canadian-owned Publishers

These firms are owned by Canadian residents, and have active English-language publishing programs that account for a substantial portion of their total business. Some of these firms act as agents for a number of foreign publishers along with carrying on their own book publishing.

Alive Press Guelph, Ontario
Ballentrae Foundation Calgary, Alberta
Black Rose Books 3934 rue St-Urbain, Montreal 131, Quebec
Book Society of Canada 4386 Sheppard Ave., Agincourt, Ontario
Chateau Books 615 Dorchester Blvd., Montreal 2, Quebec
Clarke, Irwin 791 St. Clair Ave. W., Toronto 10, Ontario
Coles Publishing 90 Ronson Dr., Rexdale, Ontario
Dawson College Press Montreal, Quebec
Delta Canada 351 Gerald St., Montreal 690, Quebec
Fiddlehead Books Department of English, University of New Brunswick, Fredericton, NB
Frontier Publishing 3518-3 Ave. S. W., Calgary, Alberta
Gray's Publishing P. O. Box 718, Sidney, BC
Harvest House 1364 Greene Ave., Montreal 215, Quebec
House of Anansi 471 Jarvis St., Toronto 284, Ontario
Hurtig Publishers 225 Birks Bldg., Edmonton, Alberta
Information Canada 171 Slater St., Ottawa, Ontario
Ingluvin Publications 5355 Walkley Ave., No. 41, Montreal 265, Quebec
James Lewis & Samuel 35 Britain St., Toronto, Ontario
Ladysmith Press Ladysmith, Quebec
Learning Concepts 101 Duncan Mills Rd., Don Mills 405, Ontario
McGill-Queen's University Press 3458 Redpath St., Montreal 109, Quebec
McClelland and Stewart 25 Hollinger Rd., Toronto 16
Mitchell Press Vancouver, BC

New Press 84 Sussex Ave., Toronto 179
Oberon Press 555 Maple Lane, Ottawa 2, Ontario
Peter Martin Associates 17 Inkerman St., Toronto 5
Prairie Books Saskatoon, Saskatchewan
Prism International Creative Writing Department, University of British Columbia, Vancouver 8, BC
Progress Books 487 Adelaide St. W., Toronto 133, Ontario
Sono Nis 3016 140 St., Surrey, BC
Talonbooks 202 Carrall St., Vancouver 4, BC
Tundra Books 465 St François Xavier, Montreal 125, Quebec
University of British Columbia Press UBC, Vancouver 8, BC
University of Toronto Press Front Campus, University of Toronto, Toronto 181, Ontario
Weed/Flower Press 756A Bathurst St., Toronto 4, Ontario
William Clare Ltd. Vancouver, BC

Agency Publishers

These firms are owned by Canadian residents, but most of their business is in publishing or distributing books originating in the US or Britain. Some of them do a bit of original Canadian publishing, but it is a small fraction of their total business.

Burns & MacEachern 62 Railside Rd., Don Mills, Ontario
Fitzhenry & Whiteside 150 Lesmill Rd., Don Mills, Ontario
General Publishing and Musson Book Co. 30 Lesmill Rd., Don Mills, Ontario
Griffin House 455 King St. W., Toronto 135, Ontario